So Says the Guru

SO SAYS THE GURU

VOLUME III

YodaGuru

I still go by this message of inspiration that was written
by my high school art mentor 27 years ago...

Dante you have
talent & skills
AND
CREATIVE
you don't need
anything more
to be successful,
JUST KEEP GROWING;
Mind, Body & Spirit
... CREATE... LOOK
AND DRAW WHAT
YOU SEE....
Have a great
Summer C-U-Next year
Rashid

TABLE OF CONTENTS

ACKNOWLEDGEMENTS

Thank you to the people, places, and/or things that have helped inspire what I've written and continued to be part of this mental journey. A special thank you to those who have responded in kind to those Yodaisms by sharing their personal stories to the point where those responses have been added to the book. It's considerably humbling how my writing has personally connected to so many people I've met in person and talked to online through social media who I've become friends with. Over the 27 years I've been writing down and then posting my thoughts, I've actually been encouraged publish them in a book. Well, you've got your wish. My writing journey is far from over. It's on ongoing process that is sparked from an initial idea and then a work in progress. I tip my hat to each and every one of you for the unwavering support, encouraging words, and tremendously positive feedback I've received over the years.

So Says the Guru

VOLUME III

SHOCK AND AWE

December 17, 2009

Leo F. Buscaglia once said, ~Love withers with predictability, its very essence is surprise and amazement. To make love a prisoner of the mundane is to take its passion and lose it forever.~ Without a doubt, a person can most definitely become jaded when it comes to matters of the heart to the point where it becomes not only predictable, but uneventful as well. It's a sad situation indeed when love or true love for that matter doesn't have the zing of surprised excitement it once had in the past because of how much the dynamic of relationships has immensely changed in today's society giving way to this sense of lost hope, especially for those who have constantly found or still find themselves in utter frustration and heartbreak.

Let me ask you this question ladies, how many of you have truly experienced genuine surprise and amazement in regards to a guy putting all his heart into doing something absolutely special such as planning a surprise birthday party, It's a sad state affairs for those women who have had birthdays they sorely wanted to forget because of how embarrassingly inconsiderate the guy(s) was/were to her. In any case, it makes any woman feel appreciated to have a man who takes into consideration her favorite food, flower, scent, etc. to call and invite all her gal pals instead of the other way around. For it's an amazing shock to the system to know the amount of effort a guy took to plan it all, whereby showing and essentially feeling the passion within his heart for her.

As said before, a person can surely be jaded from being in bad past relationships to where it can sometimes seem to no surprise at all to them as if the predictable actions of the past follow him/her to another relationship leaving you in all intents and purposes feeling like a prisoner sentenced to life without true happiness. Thinking about it, there are a certain number of people who are currently doing time within their own heart, in a manner of speaking, and would like nothing more than to have their feelings and emotions set free to share with someone special. You see, it's those feelings and emotions that have, in a sense, been down in the hole, so to speak, for quite some time and have never seen the light of day because of being in the cold, perpetual darkness of frustration, heartbreak, anger, bitterness, disappointment, etc.

For the question can be asked, how many of you have been so desensitized to a never-ending slew of broken relationships you gradually developed an I'm not surprised/shocked mentality. What do I mean? When you hear about infidelity involving celebrities like Tiger Woods, you find yourself going from surprise and shock to all out cynicism leaving you considerably non-remorseful to celebrities who do get caught. Let me tell you something, there is a serious lack of the pure innocence going into love and when you lose aspects of it like surprise, amazement, unpredictability you end up not with a vibrant, thrilling relationship always asking with a smile what's next but a relationship that is stale and possibly boring causing you to instead ask with a confused look what now.

Actress/Comedian/Singer Sandra Bernhard said, ~Love is the only shocking act left on the face of the earth.~ In retrospect, there isn't anything predictable about love/true love as its the people who are considered to be predictable. Guys, more often than not, tend to lack originality when it pertains to wanting to surprise/shock/ amaze a potential and/or significant other. If you think about it, as a guy you have to show your individuality setting yourself apart from other guys out there who I dare say don't have a clue as to what the real meaning of being romantic is all about...but I digress. In the end, every person wants an amazing relationship that's never predictable and will always have great surprises in store for you into the latter years of your life leaving his/her/your heart in a continual state of shock and awe.

NEVER GONNA BE ALONE (LAST YODAISM OF 2010)

December 22, 2009

The late Reggae Singer Bob Marley once said, ~Love would never leave us alone.~ Without a doubt, when it comes to experiencing the pangs of the utter heartbreak in which sadness, frustration, disappointment, etc. reside, a person can oftentimes consider himself/herself alone in dealing with the feelings and emotions that in all intents and purposes weigh him/her down. It's a tough situation indeed for any person struggling by themselves with the inner turmoil felt within their very own heart causing it to become a heavy burden not only on their shoulders, but on their heart as well. Thinking about it, to put it into words can most definitely leave a person with this sense of not being able to have someone who can truly understand the sheer magnitude of what he/she is personally dealing with.

Let me ask you this question to those who are or have been heartbroken, are you feeling/did you feel like the issues you're facing now or have faced in the past caused you to keep your emotions and feelings isolated to the point where it's better to be closed off than to talk openly about it? I think it would be safe to say there are girls, as well as guys out there who portray a happy go lucky, I'm fine with a smile on their face facade, but behind the smile lies a battle from within the very depths of his/her heart/soul. For it's a battle they're enduring alone where he/she is fighting against being stuck in the rut of sorrow, hopelessness, drama, negativity, sick of being sick and tired, etc. which has made people nearly or coming close to giving up.

If you think about it, when it comes to the unfortunate feeling of being alone and unloved because of being hurt in the past a person can find himself/herself clinging on by their fingertips, in a manner of speaking, to the edge of his/her heart. A person can come to a point where he/she can either keep hanging on or just let go and for a certain number of people they know the feeling of trying to pull themselves up but can't because of personal issues of the past trying to pull him/her down. It's a sad state of affairs for those who they once trusted to catch him/her when they couldn't bear the weight of it all to where they end up letting go and instead of falling into the loving arms of their best friend, they fall back hitting something considered their worst enemy...reality.

For the question can be asked for those who felt alone within their heart, did you have anyone to be there for you to talk to or have as a shoulder to cry on? We all know someone or are that someone by the look on his/her/your face can tell one has a lot bottled up inside and he/she/you want nothing more than to express whatever is eating at him/her/you to where possibly tears are shed. You see, to have someone who not only is able to somehow understand what you're going through and can provide sage wisdom to hopefully help in one's time of need puts a smile on your face. Women, more so than guys, are greatly appreciative of this and do not have that worry/fear/doubt as to whether or not the guy they're talking to/crying on their shoulder will take advantage of the situation showing he genuinely cares.

In retrospect, there is a positive presence in love and whether it's in person or in spirit it has the ability to never cause you to feel alone and cold. It can hold you tightly with both hands, whereby showing you that no matter how tough relationships are/can be he/she will not let you go or let you fall. To have that positive, warm presence in the form of a guy/girl represents a whole new world where you always look forward to living every single day filled with unknown surprises. Hey, how many people would want that type of true happiness and how many actually have it? In end, when you have the love of possibly someone special in your life along with friends, family, God by your side you're never gonna be alone, which is a song by a group/band who got recently nominated for their newest album Dark Horse in 2010 Nickelback.

WHERE ARE YOU (1ST YODAISM OF 2010)

January 6, 2010

Someone once said, ~Ask questions from your heart and you will be answered from the heart.~ Without a doubt, a person can have so many questions when it pertains to the who, what, when, where, why and sometimes how of their own heart. Yet, it's not so much the questions but the answers you try at best to wait patiently for, which is considered a difficult task. You see, it's those unanswered questions that can become a source of utter disappointment causing one to be absolutely frustrated as you find yourself continually asking the right questions but unfortunately getting the wrong answers or not answers at all. For those who are living the single life, it can be a tough situation indeed to feel as if true happiness may never be answered for themselves, whereby leaving a permanent rather than temporary question mark within their heart.

If you think about it, when it comes to love/true love one of the questions that is frequently asked is who am I going to spend the rest of my life with? For it's the question of who in which a number of people have asked or are still asking in regard to their quintessential guy/girl of mystery. Who will this person be to have you experience endless amounts of happiness and joy instead of experiencing endless amounts of sorrow and pain? Who will this person be that will have you never doubt myself as a person leaving my self-esteem in shambles? Who will this person be to show you how much of an incredible individual you truly are in his/her eyes? Who will this person be to put my entire trust in and having faith he/she will never break it? Who will this person be that the commitment he/she has for you will be strong and everlasting?

Oftentimes, the question of what tends to be asked when it involves the more detailed aspects concerning matters of the heart. A woman, more so than a guy, thinks at length on the question of what pertaining to the guy they hope to meet or possibly have met. What is his name? What will he look like? What qualities/attributes can he show her that tells her he is not a guy who is immature and needs to grow up but rather a guy who is mature and is continuing to grow? What makes him different from all the others she's met or were in a relationship with in the past? What is his family like, and does he have a relationship with them or lack thereof? What is his sense of values and morals, or does he even have any? What kind of emotional security will he be able to provide her when she's feeling down in the dumps. What type of husband/father will he be?

Let me ask you this question to those who are living the single life, how many of you are wanting to know the question of when will you finally be happy in love? Thinking about it, it can be exciting to want to know the answer to the question of when love will happen for you but at the same time it can be mentally exhausting. When is my time to be truly happy going to happen? When can I be able to breathe easier knowing all the drama of a past/current relationship is no longer weighing down on me? When can I have a permanent smile on my face instead of finding myself in tears? When can I be surprised by acts of stupidity that are honestly genuine rather than the constant stupid acts of infidelity that tend be not at all surprising? When am I going to meet the right guy/girl instead of meeting the wrong ones?

In retrospect, there comes a point while pondering the questions of the heart your left wondering how long you can keep asking them until you've reached the point of possibly going completely insane. Personally speaking, I've enjoyed asking the challenging questions and hopefully they will be answered in the form of a special lady whoever she may be. In any case, it's nice to know that while asking the seemingly tough questions on your own you have your best buds/gal pals there by your side to try to at least provide the helpful answers knowing they care about/

love you and don't want to see you giving up. In the end, love/ true love has been answered for some as they say to that certain someone with a smile on their face there you are but for others they still have question about that certain someone out there one of them being where are you, which is a song that tends to reflect this thought by Justin Roman feat. Soluna.

ARE YOU READY

January 15, 2010

Stephen R. Brad once said, ~I think there are some valuable lessons we can learn from the game Simon Says. In a nutshell, the game is all about obedience.~ If you think about it, Simon Says is not only a fun game we've all played back in the day, but it's also considered a metaphor for life. As said before, the game in a nutshell is all about obedience and you have to basically play by the rules and obey what the person is telling you to do knowing full well he/she is going to attempt to trick you in order to take you out of the game. For it's a matter of staying focused and trying not to make any mistakes in the process but they will unfortunately be made in regard to friendships, love, and in one's spiritual walk with God.

Without a doubt, when it comes to the game of life that is Simon Says, the friends we hang with on a semi daily basis can be influential either in a positive or negative way. I think we can all agree, there are a certain number of friends who have that if we tell him/her to jump he/she will jump with no questions asked mentality where they will get you to do something knowing full well you may end up looking like a complete fool, especially if alcohol is involved. It can be a difficult situation indeed to know you've royally messed up as you listened to certain friends who seemingly have the ability to do whatever insane, illegal, dangerous, or just plain stupid activity that causes you much pain and regret afterwards not just to yourself but to others as well.

Essentially, Simon Says is a game of deception and you have to have excellent listening skills because if you don't you will find yourself wishing you paid closer attention. In some aspect, the sense of deception in the game of Simon Says can also be found in matters of the heart in regard to a relationship you truly regretted being in. Oftentimes, a guy/girl can be so focused, or should I say blinded by the love of a potential and/or significant other that they don't unfortunately catch what they're actually doing using deceptive actions going on right in front of him/her until it's too late. For some, most, or people know all too well the feeling of being absolutely deceived by a particular guy's/girl's words and actions, leaving him/her wishing they should have listened to those who saw it clear as day.

Joshua 1: 7 says, ~Only be thou strong and very courageous, that thou mayest observe to do according to all the law, which Moses my servant commanded thee: turn not from it to the right hand or to the left, that thou mayest prosper whithersoever thou goest.~ Let me ask you this question, does it seem like you're in some ways playing a game of Simon Says as you're challenged by what the world says and what God says leaving you to struggle in your spiritual walk with God? You see, to listen to what God wants you to do rather what the world wants you do shows absolute trust and obedience in Him. Thinking about it, there are times where you may not be listening or refuse to listen to Him, whereby succumbing to the desires you want in life and that's when God in his own way shows you, he's in control telling you you're out.

In retrospect, life is a fun game to play and at the same time can be very hard if you play the rules. Every person has been or is currently in a Simon Says situation concerning their own life and whether it's work, marriage, getting out of debt, illness, or whatever the case may be you try to play by the rules even though they stink sometimes. Of course, you break the rules and try to avoid being seen/caught but you inevitably pay the consequences sooner or later, which hopefully valuable lessons were learned/ continue to be learned from. Hey, nobody is perfect as we will mess up from time to time. In the end, you have to thank God for being with you every step of the way in life and will continue to be with you as you face Simon Says challenges/situations ahead to where He will say to you are you ready?

ENJOY THE RIDE

January 20, 2010

Kenny Ryan once said, ~Facebook is the Disneyland of the internet.~ Without a doubt, one of the most or THE most popular "attractions" in the world of social networking is Facebook and each time you log on you never know what you're going to encounter making it at times a truly enjoyable experience. For it's an experience in which you in all intents and purposes "step" into a world where you can spend hours on end reading the high/lows of everyday life, posting notes, adding friends, unfriending, tagging photos, poking people, etc. I think we can all fully agree that many of us have become highly addicted to the nonstop entertainment each one of us gets from the countless number of interesting people who we personally consider as our friends.

As said before, you never really know what you're going to encounter each time you log into Facebook, especially after updating your status message. In some aspect, one's status message is like a proverbial public announcement system where instead of verbally announcing your activities for your friends to hear, they read it. It's a humorous situation indeed as there are times where you tend not to think about what you're going to write and as soon as you share it for others to the point where the "news" spreads like wildfire. Let me tell you something, I've had more of my friends/family message/text/call/ talk to me in person concerning status messages concerning my social life in regard to hanging out with a female, which is apparently interesting news for curious people out there.

If you think about it, one of the things we all tend to do from time to time while in Disney is people watch and you can't help but be fascinated by such a diverse group of people to where you're either in utter disbelief or totally amused. Thinking about it, we all have the comfort of people watching as classmates, co-workers, and longtime friends who we've known for quite some time post and share videos giving us a glimpse into their life with family, as well as friends. You see, it's within those videos you witness the happiness of unveiling a new addition to the family, a baby's first words/steps, family having fun singing karaoke, showing off a new pet, sharing their skydiving experience, friends just being stupid together, or whatever the case may be.

Let me ask you this question for those who have been to Disney, what do you most look forward to when you go? If you said the rides you would be 100% correct. Space Mountain, It's A Small World, Splash Mountain, Rock and Roll Rollercoaster, Tower of Terror, Mr. Toad's Wild Ride, Pirates of the Caribbean, etc. are rides we've all stood in line for. Essentially, there are a plethora of "rides" on Facebook you don't have to stand in line for that suit individual tastes none of which I am currently riding on, so to speak, so please stop sending me invites...but I digress. In any case, you can witness for yourself firsthand not only the popularity of these particular rides, but the all out intense fervency for "rides" such as Cafeworld, Farmville, Castle Age, Pet Society, Yoville, Sorority Life, and Mafia Wars which is pretty intense to say the least.

In retrospect, Facebook is one huge amusement park where you can play to your heart's content. It's a place where dreams can possibly come true by way of networking in order to find a career/job, chat with old friends/classmates, get up to date on reunions, become fans of particular people, places, or things, share in causes like Haiti relief, and make connections both literally and figuratively with certain people. Hey, we all spend time in this place, some more than others, to where we end up eventually feeling like 5 of 7 dwarves in which we can be Happy, Grumpy, Sleepy, Dopey and have moments of being intellectual like Doc. In the end, the one thing we can take out of being on the popular attraction known as Facebook is you don't have to pay for anything so have fun and enjoy the ride.

MY PROMISE

January 29, 2010

John Lennon once said, ~Love is a promise, love is a souvenir, once given never forgetten, never let it disappear.~ Let me ask you this questions to those who are in strong significant relationships, how many of you have not only made promises to your husband/wife/bf/gf/fiance, but have been able to keep his/her word in making those particular promises happen for matter? You see, the promises made to someone you truly love are considered absolutely priceless to the point where if it comes to fruition its closely held in a very special place within their heart. Essentially, when it comes to love/true love you want a guy/girl who can look you in the eyes and will make a solemn vow/promise to you to always lie, cheat, and steal in a good way of course.

Without a doubt, to make the solemn vow/promise to always lie to your best friend wouldn't necessarily sound appealing especially in matters of the heart but to always lie with your best friend gives it a whole new context don't you think? I think it would be safe to say every person who is in a strong loving relationship would most definitely appreciate lying with their best friend for life who loves him/her with all his/her heart. For it that someone who you can happily lay together with on the couch either watching a movie, tv, reading books, simply taking a leisurely nap, or help keep you company when you're sick. You have to agree, its a comforting situation indeed being wrapped in each other's arms knowing the sense of peace felt as both of you become lost within the warm embrace with the love of your life.

If you think about it, not too many people would tolerate being cheated on and for a certain number of people they have unfortunately experienced it where even thinking about it brings about a plethora of emotions. Yet, when you have someone in your life who you can trust to never break your heart with acts of infidelity, your only concern to actually worry about is whether or not he/she will cheat on you when you're playing video/card/board games. Thinking about it, to have your significant other cheat on you when playing a game like Uno or Scrabble is far less disappointing than cheating on you with another man/woman. Let me tell you something, I've witnessed many married couples having fun cheating when it pertains to games and hope they continue to do so for many years rather than the latter.

For the question can be asked to those who have had a bad past relationship, how many of you believe that a certain guy/girl in a sense stole something from you? Oftentimes, when a person experiences utter heartbreak he/she feels as if part of themselves has been stolen from him/her. In some aspect, their own identity isn't fully complete because a part or possibly all their heart containing caring, compassion, trust, faith, honesty, innocence, love, etc. has in all intents and purposes been stolen away from you. However, to have a guy/girl who can steal your heart every single day till the latter years of life and continues adding to what is inside adding more to what is already in there instead of taking away is something quite honestly so very rare to have or even find these days but it's out there.

In retrospect, promises are easily made in relationships and at the same time they can easily be broken. It's a sad state of affairs when the promise to never lie is broken, causing you to no longer feel someone by your side physically lying next to you because of being lied to so many times over. To know the promise to never cheat on you is broken leaving you feeling mentally betrayed as you believed what he/she did/said causing you to think you're worth it only to find yourself feeling worthless. To not experience the happiness that brings a smile to your face and have it be taken away from you because of a promise being broken leaves you feeling violated in a way. In the end, as strange as this sounds, I say to that certain someone out there whoever she may be my promise to you is to always lie, cheat, and steal in the best way possible.

YOU MAKE ME

February 14, 2010

Someone once said, ~Love, an emotion so strong that you would give up everything; to just feel it just once, to know that you are part of something special. To know that you can feel what love is really is; to know, to feel, to love.~ Without a doubt, when it comes to matters of the heart you can most definitely experience a plethora of emotions from that quintessential warm fuzzy feeling you get inside oftentimes described as butterflies to falling head over heels. For it's those emotions a person experiences can in all intents and purposes be considered a rollercoaster as he/she goes through highs and lows within their heart. Essentially, its the genuinely honest and real emotions one feels for another that causes you to say the following three words: you make me.

You make me feel good both inside and out. If you think about it, when you meet someone who makes you feel absolutely comfortable not only in your own skin, but in your heart as well you just feel on top of the world. I think it would be safe to say when you're in this heightened state of euphoria you find yourself completely unaware of doing certain things such as forgetting how to breathe, singing/humming a tune to yourself, having a glow about you, having a kick in your step to the point of doing a little dance, or whatever the case may be. It's quite an amusing and at times considerably annoying situation indeed for those witnessing the display of true happiness and yet deep down inside it's what single people like myself want to experience.

You make me crazy. Love and being crazy are synonymous with each other as you can go through a mixed bag of emotions over someone such as frustration, anger, bewilderment, confusion, etc. Thinking about it, every person who is in a potential and/or significant relationship knows all-too-well how crazy their gf/bf/

husband/wife can make him/her. A level of craziness where any other person would run away screaming all-the-while tearing their own hair out but when it comes to your own "bag of crazy" you stay because even though he/she makes you want to cause him/her bodily harm you truly love him/her. Hey, how many of you can say with 100% surety you and the guy/girl you're with make each other crazy in the best possible way?

You make me a better person. Let me ask you this question to those who are in a potential and/or significant relationship, how many of you see the best of yourself every time you look into his/her eyes? Guys, more often than not, look into the eyes of their girl knowing they not only see who they want to be knowing he has the potential to be the best man she has ever known. When I say the best man she has ever known, I mean the best in being able to always provide for her emotionally, mentally, physically, and spiritually. Let me tell you something, all guys tend to think this way concerning a woman they absolutely love/care about as they strive to be that guy not knowing that in her eyes, he is already that guy.

In retrospect, the emotions that go along with love/true love is something you can't stop or even try to stop from happening no matter how hard you try. For a certain number of people those emotions can be seen as unwanted, knowing how much of a powerful force, in a manner of speaking, it is and to avoid experiencing any kind of emotions they bury their feelings deep inside. However, you can't bury how you feel for long because sooner or later they will gradually surface as he/she finds himself/herself with someone who will be worth letting their guard down and not being afraid to risk their heart. In the end, when you finally experience the emotions of love/true love you say to that certain someone you make me so many things from being happy to sad but most of all you make me smile, which is a song from a former member of Kid Rock's entourage Uncle Kracker.

THE SIMPLE LIFE
March 7, 2010

Robert Louis Stevenson once said, ~The best things in life are nearest. Breathe in your nostrils, light in your eyes, flowers at your feet, duties at your hand, the path of the right just before you. Then do not grasp at the stars, but do life's plain, common work as it comes, certain that daily duties and daily bread are the sweetest things in life.~ Ultimately, it's been 23 years since my last visit to the Philippines and the difference as a 9-year-old then to now as a 32-year-old is perspective. You see, as a 9-year-old you pay more attention to your own self-interests than the surroundings before you, causing you to miss out on a truly wondrous experience. For its an eye-opening situation indeed when you take in not only the positive aspects, but the negative aspects, as well as I focus on the following three topics: traffic, family interaction, and poverty.

Let me ask you this question to those who live in an area where traffic is highly prevalent such as New York and Los Angeles, do you think your neck of the woods is totally outrageous? During my time in the Philippines, I witnessed traffic that went beyond totally outrageous as there are no rules. Essentially, a two-lane street becomes 5 lanes and there is no such thing as who has the right of way leading to witnessing an absolute standstill in traffic at a 4 way stop where nobody wanted to move to the point where an altercation nearly ensued. Yet, as much as there is complete chaos on the roads there weren't any accidents whatsoever while I was there. Let me tell you something though, as much as it was an enjoyable experience I wouldn't want to drive there because I know I would have/suffer high blood pressure, an aneurism, and/ or a heart attack.

Without a doubt, part of what made my trip in the Philippines so enjoyable other than the food and the awesome activities was spending time with family I haven't seen in years. Thinking about it, my time spent reconnecting with relatives outside on the porch rather than inside because of the lack of air conditioning was fun. The times sitting outside enjoying the entertainment of just laughing/sharing stories were the most memorable to me was when I realized that for a number of families in the states there is a serious lack of family interaction. The entertainment of the internet, tv, video games, work, etc. are just some reasons that have separated the family dynamic in the U.S. causing kids/parents/husbands/wives to see each other as strangers rather than family. Let me tell you something, U.S. families can learn a thing or two for Filipino families.

If you think about it, you never really know how good you have it until you actually see it for yourself with your own eyes. Personally speaking, I have a deeper appreciation of who I am as a person and what I have after visiting/seeing the places that many of the Filipinos call home. Whether it's living in a run-down shack next to a landfill, under an overpass, in the streets itself, or walking up to a vehicle and asking for handouts you can't help but feel for your own people, which is a sad state of affairs. However, what made me absolutely speechless was seeing both kids and adults rummaging through the trash in order to find something to eat. For the most part, that is the way of life my friend for a number of Filipinos who don't have the financial means to support themselves and have to hustle any way they can by any means necessary in order to survive.

In retrospect, my time in the Philippines was filled with excitement, fun, and not to mention food out of the wazoo, which is why I humorously named my vacation the Philippines Food Tour. Being back in the Philippines after 23 years gave me newfound insight as to what is most important. Unlike most kids in the U.S., kids in the Philippines enjoy chasing each other, playing basketball on broken down/carton made goals, or playing on mounds of dirt. In any case, a big house, fancy cars, expensive video games/video game systems, air conditioning, updated/current electronics such as DVD player or stereo system, cable, etc. are what my relatives don't have and despite that they are a extremely happy with what they have without any complaints whatsoever as they all live the simple life.

UNBREAK MY HEART

March 14, 2010

Someone once said, ~Of course, you're going to get your heart broken. And it isn't just going to happen once, but a lot. That's just part of growing up, and it makes you stronger. Then you can handle it better next time. You may not get through it yourself, but your friends will help you through it. And you'll be a stronger person because of it. Then one day someone will come along, and it'll all pay off and no one will ever break your heart again.~ Without a doubt, matters of the heart can at times be considered a cruel bastard. For it's a tough situation indeed to face heartbreak leaving you with so many unanswered questions, especially if those questions left unanswered pertain to a certain someone you are in real genuine love with.

If you think about it, when it comes to the pangs of utter heartbreak you try to make sense of the actions and/or words of the guy/girl in question who did you wrong. Essentially, when you absolutely know the reason or reasons for why you're heartbroken you can deal with it all-the-while gradually healing mentally, emotionally, personally, and spiritually. However, when you're left without any answers to speak of you deal with it by trying to search for the answers and its during the search the pain will gradually grow to the point where you inevitably become mentally, emotionally, personally, as well as spiritually numb within your heart due to the sheer impact of it all, which is an experience quite a number of people have gone through or are currently going through.

As said before, making sense of heartbreak can most definitely be difficult to even understand. Thinking about it, if I had to guess it would be like having a straight jacket strapped on to you trying to get out of it. In a sense, all your emotions and feelings are for all intents and purposes wrapped tightly around your heart and no matter what you do you can't seem to escape from it. For even the smallest function done on a semi daily basis are impaired as things such as thinking and breathing are difficult making the emotional straight jacket around your heart increasingly tighter leaving you to constantly struggle to where you;re left doing the only logical thing to do when you think nobody can truly help in your time of need...cry.

Let me ask you this question, when experiencing heartbreak from a guy/girl you're in a real genuine like with and the physical aspect of the relationship was involved, what best describes how you feel? Betrayed, disappointed, angry, frustrated, bitter, confused, the feeling of wanting to crawl out of your own skin, etc. are just a plethora of emotions one may possibly feel when you bring yourself to become vulnerable with a guy/girl and completely let your guard down. Hey, we all know someone or are that someone who is in that type of situation. It's a sad state of affairs for a person who feel as if a part of himself/herself can never be given back after sharing an intimate moment with a guy/girl who supposedly cared about him/her.

In retrospect, heartbreak is a hard pill to swallow, so to speak, and as much as it painfully hurts to not know why you can't let it become something you hold on to. You see, you have to let it go because if you continue to harbor all those feelings/emotions they will fester and when/if you do meet the right guy/girl something in that relationship will cause you to flashback leading you to throw all that baggage on to him/her, which is never a good thing. In any case, heartbreak can make you stronger just as long as you don't keep it locked away in your heart. In the end, to get through the pain you know you can rely on your best buds/gals to help you through because even though you don't want to outright say it you want them to be at your side and trust they will as you say to them help me to unbreak my heart, which is song by six time Grammy Award winner Toni Braxton that best reflects this thought.

A FRESH START

March 21, 2010

Richard Bach once said, ~Don't be discouraged at goodbyes. A farewell is necessary before you can meet again. And meeting again after moments or a lifetime, is certain for those who are friends.~ Without a doubt, working at the insane asylum aka the youth center for the past 12 years has had its highest of highs and lowest of lows. For it's a tough situation indeed to walk away from a place that has felt like home and yet I did knowing it was my time to leave. Thinking about it, I knew one day I would have to leave but the exact date was a complete uncertainty until now. Essentially, what I will most remember during my 12 long years there are the fun times, the drama, and the relationships built over a period of time that will last a lifetime.

Let me ask you this question, how many of you get paid to have fun at your job? Personally speaking, I had a blast being a big kid taking part with "my kids" in activities such as go karts, movies, bowling, pool, the beach, Waterville, counselor/kids basketball games, paintball, skating, laser tag, miniature golf, etc. Oftentimes, when it comes to certain activities like basketball games, bowling, and go karts, I have a tendency to be competitive to the point where I've been known to ram a child up against the wall during a race. Hey, my mentality is that if you're old enough to get behind the wheel of a go kart then it's every person for one's self and the counsel/kid relationship doesn't exist once the light turns green.

If you think about it, every place of business has to deal with some kind of drama and the youth center was certainly no exception. It truly befuddles the mind on how I've been able to mentally last in a place where something seems to always be heard, said, and/ or done whether its between employees/management to where problems occur. You see, not a day goes by where as soon as you step into the building you can sense something is in the air causing you to be on high alert. It's a sad state of affairs when you feel emotionally, physically, and most of all mentally exhausted/ stressed out when dealing with the drama rather than with the kids themselves. Let me tell you something, there have been times where I didn't want to go to work because of what has gone on in the past and is still continuing after I left.

For the question can be asked to those who work or have worked in the childcare/youth profession, how strong is the relationship you built with not just the kids but with the parents of those kids as well? As I've said before in a past Yodaism, you'll surely become attached to the kids who you've gotten to know, especially over a 12-year period. However, it's not just the counselor/kid attachment that can have such a strong bond as its also the established bond between parent/counselor that makes part of the job worthwhile. You see, in a way, you've become part of their extended family as you helped raise their child and when you tell him/her/them you're leaving its shockingly sad news to hear.

In retrospect, it was Mr. Mike Sidebottom who took a chance giving me my start and even went as far as saying he liked me. It seems like only yesterday that I first walked into the doors of the YC and being the newbie that I was didn't know what to expect and now 12 years later I am the first of the last big 3 of the YC with my best friend Biggie and my mentor Ms. Cindy as the last two of the original counselors to leave. Ultimately, I attain a wealth of knowledge, as well as training that will quite possibly serve me well down the road. Though I walk away from friends/co-workers and "my kids" I have gotten to know I do not say goodbye because all roads lead back to where you started from and I will pop in from time to time to say hi. In the end, it's a fresh start with a bright future of endless possibilities as I venture off into a new path and you know what I'm not looking back.

AMEN

April 9, 2010

John Bunyan once said, ~Pray often, for prayer is a shield to the soul, a sacrifice to God, and a scourge for Satan.~ Without a doubt, the power of prayer is something wondrous to behold as you put all your faith in the Lord Jesus Christ to answer what you specifically have been praying about. It can most definitely be a tough and frustrating situation indeed to continually pray for a specific need/request pertaining to your own life only to not have it come to fruition. What it primarily comes down to is waiting patiently for God to answer your prayers. For it may not be answered immediately or the next day because when it comes to Him answering our prayers its within his time, especially when it involves important decision making, family/friends, and matters of the heart.

As said before, when it comes to God answering our prayers He answers them within His time, especially when it pertains to making important decisions concerning one's life. I think it would be safe to say every person has prayed to the Lord above about a potential job opportunity or for that matter deciding to leave a job he/she has been a part of for quite some time. Each one of us have been or currently in a situation where you're either contemplating leaving a job to find something worthwhile whereas others are in search for a job that makes him/her happy all-the-while putting one's faith in Him looking for spiritual guidance. Personally speaking, I am faithfully praying that God will lead me to a job where I am not only happy, but it will be a career I will thoroughly enjoy.

If you think about it, the power of prayer works in regard to family and friends particularly when health issues occur. You see, in life there comes a point where it hands us an unexpected blow leaving us to experience a plethora of unwanted feelings, thoughts, and emotions. However, despite the turmoil you, family, and/or your friends are going through during that trying time you pray to God for strength as you leave all your worries/fears to Him. It's a sad state of affairs when a person doesn't pray and ends up blaming God for letting it even happen to the point where he/she not only gradually loses faith, but inevitably believes there is no God. Let me tell you something, don't ever lose faith or belief in Him because its not a matter of opening your eyes to see Him as it's a matter of opening your heart.

Let me ask you this question to those who are and were single, how many of you prayed to the man upstairs to send you/guide you to that certain someone special bringing absolute true happiness? As a single guy, I pray that God sends me or at least has me meet a woman who loves me for just being myself along with my geeky/nerdy quirks. Whether I have met her or not it's my faith in God as He gives me the wisdom to properly ascertain if she is "the one." On the flip side, to those who have prayed they are now in a long lasting, loving relationship in the bonds of holy matrimony with a guy/girl who has fulfilled all his/her prayers and then some. Hey, I tip my hat to all you ladies and gents out there who didn't give up praying because you are now undeniably happy with your forever best friend.

Psalm 4 says, ~Hear me when I call, O God of my righteousness: thou hast enlarged me when I was in distress; have mercy upon me, and hear my prayer.~ In retrospect, there are so many amazing and unbelievable stories that are shared from people who fervently prayed to God. Thinking about it, all throughout the Bible you've read countless people who faithfully prayed to God like Daniel who was in the Lion's Den, John the Baptist's time in prison, Job's turmoil by way of God's hand, etc. For the question can be asked, how many of us can honestly say that when it comes to our own prayer life can it compared to those men mentioned above? In the end, the prayers we say during the day or at night are requests that hopefully come true and when they eventually do one word best describes it all...Amen.

HOLD ON

April 12, 2010

Crystal Southerland once said, ~Love is like a balloon...when you push your relationship with someone forward it is like blowing up a balloon. If you blow too hard and too fast the balloon pops and likewise the relationship breaks. But if you take things slowly and let the balloon of love stretch on its own, it grows into a huge, prosperous balloon full of love. Also, if you don't push the relationship at all or at least hold it at the same level it was at, the air flows out of the balloon, deflating it, and your love will shrivel up and become flat and lifeless. So when you are in love, push the relationship forward slowly and gently and the balloon will grow comfortably into a strong immense love.~ Let me ask you this question, do you believe that you can never go too far when it comes to "blowing up" the balloon of love/true love?

As said before in the beginning quote, love is like a balloon and the amount of love you in all intents and purposes breathe into it determines whether you're committed to filling it fully or just stopping halfway. Essentially when it comes to matters of the heart you can most definitely find yourself not only mentally and physically pushing forward, but emotionally as well. For it's a scary and tough situation indeed to make the decision to go from being just a friend to wanting to be more than a friend. Every person has been or currently is in a situation where you're, in a way, breathing into the heart of a special someone slowly filling it with a certain amount of trust, security, honesty, care, hope, faith, love, tenderness, respect, contentment, etc. because too much can cause it to metaphorically pop in your face, which is an unfortunate experience quite a few people have been through.

If you think about it, there have been countless relationships in the past where the balloon of love has been deflated, in a manner of speaking, because of not pushing forward hard enough. What do I mean? You see, for a certain number of people they have given up too easily on relationships because it's just too hard to deal with whereby letting all the love he/she supposedly has for a potential and/or significant other escape causing it either end up blowing back in their face or flying around inevitably falling to the ground shriveled, empty, and lifeless. Thinking about it, it's those who give up too easily on love who aren't willing to push themselves mentally, emotionally, physically, as well as, spiritually till their red in the face. What it comes down to is putting the work in to make a relationship last, which I'm sad to say is quite rare these days.

For the question can be asked to those who are in a potential and/or significant relationship, how many of you have ever established a closeness where feelings and emotions bonded you together in the balloon of love when you first stretched out the balloon of friendship? I think it would be safe to say every person at some point physically stretched a balloon so that it will be able to not only easily inflate but make room for more air to fill it. Without a doubt, when you give time in establishing a friendship before love ever happens you have room for growth between the two of you. Oftentimes, by allowing room for growth you're able to gradually stretch, so to speak, each other's hearts to where you don't have to ever worry/fear of quite possibly over filling it with endless amounts of trust, happiness, honesty, respect, hope, faith, love, contentment, etc. that will have it burst just like a balloon.

In retrospect, when you believe you've met the right person you do your best to keep the balloon of love you have with him/her inflated. Of course, there will be times where the air will leak out because of stupid mistakes, which become lessons learned. For the most part, you just have to continue supporting and not quitting on each other when you think there is no more air left in the relationship allowing it to become all shriveled up. Unfortunately, there are people out there rather twisted and/or bored who simply enjoy popping the balloon of true happiness, wanting nothing more than to see a couple deflate right before their eyes. In the end, to those have found/met their love/true love hold on to each other not too tightly where you "pop" him/her letting all the air out but not too gently either where he/she can easily slip from your fingers to float away to possibly never be seen again.

LOVE CONQUERS ALL

April 20, 2010

Someone once said, ~I've never been in love so I guess I don't know the happiness of love. I've never been nor am I now. I'm kind of afraid to step that deep into something because I'm just tired of giving everything I've got. But it's hard when you know that you could be giving more but you're just giving what you want to give, not because you're receiving less but just because, just simply because you're afraid to admit to yourself that you would give that person your whole world. And you're just afraid that your whole world or your everything just might not be enough. You just don't want to end up empty handed and admit to yourself you want to give that person everything.~ Let me ask you this question, whether it's the first time or lucky enough to get a second chance at it, how many of you are quite honestly afraid to fall in love?

Without a doubt, love and fear will always coincide with each other causing a plethora of mixed emotions/feelings such as confusion, frustration, doubt, worry, sadness, happiness, elation, joy, contentment, etc. It's a tough situation indeed to be falling in and/or being in love with someone who at the same time absolutely scares the living daylights out of you. Why? Essentially, you're allowing the guy/girl a true glimpse of the person you truly are to where the walls you've built up gradually come done leaving at a level of vulnerability that causes you to be extremely uncomfortable. As much as you want to emotionally and mentally shut yourself off because of how uncomfortably scary it is knowing how comfortable you've become in the so-called cocoon of sarcastic cynicism, there is a small part of you that wants to experience what those around you are forever cherishing...true happiness.

As said before from the quote above, one can be afraid to step that deep into something because of being tired of constantly giving yourself emotionally, mentally, personally, spiritually, and physically but receiving nothing back in return. I think it would be safe to say a woman knows all too well of stepping in deep into a relationship with a guy only to find he hasn't committed himself into stepping in deeper causing her to in all intensive purposes sink into the depths of heartbreak as tears of sadness are shed. Thinking about it, for any woman, as well as many guys out there the fear of finding yourself deep in love can be intensely scary to where you either back off because you honestly don't know how to handle it or you move forward knowing that even though you're scared out of your mind you have that certain someone by your side who is possibly as scared as you are.

Personally speaking, I have never been in love or have never really known the feeling of what falling in love is like. Of course, I've been in the puppy love/infatuated/like stages of pre-love/true love but when it comes to falling deeply in love I can honestly say it scares me to no end. However, as a single guy who is mostly surrounded by friends who are married, you get the opportunity to learn/seek advice from them on the fears each couple has faced or is currently facing in the course of 3...8...20 years of marriage. Essentially, one of the many fears that many of them face is allowing himself/herself to be completely open and honest to their bf/husband/gf/wife without fear of being laughed at, judged, or ridiculed. Let me tell you something, there are certain things I'm afraid of that I haven't shared with anyone or even with my best friend for that matter but hope to someday with the one I love.

In retrospect, the fear of love is something that quite a few people have overcome despite experiencing their own personal relationship nightmares. It's a sad state of affairs for a certain number of people who have the inability to get past their fears of a past relationship that quintessentially has left them with emotional and mental scars that haven't been able to heal. For its those cars that have caused him/her to be scared when a guy/girl who is genuinely and honestly real steps into his/her life inevitably turning one's world upside down. In the end, matters of the heart are scary but if you keep in mind that when you meet someone special who even though scares the living daylights out of you, in a good way of course, then you'll be able to face and possibly overcome all your fears together leading you to the realization that the old familiar saying rings true...love conquers all.

WAIT FOR IT

May 4, 2010

Brian Adams once said, ~Learn the art of patience. Apply discipline to your thoughts when they become anxious over the outcome of a goal. Impatience breeds anxiety, fear, discouragement, and failure. Patience creates confidence, decisiveness, and a rational outlook, which eventually leads to success.~ Let me ask you this question, how many of you truly believe in that old familiar saying patience is a virtue? I think it would be safe to say we all have and for a certain number of people it's not a character trait that doesn't quite fit whereas its fits just fine for others. For it's a tough situation indeed to exude patience as one waits for aspects of life to come to fruition especially when it pertains to the following three things: decision making, job opportunities, and matters of the heart.

Without a doubt, the decisions each of us make on a semi-daily basis exude a particular amount of patience, depending on how big it is. It's how quickly one responds to those decisions that can essentially determine whether you're the type of person who is totally spontaneous and takes an absolute risk or thoroughly thinks it all through weighing the pros, as well as cons of said decision. What it primarily comes down to is how anxious a person is in making the decision and how high on the level of importance scale it is that you hopefully don't end up regretting it later. Hey, we've all made rash decisions in the past that have bitten us in the butt, so to speak, inevitably giving us one of many hard lessons to learn in regard to the lack of patience in the decision-making department.

As said before in the quote above, impatience breeds anxiety, fear, discouragement, and failure especially when it concerns patiently waiting for a potential job opportunity. For some, most, or all people have been in a situation where they were so impatient in getting a job that they felt a sense of anxiety, fear, and discouragement from the lack of responses despite consistently putting one's resume out there. It's those lack of responses that can mentally breed a sense of fear that will make you worry about how you will be able to pay off certain expenses. However, once you do get a response its best to get all the information concerning the job or you'll end up in a position where you're in over your head because you jumped the gun in wanting a job that oftentimes looks too good to be true.

For the question can be asked, when it comes to matters of the heart, how many of you are still patiently waiting for the right person to step into your life? As a single guy, I can attest that it's difficult to wait for the right person and yet by having patience you essentially successfully grow in confidence, decisiveness, and rational thinking. I think it would be safe to say there are many people out there who are now sure about themselves, are very decisive on not settling on the first guy/girl they're with and made rational decisions not with just their heart to where they are currently experiencing true happiness with their best friend for life. Let me tell you something, its better to wait and know it than to end up making a big mistake and blowing it.

Psalm 27:14 says, ~Wait on the LORD: be of good courage, and he shall strengthen thine heart: wait, I say, on the LORD.~ In retrospect, there is a lot in life that can test our patience as it can most definitely push us to the brink of insanity mentally, physically, emotionally, and spiritually as well. It's a sad state of affairs when a person doesn't have the courage or strength for the matter to have patience when it comes to certain aspects of life, especially when it involves matters of the heart. What it primarily comes down to is knowing its in God's timing as he guides you to the right decisions, the right job you're suited for, and the right guy/girl who will make you truly happy. In the end, I say this to you as it has been said to me many times over, which is pray to God and wait for it.

FACE-OFF

May 9, 2010

"Mr. Hockey" Gordie Howe once said, ~You've got to love what you're doing. If you love it, you can overcome any handicap or the soreness or all the aches and pains, and continue to play for a long, long time.~ If you think about it, life can oftentimes be compared to Canada's favorite sporting event and that is the game of hockey. In a sense, we're all on the so-called ice rink of life all suited up with hockey stick in hand and ready for battle each time we wake up in the morning. For it can be a tough situation indeed to get to one end of the blue line to the other knowing full well you're going to quite possibly encounter obstacles in front/all around you in order to reach and slap the puck that represents our own individual goals, ambitions, aspirations, dreams, etc. between the pipe.

Let me ask you this question to all you hockey fans out there, what aspect of the game itself do you thoroughly enjoy? For some, most, or all people its rooting for their favorite team such as the Red Wings, Canucks, Rangers, Islanders, Kings, Habs, and the list goes on. Though each of us may not be on a well-known professional hockey team being cheered on by the crowd, we do however have groups of people rooting us on as we skate with the puck in our possession towards the pipe in hopes of hearing the blaring siren of sweet success. You see, no matter how many mistakes made, losses suffered, close personal/professional victories taken away. etc. it's your "fans" known as family/friends who will always cheer you on whether you win or lose.

Without a doubt, there are times in life where we metaphorically find ourselves in the penalty box of life, so to speak. I think it would be safe to say where we've all experienced those stressful days where absolutely nothing goes right leaving you with a plethora of emotions to the point where you want to just drop your gear in order to throw down. When I say throw down it doesn't necessarily mean in the physical sense when taking your "opponents" jersey, pull it over their head, and just beat the living snot of him/her. It can also be in the verbal sense as well. Let me tell you something, there have been days where I've wanted to and actually at some point have body checked certain people through the plexiglass and felt good doing it afterwards.

For the question can be asked to those who are single, how many of you have felt or are feeling as if you're always being tripped, trapped, speared, slashed, roughed up, penalized, kneed, high sticked in the face, head butted, elbowed, cross checked, and/or have found yourself triple decked when it pertains to matters of the heart? Thinking about it, hockey is physically a tough sport and yet when it comes to your own heart there is an emotional toughness you go through as one will metaphorically be beaten up, battered, and bruised trying to maneuver your hockey puck of a heart into the five hole of someone's heart, whoever it may be, all-the-while up against "opponents" who try to stop you seemingly by any means necessary from accomplishing that goal.

Gordie Howe said, ~You find that you have peace of mind and can enjoy yourself, get more sleep, and rest when you know that it was a one hundred percent effort you gave - win or lose.~ In retrospect, in the ice rink of life we're going to be up against "opponents" that will try to take you out either in a mental, physical, emotional, or spiritual way. Hey, like the saying goes when life hits you then you hit it back. We all may not be a Mario Lemieux, Brett Hull, Patrick Roy, Eric Lindros, Jaromir Jagr, Mark Messier, or the great Wayne Gretzky but we use the skills we have to overcome life's obstacles in order to not only get our puck into the net but win our proverbial Stanley Cup. In the end, every day we find ourselves at center ice in a face-off with life itself and win or lose we hope to leave everything on the ice giving 110%.

IF IT AIN'T BROKE...

May 14, 2010

Mary Schmich once said, ~The movies we love and admire are to some extent a function of who we are when we see them.~ Without a doubt, we all grew up watching cartoons to where they have not only become pop culture, but also a staple of our own childhood. Essentially, when the cartoons we watched as kids end up on the big screen you can most definitely be a bit weary and yet at the same time excited as well. I think it would be safe to say every person who grew up watching the original animated series Transformers were stoked when it was made into a movie, which I personally saw at least 3 times. However, there are certain cartoons made into movies that just didn't/won't live up to the hype such as Masters of the Universe, G.I. Joe, and the upcoming 4th Spider-Man reboot.

Let me ask you this question, did anyone think that Masters of the Universe starring Dolf Lundgrin lives up to your own personal standards? Personally speaking, it didn't for me because it quite frankly fell way short of the mark when compared to the cartoon series for several different reasons. First off, the cartoon series focused on Prince Adam turning into He-Man whereas the movie never shows it or mentions his other persona for that matter. Second is Battlecat...nuff said. Thirdly, one of my favorites in the cartoon was never shown, leaving me disappointed indeed and I think you know who I'm talking about...Orko. Let me tell you something, there are so many things I can rant off about, but I must move on.

If you think about it, there are certain cartoons that will forever be part of our childhood such as the series G.I. Joe. For it's one of those cartoon series that every young boy like myself possibly yelled out "Yo Joe" and bought the toy merchandise...but I digress. When the movie G.I .Joe: The Rise of Cobra came out last year I was stoked but coming out of the theaters I was left confused and perplexed not about the movie but the decision on pairing characters up that didn't make any sense at all. If you know your Joe cartoon history, Scarlett is with Duke and Baroness is with Destro but for some reason Duke is Baroness and Scarlett is with Rip Cord....Rip Cord! Personally speaking, I was too preoccupied with trying to figure out why my enthusiasm for the movie slowly went away.

For the question can be asked how, many of you watched Spider-Man and his Amazing Friends as a kid growing up. It would be only a matter of time before it became a movie starring Toby Maguire who is and will be Peter Parker. The first 2 movies were outstanding, but the 3rd installment was ok. There is news that the 4th installment will be a complete reboot where it goes back to his high school days, which sounds promising until I found out that 3 key people are not returning. The Director Sam Raimi, Kirstin Dunst, and Toby Maguire have signed off on the picture leaving fans like myself to speculate that picture will royally fail because to be perfectly honest Kirsten Dunst and Toby Maquire will always be in my eyes Mary Jane and Peter Parker.

In retrospect, many movies based on comic book/cartoons have made it to the big screen that have either failed miserably or have been an absolute success. Daredevil, Fantastic Four, Steele, The Incredible Hulk, Iron Man, Ghost Rider, Spider-Man, Superman, Batman, Catwoman, Scooby Doo, Josie and the PussyCats, X-Men, Wolverine, the upcoming Avengers/Thor movie, etc. are just a long line of characters that many of us have seen jump of the pages of our comics or televisions on to the big screen. Yet, as fans we have a right to voice our opinion when a douchebag director makes the decision to remake "The Crow" in order to be more realistic is a very bad idea for so many different reasons. In the end, when it comes to turning cartoons from our childhood into big screen blockbuster movies I can speak for my fellow peeps and say if it ain't broke don't fix it.

WITH YOU

May 17, 2010

Someone once said, ~Sometimes you meet somebody and you know that whatever you did before, it must have been right...nothing could've have been too bad or gone too wrong because it led you to this person.~ If you think about it, when it comes to matters of the heart, you don't necessarily know what you did or how you ever pulled it off but you're in a relationship with someone who love/ cares about you. Guys, more often than not, have a tendency to not have a clue as to how they ended up meeting, falling in love with, and inevitably marrying an absolutely beautiful woman. For it befuddles the mind of any guy when he's chosen by a woman who not only one believes is totally out of his league but has no earthly idea as to what she sees in him, which merits a sense of disbelief.

Without a doubt, guys like myself aren't considered the hero when it pertains to "saving" a woman from finding themselves in a perilous situation involving their own heart being broken or shattered into a million pieces. For it's a tough situation indeed to cautiously enter/approach when heartbreak happens knowing the words we say in order to comfort her may not at times be what she wants to hear causing us to possibly be seen as the proverbial bad guy because of how harsh the truth is. Yet, as much as the truth hurts coming from our own mouths, women can't deny the fact that there is actual merit as to the points/facts we're trying to guide you towards, which can be quite difficult to do because half the time we're simply shooting from the hip, so to speak.

As a guy, you can most definitely be surprised when a beautiful woman who is totally out of one's league chooses to spend time/ hang with the likes of us who don't normally exude rugged looks and the physically fit physique. It's so surprising mind you that one can do a literal double take as to whether or not you're actually with her causing you to think it may possibly be a dream because if it is you don't ever want to be woken up. Thinking about it, there are plenty of guys who have this mindset that they aren't the dream come true for their significant other knowing full well in their woman's eyes he is. Let me tell you something ladies, if you ever notice your bf/husband look at you and has a completely dumbfounded look on his face he's wondering why you're even with him or why you chose him.

Let me ask you this question to you ladies out there, have you ever been at a crossroads within your own heart when it came to making the decision between a guy who can provide you with everything you ever wanted in life or a guy who can only try to give you all that he can provide knowing its not going to be easy whatsoever? It's a sad state of affairs when women choose a luxurious life only to find themselves absolutely miserable. Essentially, if you chose the guy who isn't a miracle worker, doesn't make your dreams come true right away, or doesn't have the capacity to be the key that opens every door BUT is able to give you something special to hold on to where you're experience absolute true happiness then you made the right decision.

In retrospect, women will find love/true love for that matter in a guy who is oftentimes the least likely to be the man of their dreams. For the most part, it's a guy who at first may not think of himself as someone who is the quintessential knight in shining armor or doesn't feel he can measure up in a physical way to other guys out there. Yet, despite that he makes it up with a sense of morality, genuine honesty, being real instead of being/acting like someone else, and having a big heart, which is rare for women to even find these days. In the end ladies, remember there are guys out there who aren't like the rest and when you meet him, he'll say to you I may not be what you expected but I'll always be the man in love with you, which is a song by actor/country singing legend George Strait.

THAT'S REAL

May 22, 2010

Someone once said, ~Real love hurts, real love makes you totally open and vulnerable. Real love will take you far behind yourself, and therefore real love will devastate you. If love doesn't shatter you, you will not know love.~ Without a doubt, real love is something every person like myself is anxiously waiting for. For a certain number of people they are currently experiencing the euphoric bliss of real love that has taken them to places within that is remarkably amazing and too few people have traveled, so to speak. However, for some people they've experienced the utter misfortune of fake love that hasn't taken their heart anywhere except to an all too familiar place where broken hearts and shattered dreams of true happiness reside.

If you think about it, when it comes to the aspect of real love it gives a person the opportunity to willingly put their heart on the line for each other by opening themselves up not just in the physical sense, but in the emotional sense as well. It's a tough situation indeed to open up emotionally as you're allowing yourself to be seen as the person you truly are rather than the person you're not. Thinking about it, you can most definitely close yourself off to certain aspects of your life that you're afraid to share because it's just either too embarrassing or too painful to talk about. Let me tell you something, real love sits right by your side crying/laughing along with you and not at/because of you, whereby making the relationship between the two of you a much stronger dynamic

As said before, experiencing the misfortune of fake love leaves you for all intents and purposes stranded alone in the middle of nowhere within your heart. It's a sad state of affairs for those who have been in a past relationship where what they thought was real love was in fact just a mere illusion on his/her part. Essentially, love is capable of being real if two people work hard in order to make it that way. However, when you have a guy/girl who acts as if its real, doesn't put in the work, and only in the relationship for superficial reasons then it makes the reality of being used than loved all the more devastating, which is seemingly prevalent these days with the rise of the break up rate in couples not only in the dating world, but also in the marriage world in regards to divorce.

Let me ask you this question to those who are in significant relationships, has there ever been a situation that both of you experienced where it tested how real your love for each is? Oftentimes, one of the biggest challenges in a relationship to face is having arguments that test you're willingness to actually listen to each other in order to work through/solve the particular problem or just sit there acting like you're listening but all you're doing is thinking up what're going to say to make your point known, which quite frankly makes matters even worse. Hey, when you really love someone, you take the time to sit down, opening both your heart and your ears to listen, taking everything that he/she has to say because if both aren't open then you're not communicating properly.

In retrospect, the difference between real love and fake love boils down to many things but for me personally it's about one thing... not being selfish. You know you have a love that is truly real when the sincerity of one's thoughts and actions are shown from his/her own heart in an unselfish way for one's significant other. In the end, love isn't some make believe fairy tale fantasy that always has relationships ending happy ever after because that's not real; but if you accept the harsh reality of how seriously hard relationship can be and how it takes constant hard work in being able to open up, being fully present, and communicate with each other when arguments occur whereby making the story love or true love for that matter so special then my friend I say to you now that's real.

LET IT FLY

May 28, 2010

William Wordsworth once said, ~ Fill your paper with the breathings of your heart.~ In some aspect, love is like a paper airplane and there is most definitely a process you go through in order to create something you want to see fly to the point where it never falls to the ground. Thinking about it, the paper is a representation of our own heart as each fold made in regard to our own thoughts, feelings, and emotions helps in always keeping our hopes of true happiness up in the air. Essentially, there is a sense of fun, joy, and excitement in the creation of a paper airplane as a kid back in the day. For its that same sense of fun, joy, and excitement can also be found in creating something absolutely special involving matters of love/true love.

If you think about it, making a paper airplane isn't as easy as it looks, as each fold you make determines how much detail and effort you put into something so worthwhile it lasts a lifetime. In a way, that is what every person wants when it comes to being in a strong, loving relationship as the folds of trust, contentment, hope, faith, communication, respect, honesty, intimacy, security, patience, caring, tenderness, understanding, etc. are considered key steps in creating in all intents and purposes an aerodynamic, smooth flowing bond. For it's a tough situation indeed to try to experience love in which a guy/girl is able to correctly fold areas of his/her/your heart that either have special meaning or are sensitive in nature.

Without a doubt, there are men and women out there whose hearts have become crinkled beyond recognition because of being folded and unfolded so many times over. It's a sad state of affairs for any person to find themselves constantly starting over again, unfolding their heart or flattening it out after it's been crinkled/ crumpled up and tossed in the garbage, in a manner of speaking.

For some, most, or all people know all too well the feeling as if their heart will not be able to take much more "abuse" before it ends up tearing up or quite possibly has already torn up. Let me tell you something ladies and gents, the human heart can endure the pain of utter heartbreak as it just takes the tape of time and close friends to help mend/heal your heart.

Let me ask you this question to those who made paper airplanes as a kid, did you ever try to add or be fancy with it by doing something such as making two small tears on either side of the back of the wings to create flaps? Here's another question, did it actually help any? Oftentimes, when it comes to love there comes a point where a person will try to add on/be fancy by tearing or should I say enhancing the relationship in order to make it better but ends up making it worse to the point where you're left not only holding part of the relationship in one's hand that's been unfortunately torn off, but also a part one's heart that has been torn off as well. Hey, what it comes down to is knowing that you don't need to make any changes whatsoever to love because it's perfect just the way it is.

In retrospect, each one of us wants to experience a type of love/ true love where you don't want to be in a relationship that's haphazardly put together to where you end up with uneven folds leading to one wing larger than the other or whatever the case may be. You see, it takes a step by step process involving folding areas of you heart that are what's most important in a relationship all-the-while keeping the creases of your thoughts, feelings and emotions nicely aligned that when you meet/find someone who is also taking that same step by step process you know he's/she's genuinely real, which is rare to find these days. In the end, I say to those of you who are currently creating/have created together a paper airplane of love in which both of you are breathing new life into each other's heart let it fly.

A NEVERENDING STORY

May 29, 2010

Someone once said, ~True Love. It isn't some insignificant passing thing. It's lasting and it's solid-it doesn't change just because things around you do. It doesn't waver or disappear just because you're faced with problems. It doesn't fade away just because you get older. Its fixed, its sold, and it doesn't change-its the bright point of someone's life, brings them back on their path in life when they're lost Its endless.~ Without a doubt, we all want to experience our own story of true love that is able to stand the test of time and for a certain number of people they're fortunate enough to be living it. For it is indeed a story like any other of patience, triumph, disappointment, tragedy, moments of frustrations, times of regret, sadness, joy, and everything in between that make finally experiencing true happiness such an absolute epic tale, so to speak.

As said before, we all want to experience our own story of true love that we can essentially pass on from generation to generation that is most definitely worth hearing. I think it would be safe to say we've all heard the stories told by our grandparents/great grandparents who truly knew the meaning of what true love is all about to the point where it can bring tears to your eyes. It's when you sit and listen to them telling their story you see the light shining brightly in both their eyes as they not only continue to look lovingly at each other with the same burning passion they have for one another when they first met, but are able to still see the young/ man woman they fell in love with 50, 60, 70 years ago. Let me tell you something, it's those kinds of heartwarming stories of true love you don't get to hear all too often and I'm sad to say are very rarely heard these days.

If you think about it, when it comes to the epic tale that is true love, problems will be encountered, which is to be expected in any relationship. Yet, its how those particular problems are handled that determine whether or no the both of you want to continue the story knowing the work the both of you put into the relationship wasn't an easy process by any means whatsoever or end up just another sad story of a broken relationship where it's easier now a days for two people to just walk away/give up/quit than to get to the root of the problem in a relationship. What it primarily comes down to is pride and oftentimes you have to set aside one's foolish, selfish pride and deal with the unresolved issues possibly involving fears/insecurities face to face for the sake of the relationship or the story you've imagined wanting for so long within your heart will never come true.

Let me ask you this question to those in a significant relationship: how many of you truly know that the story your bf/husband/wife/gf are writing together will always be filled with endless amounts of happiness and excitement? In all honesty, you can't know and that is what makes true love such a tremendous story as the both of you will find ourselves in situations that are so unbelievable you can't help but laugh. A sense of humor is vital because it helps you get past the seriousness of life that tends to throw at you from time to time to where it leaves both of you so stressed out you want to kill each other. Thinking about it though, to look back at past chapters of your lives together with your forever best friend and being able to laugh through it all, the good and most certainly the bad, makes life worth living don't you think?

In retrospect, stories of true love never change but it's the people and circumstances concerning those people that do. It's solid and can completely change a person's life to where it can metaphorically erase chapters of past heartbreak. Granted, each of us have been in the past or currently finding ourselves lost because of the pain leaving us wandering around within our own heart but through faith, hope, the love of friends/family and fervent prayer to God you'll be guided on the right path to true love. Stories of true happiness. always have a beginning, a middle, and an end, which is a formula that has always worked. In the end though, when it comes to your own personal story there will always be a beginning, a middle, but no ending for you because the epic tale of true love you're currently writing together/hope to write someday with someone special is/will be a neverending story.

FALLING SLOWLY
June 3, 2010

Robert Frost once said, ~Two such as you with such a master speed cannot be parted nor be swept away from one another once you are agreed that life is only life forevermore together wing to wing and oar to oar.~ If you think about it, when it comes to matters of the heart a person can either fall instantly in love or gradually have it happen over a period of time that may take months or even years. It's a fascinating situation indeed to observe both sides of the spectrum in which a number of people experience an instant connection whereas for others the connection was/is a gradual process towards true happiness. Essentially, it causes those who are single like myself to think/wonder if one should live by the mentality that life is too short to think/wonder in regard to love or is it truly worth taking your time for.

Without a doubt, the feelings and emotions you have for a certain someone, even one you haven't met yet can most definitely stir within your heart. For it's that person who is an absolute unknown but as soon as you meet him/her you somehow have that feeling you've known that person for quite some time. Oftentimes, there are moments where you do meet someone causing all your emotions and feelings to quickly rise to the surface of your heart to the point where your thoughts become actual words said out loud to yourself, which has possibly happened to every person in the past or is currently happening for a many number people as we speak. Thinking about it, it's those words that can cause you to react to where you can either find yourself walking a slow, steady pace towards true happiness or run fast and run the risk of making a total fool of yourself.

As said before, there are people out there who have the mentality that life is too short in regard to love so you have to make it happen and create that connection. However, the connection that is quickly established one moment can unfortunately be broken the next because there wasn't anything solid to hold on to, in a manner of speaking. It's a sad state of affairs when guys/girls don't have any sense or realization of who they're with because they are so focused on both the physical, as well as the superficial aspect of the relationship leading to the person's whole mood to change. For a number of people, they know all too well the fast downward spiral of suffering utter heartbreak and then experiencing the slow painful process of completely erasing any sign of him/her not only from their mind, but their heart as well.

Let me ask you this question to those who have suffered a painful heartbreak, when you eventually found love again that is genuinely and honestly real was it instant or did you take time for it to happen? In some aspect, one's heart is like a ship and when you go through a hard breakup/divorce your heart, in a sense, sinks fast or slow into the dark depths of sadness depending on the relationship itself with the guy/girl in question. For the hearts of a number people are metaphorically located at the bottom of the ocean or currently sinking because of being hit by a cannonball that they didn't see coming. You see, ladies and gentlemen, there comes a point where your heart will eventually see the light of day or stop sinking as you meet someone who repairs the hole within your heart causing your hopes of a brighter and hopeful future to slowly rise once again.

In retrospect, love/true love is something that not too many people have been lucky to find because of unfortunate experiences they've had in the past. For some, most or all people they feel as if they're seemingly on the fast track to heartbreak despite taking it slow with that supposedly special guy/girl. In a way, it's like they're always on the losing end of the battle and are so sick and tired of it that just once he/she would like to know the feeling of finally being able to win one for a change, which is an experience that from what I hear/have been told by friends who have been through it is worthwhile. In the end, I know I will fall in love someday and when it comes to the speed at which it happens, I hope it doesn't have me falling fast but rather falling slowly, which is a song from the movie Once by Glen Hansford and Marketa Irglova that reflects this thought.

POWER TO THE GEEK

June 11, 2010

What is a geek? By definition it's a term that refers to an individual who has a fair amount of knowledge when it pertains to certain things like music, video games, comic books, Japanese anime, books, television, movies, etc. Without a doubt, every person is considered a geek and whether you don't want to admit it to yourself to the point of continually denying it, don't because you are in fact one. You see, geeks are everywhere, and it may be a surprising situation indeed to know there are those who don't necessarily fit the typical geek persona, whereby breaking a longstanding misconception. For a number of people like myself have embraced their geeky side and quite frankly are not ashamed in revealing the extent of our geekiness.

Let me ask you this question, how many of you randomly quote movie line on any given day at work with your co-workers, with friends, and/or with family? I think it would be safe to say we all do it to the point where friends/family/co-workers join in and try to stump each other, especially if its about one particular move. Thinking about it, there are so many quotes from well-known movies that geeks like myself can say certain ones off the top of our heads without even thinking about it. Monty Python and the Holy Grail, Star Wars, Spaceballs, Napoleon Dynamite, Airplane, Airplane 2, Happy Gilmore, any Arnold Schwarzenegger movie, Braveheart, 300, The Princess Bride, etc. are just a handful of movies that geeks everywhere not only quote by heart but enjoy quoting them to no end.

If you think about it, there comes a point as a geek where reminiscing about old tv shows you grew up with back in the day amongst friends is considered an enjoyable experience. If you grew up in the 80's/90's, shows like The A-Team, Knight Rider, Airwolf, Streethawk,

The Highwayman, Simon and Simon, T.J. Hooker, Quincy, Columbo, Magnum P.I., The Fall Guy, Starman, Alien Nation, Remington Steele, Hart to Hart, Scarecrow and Ms. King, Miami Vice, Perfect Strangers, Quantum Leap, Hardcastle and McCormick, Moonlighting, Spencer For Hire, etc. were considered absolute entertaining. For instance, in what show can the bad guys not get shot but instead have a trail of bullets chasing them in The A-Team, which was awesome when you're a kid but as an adult it's considered pretty lame.

For the question can be asked, when it comes to your favorite celebrities/singers who do you think is considered a geek? The answers may surprise you. Essentially, every guy fell in love with or had a crush on Winnie Cooper aka Danica McKeller from the Wonder Years. She not only considers herself a geek but also America's Best Dance Crew's Layla Kayleigh who is an avid gamer. Who else is an avid gamer? Actor Robin Williams and Chuck stars Zack Levi and Josh Gomez. Robert Downey Jr, is a comic book geek. Queen Guitarist Brian May is a rock & roll geek who was appointed Chancellor of Liverpool at John Moore University. Mr. Fast and the Furious Vin Diesel, whose real name is Mark Vincent, is a down and out Dungeons and Dragons geek, which may be surprising to many of fans of his out there.

In retrospect, geeks are cool and always have been. In the past, they would be described as a person with bad hair, always sweaty, and uncoordinated. Not now as the stereotype has changed immensely. It's not how much knowledge that we have when it comes to certain things like quoting countless movie lines off the top of your head or reading all the Harry Potter/Twilight book series, it's how much you enjoy sharing it with others even though they may not share your enthusiasm. Hey, geeks are not just considered cool but from what I've read they are also considered attractive, as well as sexy qualities for a certain number of women. Question, where are these women? In the end, I say to my fellow geeks all around the word power to the geek.

LIVE LONG AND PROSPER

June 15, 2010

Italian film actress Sophia Loren once said, ~There is a fountain and youth: it is your mind, your talents, the creativity you bring to your life and the lives of people you love. When you learn to tap this source, you will truly have defeated age.~ Let me ask you this question, how many of you are looking forward to your golden years spending it not only alongside your significant other, but with children/grandchildren, as well as your partners in crime otherwise known as your gal pas/best buds. For it's indeed an interesting situation indeed to imagine ourselves in our formative years causing each one of us to wonder if we're still going to be the same person and do the same things like we used to back in the day when we were younger.

Without a doubt, people who are in their 30's like myself tend to complain or should I say joke around about how we're getting old. All joking aside though, the fact we've made it to/past our 30's is a testament that we've thankfully moved from our life is unfair hormone ridden drama filled searching for our own identity teenage years past our early 20's where one has the study hard/ party even harder mentality to reaching the thirty something stage of life, which for most women is not a pleasant age to reach. In any case, for those of us who are in our 30's you can't help but look back and find humor in the fact that when we were younger, we used to make fun of the so called "old people" and now we've become the "old people" that these young kids today make fun of.

As said before in the quote above, there is a fountain of youth and it comes from our mind, talents, and the creativity you bring not only to your life but to other people's lives as well. Thinking about it, even though a person grows older physically the mind can still be sharp as ever as he or she creates something so spectacular/

breathtaking/awe inspiring/ that it touches your heart and soul. Whether its in written form like a book/poem/essay or something made with one's hands like a painting/sculpture/drawing you are simply amazed at not only the imagination coming from within the mind of someone older, but the absolutely creativity in which it's created causes you to have even greater respect for those who paved the way for us.

For the question can be asked to many of you out there, have you thought about what it's going to be like when you reach your golden age whenever that may be for you? If you think about it, there are certain advantages to getting older as you can get the senior discount whenever you eat out and you practically say anything you want that comes to mind because you deserve the right to speak your mind. For us guys, we can flirt/make jokes with young women we meet, possibly stealing a dance with them and the same can be said for women as well with strapping young men who they just want to pinch their cheeks. What it comes down to is that age doesn't have to define you when you reach the latter part of your life and if you can still think it/say it/do it then go right ahead.

On Saturday May 8th, 2010, Betty White became the oldest person at the age of 88 to ever host the sketch comedy show Saturday Night Live giving the show itself its highest ratings ever in the history of their show. Fans made it their mission to have her as host started through Facebook when she did a Snickers football commercial that also involved another ageless actor 89-year-old Abe Vidgoda...yes, he's still alive. The entire show was absolutely hilarious to the point where the SNL cast sang The Golden Girls theme song in honor of her, but she flipped it turning it into thrash metal. In the end, you're only as old as you feel and though at times, I feel like Betty White's age I hope, along with many of you, to live long and prosper as she has with the vibrancy/sense of humor/sharp wit that she hasn't lost throughout the years.

A THIN LINE

June 21, 2010

Alice Walker once said, ~Love is big. Love can hold anger, love can hold pain, love can even hold hatred. It's all about love.~ Without a doubt, a person can have a love/hate relationship when it comes to matters of the heart, especially for those who are living the single life. For it can be a joyful and exciting situation indeed for those who would like nothing more than to experience the euphoric bliss of true happiness with a guy/girl who brings out all the right emotions within your heart to the point where you always have a smile on your face. However, when heartbreak occurs, you're left to deal with all the wrong, unwanted emotions that are considerably dark in nature causing you to express more than just anger and hatred towards a past relationship.

Let me ask you this question to those who are single or have recently become single, if you were given the opportunity to talk no holds barred about the love/hate relationship you have with matters of the heart would you be able to keep your emotions in check? I think it would be safe to say that for the most part one is able to keep their composure in the beginning but will find it increasingly difficult to keep it subdued before emotions run rampant. Frustration, disappointment, irritation, annoyed, bitterness, sadness, confusion, anger, hatred, regret, etc. are a handful of emotions that can well up within your heart reflecting back on a past relationship in which the guy/girl betrayed your trust to where your whole outlook on love progressively changes.

If you think about it, when it comes to the love/hate relationship in regards to matters of the heart involving getting your heart broken you can end up being angry at yourself. Why? You see, even though the cause of the broken relationship isn't your fault, a part you can metaphorically beat yourself up to the point of asking questions that pertain to the who, what, when, how and why's concerning the emotional pain of love, but the mental pain as well. Who will I be able to trust with my heart again? What am I doing wrong? When will I experience the happiness I deserve? How do I end up picking the wrong guys/girls? Why do I set myself up for getting hurt? It's those questions and much more that can lead you to the brink of insanity if you dwell on it.

For the question can be asked to those who have had a painful breakup, how many of you have a love/hate relationship with your ex? Thinking about it, there is a certain amount of hatred you have for the guy/girl you loved with all your heart in the past and yet part of you may possibly love/care about him/her. It's natural to feel that way because on one hand you experienced great memories with someone who made you smile inside and out but on the other hand, it's that same person who caused you great pain, frustration, stress, sadness etc. Essentially, there comes a point where the decision is made to finally break ties with him/her in order to move on from the past and focus on the present leading to a better future for yourself filled with happiness and if kids are involved for them too.

In retrospect, there's always going to be a love/hate relationship for those who are sarcastically cynical people such as myself who hope to fall in love someday but the hope, we have tended to have, has its ups and downs causing our enthusiasm to be considerably affected as well. It can be hard to exude a positive outlook about the possibility of experiencing true happiness for yourself when you're inundated with news of infidelity combined with friends who are in happy relationships. It can get annoying, which causes you to want to bang your head against a hard surface. In the end, there's a thin line that separates the love/hate relationship with matters of the heart that can initially have us teeter tottering on the side of true happiness or the side of absolute misery, which begs the question what side are you mostly on?

SILENCE IS GOLDEN

June 29, 2010

Erma Bombeck once said, ~Some emotions don't make a lot of noise. It's hard to hear pride. Caring is real faint-like a heartbeat. And pure love-why some days it's so quiet, you don't even know it's there.~ If you think about it, when it comes to matters of the heart every person wants to experience a sense of peaceful silence with someone special and for a many number of people they're experiencing it right now as we speak. It's a type of peaceful silence in which the serene sounds of true happiness aren't necessarily expressed out loud but rather in a quiet, relaxed manner. For it's a calming situation indeed to be in a truly happy relationship where so many emotions/feelings sound off like silent fireworks within your heart that you alone can hear loud and clear.

As said before, there is a sense of peaceful silence when experiencing true happiness to the point where a soft distinct sound is heart that can initially describe the feelings/emotions you have for a potential and/or significant other without even saying a single word. A simple soft sigh may not make a lot of noise but if it's followed by a smile, it can most definitely get your attention. You see, a simple soft sigh can express out loud emotions/feelings of contentment, happiness, joy, caring, tenderness, commitment, trust, respect, excitement, trust, honesty, etc. Thinking about it, it's those particular silent sounds of love/true love that considerably drowns out the noisy drama to where it's no longer heard, which is what one wants in a relationship.

Without a doubt, when drama happens it does make a lot of noise causing a person to be unable to hear, so to speak, not only emotionally but mentally as well. It's a sad state of affairs when you're not able to think straight or describe what you're feeling because of how noisy the drama is, especially if it involves heartbreak causing you to let out a sigh. Essentially, it's that sigh in which emotions/feelings such as confusion, frustration, bitterness, utter contempt, disappointment, anger, apprehension, indecisiveness, doubt, worry, sadness, etc. can clearly be heard by others. I think it would be safe to say that for those who are dealing with issues involving heartbreak, your head, as well as heart are filled with so much noisy negativity that it's difficult to keep a smile on your face.

Let me ask you this question to those who are in a significant relationship, how many of you are enjoying the silence of love/true love with a guy/girl who gives you peace both mentally and emotionally. Oftentimes, being able to be together alone and doing something like sitting on the beach watching a sunset are considered treasured unspoken moments of silence. For a certain number of people, the inner solace that is shared together with their best friend even when separated from him/her shows that their presence is always felt within their heart no matter where he/she is. Let me tell you something, to have that strong peaceful connection with someone where instead of hearing the noise of drama within your heart you hear the steady, tranquil sound of two hearts beating as one.

Someone said, ~Life is so ironic to understand fully. It takes sadness to know what happiness is. Noise to distinguish silence and a broken heart to find true love.~ In retrospect, to those who have found/met the person who makes him/her happy, they have God to thank for being able to keep them from not letting the soothing sound of hope and faith be drowned out by the oftentimes loud sound of sarcastic, cynicism that tends to ring very loudly in the ears of those of us such as myself who would like someday hear what true happiness actually sounds like. In the end, silence is golden for those lucky enough to have a kind of love that continually makes noise, in a good way of course, in the quiet comfort of each other's heart.

I PROMISE

July 10, 2010

Percy Bysshe Shelley once said, ~Love is free; to promise forever to love the same woman is no less absurd than to promise to believe the same creed; such a vow in both cases excludes us from all inquiry.~ Without a doubt, love is indeed free and we all have the right to be with someone who we generally like being around or interested in. As a guy, it's in our nature to enjoy the company of a beautiful woman or several beautiful women for that matter who can most definitely visually capture our attention. Yet, it only takes one woman who can't just visually capture our attention, but can be able to also emotionally and mentally capture the attention as well for many years, which is what guys like myself want as we promise our heart to her.

If you think about it, to make that promise to be totally committed to one woman for the rest of your life can actually scare a many number of guys to the point where they freak out, but for others it's something that they look forward to. It's rare but not uncommon for a woman to meet a guy who can actually be and is able to stay faithful to her to where commitment, trust, respect, dignity, honesty, hope, joy, excitement, honor, loyalty, appreciation, etc. continue to stay unbroken within her heart. For its a guy who knows what he wants in a relationship, doesn't play mind games, isn't narcissistic, doesn't drag her down in order to build himself up, thinks about her needs over his, doesn't treat a woman with disrespect because he knows the value of a truly great partner in crime in front of him.

As said before in the quote above concerning promising forever to love the same woman has become a rarity these days with acts of infidelity running rampant to where the list of promises verbally made by the guy just become hollow words that no longer have meaning. It's a sad state of affairs when a woman doesn't have the capacity to trust the promises made due to past heartbreaks. The promise to make her his first priority in his life; promising to never make her feel alone in the world because he will always be there right by her side; to promise to not ever intentionally hurt her by his words or actions; promising to never make her look like a fool; promising to be always be appreciative and not take her for granted, etc. are just a number promises that were unfortunately broken by a past relationship.

Let me ask you this question to all you ladies, how many of you have a guy or hope to have a guy in your life who has been/is able to keep the promises made to you? I think it would be safe to say that many women are tired of believing one promise after another only to find themselves once again being hurt, let down, and/or fooled into thinking he's different from all the rest. Thinking about it, every woman deserves to hear promises from a guy that will never be broken or sound empty, in a manner of speak, because he is true to his word unlike past relationships Let me tell you something ladies who are single, the guy you've been waiting for is out there somewhere and when he steps into your life all the promises you've wanted for your heart will assuredly be fulfilled.

Robert M. Hensel said, ~Build your world around me, and promise to never let me go, and if ever there comes a time it may seem crowded, may we expand so love may grow.~ In retrospect, a guy who can make the promise to be with one woman for the rest of his life and prove it when so many temptations are placed in front of him shows how much he truly loves her. For it's a guy who can open his eyes to see a life filled with true happiness built on love that is permanent rather than temporary to where he can look back and say to her thank you. Guys like myself hope to one day be lucky enough to meet that special someone. In the end, I won't let her go and she can look me in the eyes, truly believing the two words that tend to not be taken seriously these days...I promise.

SAFE WITH ME

July 18, 2010

Carl S. Avery once said, ~Love enables you to put your deepest feelings and fears in the palm of your partner's hand, knowing they will be handled with care.~ As said before, love enables you to put your deepest feelings and fears in the palm of your partner's hand. Thinking about it, when it comes to love or true love for that matter it can be quite difficult to place your heart, so to speak, in someone else's hand even if that particular guy/girl has the same mutual feelings and fears as you do. For it's a tough situation indeed to just hand over what each of us metaphorically hold tightly within our heart because in the back of our mind there is the possibility it won't be handled carefully to where you're left holding the crushed remnants of what was true happiness.

Without a doubt, one of the most important aspects of a loving relationship is to have someone who can most definitely carefully handle with care in their capable hands all that you're thinking, feelings, and are sorely afraid of in matters of the heart. Trust contentment, honesty, caring, respect, commitment, understanding, happiness, faith, honor, loyalty, worry, doubt, fear, frustration, disappointment, anger, bitterness, confusion, etc. are just a number of things that a person who is in love can at time be weary of placing in a potential and/or significant other's hand. Why? Essentially, past relationship experience has taught him/her that when it comes to opening yourself up emotionally, mentally, and physically their heart will end up being crushed in the palm of a guy's/girl's hand.

If you think about it, there are those out there who know all too well of having their feelings and fears along with the emotions associated with it crushed in the hand of a past relationship. Its a sad state of affairs when women, as well as men, feel as if their entire being has been crushed to the point where all that you shared with him/her is completely thrown back at your face. In a sense, having those crushed remnants of what was in your heart thrown back at you can be, in some aspect, like a hard slap right across the face with the same hand that you thought would keep your heart safe leaving you to deal with the sting of utter heartbreak. Let me tell you something, for those who have felt or are currently feeling it the sting will go away as it just takes time.

Let me ask you this questions to those who are in a potential and/or significant relationship, have you placed your heart in his/her hand and fully entrusted him/her to take care of it knowing that he/she may not only crush it but drop it on the ground in order to stomp all over it but chooses not to? Hey, it's what relationships are all about as the concerns you have within your heart will always be taken care of as best they possibly can and will not be intentionally dropped by your partner in order to hurt you. What it primarily comes down to is finding/meeting the right guy/girl who will hold your heart in the safety of their hand and in turn he/she will entrust his/her heart in yours, which is considerably rare to find because of how incredibly selfish certain guys/girls are these days.

In retrospect, every person wants to feel secure in the fact that their feelings and fears will always be in good hands with someone they love. Unfortunately, that isn't the case as there are people out there who don't know how to hold a person's heart causing one to constantly be at the ready in case, they have to catch what slips through their fingers, which can be mentally and emotionally tiring. For a certain number of people, they have found/are finding themselves in this type of situation where they don't feel that innate security in a partner who is able to safely hold their feelings and fears within heart and never drop it. In the end, to those of you who are single you'll eventually meet your trusted partner who'll reach out saying to you put your heart in my hand and it will be safe with me.

ONE CRAZY RIDE

July 24, 2010

Someone once said, ~Life is like riding a bull. You get bucked off and climb right back on and do it again.~ As said before, life is like riding a bull and on a seemingly daily basis we find ourselves strapping tightly in as we experience situations both known and unknown that can not only metaphorically throw us around like a rag doll, but also test how long we can emotionally, mentally, physically, as well as spiritually endure the ride, so to speak. You see, every time we open our eyes and step into the bull riding arena of life we're locked in the chute ready to face with absolute focus, courage, and determination challenges that are tough and instead of being given 8 seconds to see what each of us are made of we're given an unlimited amount of time.

Without a doubt, when it comes to riding a bull, it takes a lot more mental rather than physical strength to keep yourself from being thrown off such a huge beast. Thinking about it, life is truly considered one huge beast and it can most definitely be a challenge to take on what is considered a behemoth of an unknown. For it can be a scary situation indeed to face the metaphorical bull each of us is riding in order to achieve or should I say conquer our own individual hopes, dreams, goals, as well as possible achievements you personally set for yourself. What it primarily comes down to is having a firm, tight grasp on what you want to do and where you want to be all the while making the smartest decisions possible.

If you think about it, one of the most dangerous aspects of riding a bull is getting your hand caught in the rope or being thrown off and getting injured from being trampled on. I think it would be safe to say, an aspect of life that is not so much dangerous but rather annoying is being caught up in the rope of drama and as much as you want to walk away cleanly without getting hurt you unfortunately do. For a certain number of people know all too well what it's like to in all intents and purposes be thrown off a relationship and then suddenly find themselves not only being emotionally stomped/trampled on, but also being gored by the horns of betrayal leaving them to deal with the pain that can either take weeks, months or even years to recover from.

Let me ask you this question to those who are avid watchers of bull riding competitions, what is the most important thing to have when attempting to ride a bull? If you said a team to back you up, you're absolutely right. Oftentimes, life tries to do everything in its power to dismount/throw/buck us off and leaves you feeling absolutely defeated. However, it's nice to know each of us has a supportive team to back us up in the form of friends/family who jump in and are able to be an awesome distraction from all that is going on in your life. For it's those same people who are able to catch us when we fall, help us back to our feet, brush the dirt off our clothes, and provide us with words of encouragement so we can get back on the bull once again.

In retrospect, every person has heard the saying you got to take the bull by the horns and for some, most or all people they 're doing just that. Essentially, that is what life is all about as you encounter situations that will have you shaking in your proverbial boots because of the sheer size of the "bulls" we're facing, but we get on any way in order to take control of it and not the other way around showing that we have the confidence, determination, courage, and faith in God to see us through to the end. Marriage, friendship, work, etc. are just a number of things that many of us are staying on top of as best as we possibly can knowing full well, we'll fall over to the ground every now and then. In the end, when you're on the bull of life you know you're going to be in for one crazy ride after another.

LEAD BY EXAMPLE

August 3, 2010

Tim Foley once said, ~The most important role models in people's lives, it seems, aren't superstars or household names. They're everyday people who quietly set examples for you - coaches, teachers, parents. People about who you say to yourself perhaps not even consciously, 'I want to be like that."~ Let me ask you this question, when it comes to having role models who did you look up to when you were growing up as a kid and now as an adult? For it's rare these days to have role models who don't end up constantly letting you down but they're out there. I think many would agree that by having a positive role model in your life whether it be male or female can help you not only grow and gain perspective about yourself, but also the world around you.

Without a doubt, each of us is given the choice to choose who we not only want to look up and admire, but also aspire to be. Thinking about it, the decisions we make in the way we act, think, see, speak, and/ or dress are oftentimes instilled in us by our parental units, mainly fathers who can most definitely be a positive influence as we're provided with sage wisdom that is truly beneficial for us. For it's a tough situation indeed for any single mom out there who hopes to one day meet a guy who will be able to be that strong positive male role model in their child's life, especially if he she has a son or sons. Let me tell you something, there are many young men out there who are sorely lacking the positive male presence in their lives and yet for some guys they've turned out okay without one.

As said before, the most important role models aren't superstars or household names because a true role model has the ability to make you want to become a better person and not the other way around. Lindsey Lohan, Paris Hilton, Tiger Woods, Mel Gibson,

Jesse James, etc. are just handful of people who you wouldn't want to necessarily look up to as they have certainly gotten themselves into trouble to the point where they served time in jail or suffered public scrutiny and yet you're able to learn what not to do by the mistakes they have made. Hey, in their own right Tiger Woods and Jesse James are great at what they do in their respective fields to where you want to learn from them, but you wouldn't want to go to them for advice on how to have a successful, happy marriage.

If you think about it, there are people out there who don't even know they are role models, and it makes you proud to know they are making a difference. Elmer Writman may not be a well-known name, but he is considered a role model to the many kids in his neighborhood. Elmer would take long walks and would always be accompanied by kids who simply enjoyed him talking about world events, chemistry, and the importance of staying active. He taught countless kids in his neighborhood that not only thoughts and opinions mattered, but he also taught them to think more broadly and treat each other with dignity, as well as respect. For the question can be asked, do you know a person like this living in your neighborhood?

In retrospect, when it comes to role models, they have to be the type of person who is able to affect us in a way that helps us realize how fortunate we are to have him/her/them in our lives. In addition to that they teach you the value of respect, integrity, honor, kindness, morals, honesty, and true friendship. It's a person or persons who has helped or continues to help shape, challenge, support, and encourage you when you need it the most. As scary as it is, each of us are role models causing us to be careful at what we say or do especially around young kids because they are very impressionable and can be easily influenced. In the end, a great role model is someone who tries his/her best to lead by example and even though mistakes are made he/she does their best to fix them.

MY MARK (600TH YODAISM)

August 8, 2010

Someone once said, ~Leave your mark where others can only dream of going.~ Without a doubt, a person can oftentimes wonder what kind of impact/mark you're meant to or want to leave in this world. For it's a tough situation indeed to stamp out a life you can look back on and be absolutely proud of but you do your very best. I think many would agree that each one of us would most definitely want to set out to achieve our hopes, goals, and dreams all-the-while meeting people who have helped support and encourage you all the way. Thinking about it, as we all go about our individual lives you find yourself asking whether or not you've been able to leave a lasting impression to where others may quite possibly become better people for knowing you.

If you think about it, being able to be a giver rather than a taker is considered one of the ways to leave your mark on this world. When I say giver, I don't necessarily mean starting charities for important causes. Instead, be a giver of your time as you're there for people in your life who can always count on you to be there for them when they need it the most. An encourage word, a shoulder to cry on, words of wisdom/advice, much needed prayers, sharing the word of God, etc. are just a handful of ways where you can most definitely achieve a positive lasting impression to where your presence will not only be felt in their heart but also be a long lasting memory that will never fade away. So does anyone immediately come to mind for you?

As said before, you can find yourself asking whether or not you've been able to leave your mark in this world to the point where others may quite possibly become better people to know you. I think it would be safe to say we all would like to leave a mark in which the people who have gotten to know us didn't regret the friendship established for quite some time. You see, the mark of a great friendship is striving to be that guy/girl who brings you up instead of tearing/knocking you down emotionally, mentally, physically, and spiritually. Plus, when it comes to drama you try your best to avoid it rather than starting it causing unwanted conflict. In other words, you take the high road knowing full well you have the respect of many of your peers.

Let me ask you this question to those who are considered talented in their own right, do you think you will leave your mark with the abilities you have in a certain skill set in regard to what you enjoy or love doing? Music, singing, photography, entertainment, painting, poetry, drawing/sketching, books, etc. are just a number of things that on an individual basis are considerably good at because we believe in our abilities so much so that you're able to receive public recognition for your hard work. However, if you don't then it's okay because the simple joy of doing what you do will for all intents and purposes rub off on those around you. Let me tell you something, nothing is more gratifying than having some be inspired because of something you did and in turn they do it themselves.

This particular Yodaism marks my 600th and when I first started writing 14 years ago, I never really knew how mentally far I would be taking my thoughts. It truly befuddles my mind on how much I've written down in the past that I think are relevant subjects matters and how, in some ways, it has affected people who have read them to where they respond to what I've written by sharing info concerning their own personal life. Ultimately, it's those readers who end up writing themselves and its flattering to know you, in some way, had a part in it. In the end, to those who continue to read what I write I hope I have been able to somehow leave my mark on you and whether you've possibly become a better person for knowing me that is for you to decide.

CROSS THE STREAMS

August 16, 2010

Francois de La Rochefaucauld once said, ~True love is like a ghost, everyone talks of it, few have seen it.~ As said before, true love is like a ghost and its undeniable presence can in all intents and purposes haunt a person's heart, especially if their living the single life. For a certain number of people know all too well the feeling of being, in a sense, haunted by matters of the heart either emotionally and/or mentally to the point where it can be viewed as a pesky poltergeist or a harmless apparition. For it can most definitely be a tough and oftentimes annoying situation indeed to experience a type of paranormal activity going on within your heart to where it causes you to become a ghostbuster of sorts in order to investigate and/or capture it.

Without a doubt, when you're a so-called ghostbuster one of the main things you need in regard to equipment is a portable particle accelerator proton pack with a hand-held wand/particle thrower to capture a ghost. However, unlike the fictional proton pack/thrower that essentially drains the psychokinetic energy from a ghost, the proton pack known as the human heart is capable of giving energy/strength that is able to last more than just 5,000 years. For those who are living the single life, they would certainly want to find/meet someone who is capable of strengthening rather than draining all the love, honesty, faith, hope, contentment, happiness, caring, compassion, etc. within the energy cell of their heart.

If you think about it, when it comes to the ghost that is true love you know it does exist based on personal accounts of witnesses who have/are encountering it but in the course of one's own investigation it's difficult to know where it actually is. You see, for those who are still investigating like myself we're equipped with our own proverbial PKE meter that helps us locate where it may possibly be. Essentially, the PKE meter we all have in our possession is again our own heart and though it has the capability to detect where the possibility of true love is it's not always accurate. I think it would be safe to say there's a number of people who have tracked, in a manner of speaking, a relatively strong signal to a potentially worthwhile relationship but unfortunately it ended up being a weak signal.

Let me ask you this question to those who have watched the movie Ghostbusters, how many of you are familiar with the scene where Dr. Peter Venkman played by Bill Murray gets slimed by Slimer? Thinking about it, when you come face to face, in a manner of speaking, with the ghost that is true love you find yourself not only unable to move or think for that matter, but it also causes you to become afraid. Why? What it primarily comes down is the fear of being slimed or in this particular case becoming vulnerable as you open yourself up and the closer you get to true love the possibility of getting emotionally hurt leaves you with two options which is either to stand your ground facing it head on or back up/turn around in order to run as fast as you can.

In retrospect, we're all in some aspect the quintessential gatekeeper hoping to meet our very own keymaster or vice versa. In other words, each of us shouldn't be aimlessly wandering around constantly focusing on/looking for true love but instead just live our lives doing our own thing. However, when we need that much needed support when you're reminded of how lonely you are you know who you're gonna call which are your best buds/gal pals. If you just happen to meet that certain special someone who is truly genuine instead of someone who has Gozer-like qualities, then it's kudos to you. In the end, I say to those of you who have found your ghost busting partner for life I hope the two of you together continue to cross the streams.

WHAT SHE GETS
September 2, 2010

George Eliot once said, ~Oh the comfort, the inexpressible comfort of feeling safe with a person; have neither to weigh thoughts nor measure words, but pouring them all the right out, just as they are, chaff and grain together; certain that a faithful hand will take and sift them, keep what is worth keeping, and then with the breath of kindness blow the rest away.~ Without a doubt, its considered rare these days for any woman to be in a relationship with a guy who can most definitely be and stay faithful. For it's a tough situation indeed for them to truly experience absolute comfort within their heart when it pertains to a guy's faithfulness causing her to be doubtful as to whether they're any good ones left to which I simply yes...but I digress.

Let me ask you this question to you ladies who are in a potential and/or significant relationship, how many of you are certain that the man in your life is faithful to you? Essentially, what I'm asking doesn't just involve being/staying committed to you. You see, it's in the little things he does that show you he's there for the long haul and oftentimes he doesn't have to say anything but just be there even when you didn't ask him to. Ladies, think back to a particular moment in time when your boyfriend/husband surprised you when you least expected it concerning something important to you. For you to know he was there supporting you can be very touching to the point where it literally leaves you at a loss for words.

If you think about it, when it comes to the faithfulness of a guy a woman doesn't necessarily want the type who is talked about in fairy tales because in their minds they tend to not exist. Thinking about it further, it's those types of guys who are merely dreams conjured up from within their subconscious or a possibly a hopeful wish made at the bottom of a wishing well that has never really come true. It's a sad state of affairs when a woman gets everything she ever wanted from a guy when it comes to material objects but doesn't get what she truly wants from him. Communication, contentment, intimacy, emotional/mental security, faith, hope, honesty, trust, caring tenderness, etc. are the little things she most wants that undoubtedly make a big difference with her.

For the questions can be asked again to you ladies, how many times have you been able to count on your potential and/or significant other to be faithfully by your side when it matters most. Here's another question for you, are you able to count those times on just one hand, two hands, or are there so many it's difficult to keep track of? You see, to have a guy in her life who doesn't have her thoughts concerning him weighing her down because of his shady actions or cause her to over analyze every word he says that seem suspicious to where it brings her to the brink of insanity is an absolute for any woman to experience. For a certain number of women, they currently have that guy in their life while others want to know where he is and to that I say patience is a virtue.

In retrospect, in the faithfulness of love or true love for that matter every person wants to feel the comfort of feeling safe not just physically and mentally, but emotionally as well. Women, more so than guys, want to experience the gentle touch both literally and metaphorically knowing they are absolutely the one woman he is going to spend the rest of his days with. What it comes down to is the comfort of being uncomfortable as you completely open yourself to a guy who is quite possibly feeling the exact same as you are. In the end, for any single woman out who finds herself in a great relationship with a faithful guy because that's not only what she gets to her surprise but it's also what she deserves as well, which is a song by country legends Brooks and Dunn that reflect this thought.

NEVER RUNS OUT

October 28, 2010

Jules Renard once said, ~Love is like an hourglass with the heart filling up as the brain empties.~ As said before, love is like an hourglass with the sand representing our own thoughts, feelings, and emotions concerning matters of the heart. For its the sand in regard to love or true love for that matter can most definitely be viewed as either as a fleeting existence or absolutely never ending. Hey, its all a matter of one's own perspective as some people view the sand within the heart-mind hourglass as time running out in ever experiencing true happiness while others simply view it as having all the time in the world sharing it with their significant other.

Let me ask this question to those who are experiencing all the time in the world with their significant other: when it comes to sharing the sand of our own thoughts, feelings, and emotions to where it fills up each other's heart, what keeps it continually flowing between the two of you? Trust, faith, honesty, contentment, communication, understanding, commitment, security, respect, intimacy, hope, love, caring, tenderness, compassion, etc. are essentially what keeps the sand continually, as well as steadily flowing from one heart to another. It's a tough situation indeed to keep what are considered important aspects of a relationship flowing at a constant rate but it's all truly worthwhile.

Without a doubt, there are those who have this certain mindset that time is slowly but surely running out in ever experiencing true happiness. Essentially, the sand of their own thoughts, feelings, and emotions tend to feel as if they're flowing much faster, especially when experiencing times of utter heartbreak leaving one to deal with asking the oftentimes difficult questions. If you think about it, it's while trying to answer those particular questions one will flip the hourglass because he or she doesn't want to end up having one's heart filled with grains of sand that represent disappointment, frustration, bitterness, anger, sadness, loneliness, resentment, contempt, doubt, etc.

Personally speaking, I have the perspective that when it comes to my heart-mind hourglass the sand of my own thoughts, feelings, and emotions are in perpetual limbo within my mind rather than within my heart. In other words, my mind is and will always be full of questions to ask, leaving me to continue to be the type of guy who has an analytical, sarcastic, cynical view concerning not only love, but relationships as well. What it comes down to it, the constant flow of being asked when are you getting married and being told you're next tends to leave me somewhat apathetic, but to be perfectly honest I'm not ruling it out entirely to someday experiencing true happiness.

In retrospect, love/true love has always been viewed as either fleeting or never-ending like the sand within an hourglass. Thinking about it, a person can let the sand of their thoughts, feelings, and emotions all fall to the bottom because of experiencing unfortunate times of utter heartbreak or he/she can make each grain of sand count knowing full well they'll be shared and appreciated with someone truly special. For the question can be asked, how many people can truly say they have a steady, never-ending flow of sand or should I say love with their significant other? In the end, I say to those of you who are continually experiencing the never-ending flow of sand I hope it never runs out between the two of you.

FOREVER FOR YOU

November 10, 2010

Someone once said, ~Somewhere in life you fall in love. It changes you forever whether it be bad or good. It changes you... everything, even a smile, a touch, even a simple thing as a stare in the eyes means everything to you. Pray that someday you find your special someone.~ Without a doubt, when you fall in love it can most definitely change in ways that can be viewed as either bad or good. For one's whole outlook on not only love but relationships as well completely changes when you finally meet someone who you connect with on every level. True, it may have been indeed a difficult journey to be at a place of absolute contentment within your own heart but for the most part it was truly worthwhile, which is what love/true love is don't you think?

As said before, when you fall in love it can most definitely change you in ways that can be viewed as either bad or good. Thinking about it, when you know it's good between you and your significant other everything seems to absolutely clique without any problems whatsoever. I think it would be safe to say that when you have aspects of a relationship such as trust, honesty, faith, communication, commitment, respect, etc. the problems faced together ultimately tend to work themselves out. Hey, it's just a matter of working with each other instead of against each other to the point where the word forever doesn't cause you or your significant other to cringe but rather express a smile as you both look lovingly towards one another.

If you think about it, falling in love can certainly change you forever in a bad way but in the same sense can be considered good as well. What do I mean? For those who are in a potential and/or significant relationship, how is your level of sanity in regard to dealing with not only the bad habits, but also the weird/strange eccentricities of your bf/husband/gf/wife that can truly drive you crazy? Essentially, those habits/eccentricities are what make him/her absolutely special in his/her own way. You see, even though he/she can drive you nuts when doing it unbeknownst to them, you somehow can't imagine not being able to live without it because quite frankly you're so used to it that it's simply become part of the dynamic of your relationship with him/her.

Let me ask you this question to those in a significantly strong relationship, how do you know it's going to last forever? In my opinion, you don't know because nothing is ever really for certain in this life, especially when it pertains to true happiness. Granted, love can change you when something like a simple smile, a simple touch, as well as a simple stare directed your way causes you not to remember your own name. What it comes down to is being able to keep the smile on your face when things get rough, be continually touched not just physically but emotionally, spiritually, as well as mentally, and stare into the eyes of someone you love knowing full well he/she doesn't cause you to ever doubt his/her commitment to you is forever.

In retrospect, forever is a word that tends to have two different meanings particularly when it concerns love/true love. For a certain number of people, it actually feels like forever in experiencing true happiness as you find yourself dealing with pangs of utter heartbreak such as frustration, anger, confusion, doubt, etc. However, for those who know all too well the feeling of forever in which you and your special someone is in a state of euphoric bliss I tip my hat to you both praying you'll go the distance. In the end, for people living the single life like myself we pray to God to one day meet that certain someone who we will fall in love with hoping to say to him/her I want to be a part of your life forever for you.

JUST A MEMORY (LAST YODAISM OF 2010)

November 28, 2010

Jim Cornette once asked, ~Will pro wrestling as it used to be ever return?~ As a wrestling fan for over 24 years, I've witnessed a plethora of changes in a business primarily been labeled as sports entertainment. Thinking about it, when it comes to change, especially in the sport of pro wrestling, there are times where it's actually much needed but other times you oftentimes end up scratching your head to the point where you ask the question why? I think many wrestling fans, not just myself, would agree that wrestling today isn't what it used to be causing fans like myself to not only be considerably disgruntled and in disbelief, but angry as well. Essentially, in my personal view wrestling has changed in many ways but more specifically in format, the climb to success, and rivalry.

Let me ask you this question to many of you wrestling fans out there, is it me or has there been a lot more talking segments rather than wrestling going on lately? For it's quite an interesting situation indeed the turnaround in the talking/wrestling percentage as the majority of what is being watched by many of us are wrestlers either addressing the crowd or talking/calling out another wrestler. We've all seen it and it primarily takes up 15 to possibly 30 minutes of the program. True, it's for storyline purposes in order to drive the drama that is the proverbial male soap opera for guys but unfortunately, it's getting to a point where it's becoming not only tedious for those watching in person and on tv, but dare I say boring as well.

Without a doubt, there are certain wrestlers who have paid their dues in regards to climbing the ladder of success to capture a world heavyweight championship title. However, its a sad state of affairs when the journey itself is bypassed through shows like WWE NXT/

Tough Enough as new superstars such as Wade Barrett, The Miz, Shaemus, etc. don't just attain instant stardom, but receive instant title shots. A wrestler such as Triple H paid his dues by starting out his career as a relative unknown in WCW going by the name Terra Ryzing but would later have subsequent success with a new name in the WWF as Hunter Hearst Hemsley wrestling against the likes of Henry O. Godwin in a forgettable hog pen match. Now, he's a fan favorite and a mega superstar around the world.

For the question can be asked to the wrestling fans out there, how many of you truly miss the days of the Monday Night Wars? Personally speaking, I thoroughly enjoyed the days of channel flipping from WCW to WWF, especially in the 90's with the whole Sting vs. NWO and the whole "Attitude Era" running rampant with Stone Cold Steve Austin leading the charge. I can honestly say the mid to late 90's were absolutely enjoyable to watch because it captured your attention to where it got right in your face without any apologies whatsoever. You see, it was the rivalry between these two companies that made it enjoyable to watch but unfortunately with WCW bought out and TNA trying to stay with the WWE there hasn't really been much competition or in this case a big rivalry.

In retrospect, when you're a wrestling fan you can eventually become jaded concerning the state of wrestling today. For example, when I was younger, I used to get angry when the "bad guys" got the upper hand on the "good guys" but now as I've gotten older, I'm more into figuring out the storyline and where it's leading to. In my honest opinion, the best days of pro wrestling aren't found on Spike TV, USA, or SyFy as they can be only found in one place... YouTube. Stone Cold driving into an arena in a Beer Truck spraying The McMahons along with The Rock with a hose full of beer, Sting repelling down, coming up from, or heading to the ring in order to attack Hogan/NWO, etc. are considered just a memory that in the end can't be touched or unable to be duplicated ever again.

PRECIOUS (1ST YODAISM OF 2011)

January 29, 2011

Curtis Judalet once said, ~Love is as much of an object as an obsession, everybody wants it, everybody seeks it, but few ever achieve it, those who do will cherish it, be lost in it and among all, never...never forget it.~ As said before, love can be considered an obsession for a certain number of people to the point where one can, in some aspect, become the character Gollum from The Lord Of The Rings movie trilogy or otherwise known as Smeagol. Thinking about it, there are a number of women who when it comes to matters of the heart in regard to attaining the ring of holy matrimony, their pursuit can truly become obsessive to where it can mentally, emotionally, and in some instances physically consume them.

Without a doubt, every woman has that innate desire of having the ring in their possession, especially on their ring finger. Essentially, that innate desire can oftentimes grow within their own heart when they are either a witness to or hear news of an engagement concerning an acquaintance, friend, and/or best friend. For it's a tough situation indeed for any single woman to keep the desire of having/wanting the ring in their possession in check to where it doesn't completely destroy them knowing those around her have had or are currently having their desire of absolute true happiness fulfilled, which can be at times difficult to witness causing a mental/emotional/physical battle similar to that of Smeagol against his alter ego Gollum.

If you think about it, it's most definitely hard for any woman to keep a bright smile on their face and not find herself metaphorically descending into darkness within herself. Frustration, anger, fear, doubt, envy, disappointment, jealousy, etc. are considered a plethora of emotions that a woman can experience leaving her to have a mental debate/argument/discussion going on not only in her head, but heart as well. I think it would be safe to say that among those emotions mentioned above, jealousy can most assuredly be the downfall of so wanting to experience the feeling and beauty of what the ring represents that it can cause her to slowly exude an ugly facade both literally, as well as figuratively so much so she changes into someone who is hardly unrecognizable.

Let me ask this question to all you single ladies out there: how many of you still have a small part of your Smeagol-like self that is still intact and not letting your Gollum-like self, take complete control? What do I mean? For some women, love can be seen/felt as a strong need that can become overwhelming because without it they're absolutely weak if she can't touch, see, and/or feel it, leading them to settle for relationships that are both unfulfilling and temporary. What it comes down to is just a matter of having the patience and resolve in letting nature run its course concerning matters of the heart instead of fighting/manipulating it to make it happen leaving one to continue to not only mentally, but emotionally torture themselves as well for months or possibly even years.

In retrospect, a woman's pursuit/quest of love/true love in regard to attaining the proverbial one ring can either bring about euphoric contentment leaving her with countless enjoyment within her heart or ends up experiencing the unfortunate downfall of losing it causing constant emotional/mental/physical pain, suffering, and/or heartbreak. In any case, the struggle for a single woman or any woman for that matter to stay strong when it pertains to their bright Smeagol side and not let themselves slip into the dark Gollum side of herself can be quite a tough task to undertake because of bad past relationships but it's doable. In the end, to all you single ladies out there I hope the desire to one day individually attain your precious comes to fruition and may it be unforgettable.

BULLSEYE

March 4, 2011

Minute Major once said, ~Darts is a fascinating game which takes patience, intelligence, and coordination. The problem most people face when playing darts is the challenge of being consistent and precise. It's very difficult to hit the same spot every time and its so easy to become frustrated or give up.~ In some aspect, life is like playing a game of darts as there will be/have been times where patience, intelligence, and coordination are/were needed. Essentially, the individual darts we hold represent our hopes, dreams, aspirations, etc. in regard to work, family/friends, and most definitely matters of the heart. For the question can be asked, when it comes to the proverbial dartboard of life has it been easy or challenging in hitting the target you've been specifically aiming for?

If you think about it, its a tough situation indeed to consistently be on target, so to speak, when it pertains to our own personal dartboard of life. You see, the darts each one throws aren't always going to land/hit where we want them to, causing us to experience a mixed bag of emotions. In a sense, that is how life can be as we find ourselves standing at a distance experiencing emotions such as frustration, disappointment, doubt, anger, fear, etc. I think I can safely sat we've all been in a situation concerning a potential opportunity where the initial mindset was that we're initially getting closer to hitting the target/position wanted but unfortunately it wasn't hit leaving one standing there momentarily hanging/shaking our head.

As said before, the problem most people face when playing the game of darts is the challenge of being consistent and precise. Thinking about it, the same problematic challenge in finding consistency and preciseness in playing darts can also be found in matters of friendship. Without a doubt, there are times where best buds and gal pals experience rocky times causing him/her/them to miss the mark in certain areas of seemingly strong established friendship to the point where one feels like they've been hit with the sharp pointy end of the dart. Hey, its not a good feeling whatsoever when a trusted friend or group of friends you thought would always have your back doesn't leave you to question how truly off the mark you were about him/her/them.

Let me ask you this question to those who are in the dating field, has it been easy or hard for you to hit the right areas concerning not only your heart, but the heart of that particular guy/girl you're interested in? For a certain number of people, they've there are those who unfortunately have been off the mark when it comes to past relationships and experienced being hit countless times by the pangs of utter heartbreak leaving one to feel as if his/her heart is quite literally a dart board filled with holes that represent pain, frustration, anger, bitterness, etc. However, there are those who have been able to land the right areas concerning the proverbial dart board of the heart by having the patience, intelligence, and not to mention the coordination to experience being hit by true love leading to absolute true happiness.

In retrospect, like the game of darts it's all about practice and in life we are given the chance to perfect our game, in a manner of speaking. True, it's during the so-called dart game of life we'll most likely miss every now and then, but the key is to not give up to the point of becoming disappointed, frustrated, angry, thinking we're a loser, etc. when the particular dart we're throwing doesn't specifically land where we want it to. What it comes down to is taking the information we got and learning from it in order to adjust our trajectory so the next time we throw it lands that much closer to the intended target. In the end, life is oftentimes considered a hit or miss experience and the more we continue playing the game improving our skills, hopefully having fun while doing it we'll hit a bullseye.

MUSIC OF THE HEART

June 1, 2011

Someone once said, ~In the rhythm of life, we sometimes find ourselves out of tune, but as long as there is someone who becomes our melody, the music plays on. Thanks for being one of my best songs.~ If you think about it, a person's heart is in some aspect like a musical instrument that in all intents and purposes tries to get in tune, so to speak, when it comes to matters of love/true love. For its a tough situation indeed to meet someone who in a sense has the ability to not only get in a steady rhythm with your own heart but is also able to truly listen to the melody of it as well. Essentially, what it comes down to is meeting the right guy or girl who you will never be able to be out of tune with to the point where beautiful music is always from within each other's heart.

Let me ask you this question, how many of you have the ability to play a musical instrument like a guitar or a piano? To those individuals who are musically inclined they gradually developed a good ear in being able to listen rather than hear when something isn't quite right in regards to tickling the ivories on a piano or strumming the strings on a guitar. I think it would be safe to say that a woman wants a guy who has an excellent ear, in a manner of speaking, when he's able to actually listen for the wrong notes being played in the relationship. You see, when that happens the guy in question is able to make the right corrections instead of just hearing it and not doing anything about it causing the song in one's heart to sound absolutely spectacular.

As said before, the human heart is considered in some aspect like a musical instrument and for an unfortunate number of people they've experienced sour notes involving a past relationship causing their own heart to become out of tune. For some people they're heart has been out of tune for quite some time and its been difficult to meet that certain someone who will be patient enough to take the time to find tune their heart. It's a sad situation when a person's heart is out of tune because their heart was played with incorrectly so many times in the past that they've forgotten what its like to experience listening to the soothing rhythm and melody of true happiness but instead have been constantly hearing the unbearable wrong notes of utter heartbreak.

For the question can be asked to those who are in a potential and/or significant relationship, how in tune are you within each other's heart? Thinking about it, couples who have been together for quite some time don't necessarily share the same melody or rhythm for that matter and it oftentimes leads to a strange meld of sound that it causes one to become absolutely perplexed at what their hearing, which is something that tends to happen from time to time. Without a doubt, each one of us know a couple or possibly are in a relationship with a guy/guy where the sound/rhythm are complete opposites of each other but somehow, they make it work to the point where after hearing to it a few more times you begin to finally get what they're listening to within their hearts.

In retrospect, every person hopes to find not only the right melody, but the right rhythm when it comes to matters of that musical instrument known as the human heart. Granted, it takes time to get in tune as you try to establish the right melody and rhythm with that certain guy or girl in question. For some people they have the ability to pick it up to where a song is instantly created whereas for others it's a hit or miss process that can at times be truly frustrating but they stick with it knowing they'll eventually have countless hits with certain someone whoever he/she may be. In the end, I tip my hat to you couples out there who are continuing listening for and creating the best songs with each other, but to those who are living the single life like myself, I hope you someday are able to find the music of your heart.

MYSTERY OF LOVE

August 22, 2011

Tom Robbins once said, ~When the mystery of the connection goes, love goes. It's that simple. This suggests that it isn't love that is so important to us but the mystery itself. The love connection may be merely a device to put us in contact with the mystery and we long for love to last so that the ecstasy of being near the mystery will last. It is contrary to the nature of mystery to stand still. Yet, its always there, somewhere; a world on the other side of the mirror, a promise in the next pair of eyes that smiles at us. We glimpse it when we stand still.~ Without a doubt, love or true love for that matter can most definitely be considered an absolute mystery when it pertains to making a truly genuine heart to heart connection. For its a mysterious connection that continues to peak one's interest in regards to that certain special someone in his/her life whereas for others there is unfortunately no mystery to speak of whereby the connection is totally lacking.

Let me ask you this question to those who are in a significant relationship, is there still a sense of mystery shared between the two of you? I think it would be safe to say that when it comes to matters of the heart every person wants to spend their life with a guy/girl who continually keeps you guessing in a good way of course instead of a bad way that leaves or has left you tearing your own hair out due to confusion, frustration, and/or anger not only with your mind, but heart as well. When I say keeps you guessing it's of course referring to considerably special and possibly unexpected moments that have left you thinking how unbelievably lucky you are to share your life with someone that you just end up continually asking the following three words...who are you? It's considered an absolute mysterious situation indeed when questions continue to pop up, so to speak, concerning your best friend for life leading you to attain answers that essentially give you a better spiritual, mental, and emotional understanding to the point where it always leaves you with a smile on your face.

If you think about it, for those who share a love that is a strong and deeply significant relationship there will always be a sense of that mysterious thrilling excitement one gets either from a soft word spoken, a simple gaze given, or a gentle touch. You have to give it to couples who have been married for over 40...50...60 years as they are still able to keep the mystery alive in their loving relationship. A loving relationship in which you witness firsthand that love is ageless and the thrill of being in love keeps not only both their hearts continually skipping a beat but makes them feel young at heart for each other. Unfortunately, its a rarity these days to even come across a marriage relationship where it doesn't just involve the physical aspect of love. Thinking about it, there have been couples out there who lacked any mystery whatsoever in their relationship and experienced the temporary adrenaline rush based on the mystery of superficial lust to where they learned very quickly the harsh reality that the physical aspect of love alone was not enough to sustain something truly meaningful and long lasting.

For the question can be asked to you ladies out there who are living the single life, how many of you are still hoping to meet a guy who mirrors your own heart? In other words, he reflects your thoughts and emotions within his own heart to yours and is not merely using them for his own twisted pleasure in order to share a false connection. Yet, the question remains how do women know the thoughts and emotions within that particular guy's heart are absolutely genuine? That ma 'lady is where the mystery lies, and it primarily comes down to two words...no games. For a certain number of women, they've been able to establish a strong connection free of games but for others they continue to be dumbfounded by the games being played leading them to shake their heads at the all out absurdity and stupidity of the entire male species. However, be rest assured ladies that although there is the mindset by many of you women that the entire male species are complete idiots there a number of us men that don't think or act like the guys of relationships past you tended to cross paths with.

In retrospect, it's fair to say that what's missing in relationships today is the aspect of longevity. We've all heard the saying life is considered a marathon, not as a race and the same can be said for love as well. It's a sad state of affairs when couples don't pace themselves causing them to give up on the relationship before it ever even started. Why? The mystery and the connection were quite possibly there but it totally lacked substance, as well as quality leaving the guy, the girl, or both to become down right bored because he/she stopped asking or didn't ask any questions at all. .Think about this, how many people are in deeply connected relationships because they weren't afraid to ask the deep rooted questions that would inevitably lead them to step through the proverbial looking glass of their heart and into the seemingly mysterious heart of their significant other. Ultimately, it's not that hard to figure out that when you're able to establish a strong connection of mutual commitment, trust, loyalty, support, respect, intimacy, etc. love/true become so much simpler don't you think and in the end my friend that's the mystery of love.

ALIVE

September 1, 2011

Washington Irving once said, ~There is in every woman's heart a spark of heavenly fire, which lies dormant in the broad daylight of prosperity; but which kindles up and beams and blazes in the dark hour of adversity.~ As a guy, you oftentimes wonder what sparks the heavenly fires of a woman's heart to the point where it doesn't burn out. For it can be a tough situation indeed to figure out the right spark in order to have their heart be permanently rather than temporarily illuminated by the fiery warmth of true happiness. Thinking about it though, it's considerably easy to initially bring about a spark to where it quite possibly turns into an eternal flame of love, but the difficulty lies in being able to properly handle it without getting burned, so to speak.

If you think about it, when you witness a woman truly falling in love with a guy who is not only real but absolutely genuine as well, the spark she started out within her own heart essentially grows turning it into a bright, glowing, flame of warmth. You see, to have that growth from the initial spark to the eternal flame of love a guy must be able to know how to properly kindle the emotions and feelings that can, in a manner of speaking, burn out quickly. I think it would be safe to say a lucky number of women are fortunate to have a guy who is able to correctly stir up instead of poke at aspects of love such as trust, faith, honesty, hope, contentment, commitment, communication, respect, intimacy, caring, tenderness, compassion, etc. causing their heart to continually burn longer, brighter, and hotter.

As said before, it's considerably easy to bring about a spark in a woman's heart but the difficulty lies in being able to properly handle it without getting burned. Unfortunately, there are guys out there who weren't able to quell the flames of girl's hearts because they were playing around with it and ended up getting burned by the flames of their wrath/anger. It's a sad state of affairs when the lack of care and attention certain guys have in correctly stoking the warmth of a woman's emotions, as well as feelings, causes their heart to burn out so much so, that after a period of time it's left cold and dormant. Let me ask you this question to you ladies out there who have experienced in the past the pangs of utter heartbreak, how long has your heart lied dormant?

Without a doubt, it's a beautiful sight to behold to see any female's heart continually beam and blaze with absolute fiery passion when it pertains to matters of the heart in regards to love/true love. The glowing flame of warmth they feel inwardly can most certainly be felt outwardly causing those close to or around them to be fortunate enough to not just feel it but also see it by a flash of a smile, a look of happiness in their eyes, or whatever the case may be. Yet, for a certain number of women it hasn't always been easy by any means whatsoever to finally be in a comfortable place within their heart knowing they've gone through dark periods of spiritual, mental, physical, and not mention emotional adversity. What it primarily comes down to is having a guy who can carefully handle the fire within their heart because if he can't it will consume him.

In retrospect, a woman never really loses that quintessential spark when she suffers times of utter heartbreak. True, it can be considered quite difficult to be able to ignite it when she meets someone who she is potentially interested in because of past relationship issues. In some aspect, it's like trying to light a lighter and no matter how many times you attempt to get something going the spark itself isn't quite there, which happens from time to time. However, if a spark is established it inevitably takes patience to hopefully have a long-lasting heart to heart connection that never burns out. In any case, you have to admire the strength and resiliency of a woman's heart after it comes close to completely being extinguished due to the mere stupidity of guys. Granted, not all guys fall into this particular category of stupidity when it involves the precious albeit dangerous flames that can most certainly be painful if not handled correctly. In the end, I say to you ladies whose heart remains dormant and awaits that special spark to ignite it you'll truly feel alive once you do.

THE MASTER

September 5, 2011

Professor Morely Davidson said, ~There is a universal popularity of the Rubik's Cube puzzle - it's probably the most popular puzzle in human history.~ If you think about it, life is very similar to the iconic 80's toy many of us grew up playing with as we can oftentimes find ourselves holding in our hand, in a manner of speaking, circumstances that are seemingly complicated regarding our own lives. For it's a tough situation indeed to figure out a way to solve what is considered to be at first glance considerably easy but in fact it's something truly complex involving countless twists and turns that are viewed as absolute challenges. What it primarily comes down to is having the dedication and determination to stick with it despite how difficult it is instead of completely giving up on it.

Let me ask you this question to those who grew up playing with the colorful six-sided cube, how long did it take for you to solve it? I think it would be safe to say it took a tremendous amount of time and not to mention focus to get all six colors in their respective areas. Thinking about it further, the colors we put a significant amount of time and focus into matching are a representation of aspects of life such as work, finances, love, dating/marriage, friends, as well as family. Unfortunately, there comes a point where too much time and focus is put on one particular side leaving what is left to remain incomplete. Essentially, you have to just keep your attention on all six sides of the cube of life and not worry about when it's going to be solved because you basically have all the time in the world.

Without a doubt, there are times when trying to solve the Rubik's Cube you end up wanting to throw it against the wall. The same can be said for life too as there are certain aspects of it that can cause us to become so confused and frustrated we end up throwing our hands in the air. One aspect of life that can lead to confusion and frustration is matters of the heart pertaining to love/true love because every person has experienced or is currently experiencing not only the metaphorical twisting, but the turning of their own heart in order for true happiness to be solved, which hasn't happened yet for a certain number of people. Let me tell you something, sometimes you just have to put down the Rubik's Cube of your heart, step back, and for the sake of your own sanity try again later.

For the question can be asked concerning the colorful six-sided cube, when you were trying to solve it did any of your friends put their own 2 cents into the mix giving you suggestions on how to complete the tricky puzzle? The answer, I fair to guess, is a resounding yes and I for one can honestly say the suggestions given by my friends were either utterly annoying or downright stupid. You see, in their mind they knew the best solution to solve the problem at hand and one of those aforementioned solutions was to take all the colored stickers off so you can stick them together, which is of course cheating. Hey, when it comes to solving our personal/professional problems the suggestions given by our friends who can most assuredly be annoying and stupid, but you have to give it up to them for continually sticking by your side no matter what.

Someone once said, ~Life is like a Rubik's Cube. It's ever changing, and it always seems like you can't ever get it right. A puzzle than can never be fixed correctly like it was before and yet in the back of your mind you're convinced that all can be right one day.~ In retrospect, there are quite frankly so many solution to solving aspects of life that are difficult but the one main solution is through prayer as you put the Rubik's Cube of your own life in the hands of God. True, like the cube life may not always be fun at times but the one thing you can count on is being able to look back and have a good laugh. In the end, I say to you my friend, when you do eventually solve the colorful six-sided cube of your own life with God's guidance you can proudly call yourself the master as you feel a sense of accomplishment for a job well done.

PIPEBOMB

September 9, 2011

Current WWE wrestler C.M. Punk said, ~I want to make wrestling cool again.~ Without a doubt, the sport of professional wrestling in regard to the WWE hasn't been cool and not to mention fun for quite some time to the point where it has actually become uninteresting to watch. It's a sentiment I share with many other die-hard wrestling fans who would absolutely agree with me. However, what or should I say who has brought the cool and fun factor back to the proverbial male soap opera for guys is the ever so controversial C.M. Punk. You see, the man who proclaims himself to be straight edge has single handedly kicked new life into a business that primarily deemed sports entertainment by simply speaking his mind and for true wrestling such as myself we're hanging on every word.

As said before, C.M. Punk has been speaking his mind causing true wrestling fans all around the world to intently listen to what he has to say because it's the truth. It's a refreshing situation indeed to hear him speak, inevitably pushing the envelope when it comes to talking about the issues of the wrestling business that are considered not only taboo but have given a voice to what many of us have been thinking/writing for a number of years. Essentially, he broke down or should I say destroyed the 4th wall ranting off about such taboo topics as the WWE being better off after Vince McMahon is dead, particular wrestlers being let go, the PG era, the marriage between Triple H and Stephanie McMahon, etc., are a small list of things he has the balls to say knowing he can get away with it.

If you think about it, of the list of taboo topics Punk has openly spoken about, the issue concerning the PG Era is a problem he not only thinks needs to be changed, but for many of us who grew up watching wrestling that wholeheartedly agree it needs to change as well. In his mind, John Cena is the source of the problem as he is primarily the face of the PG Era and it's the main reason why the WWE has consistently remained stagnant. Why? The reason is the WWE mainly marketing to kids who along with a certain number of the females in the audience are ruining what many true wrestling fans have grown to enjoy/love. Thankfully, the PG era is gradually returning to the prominence of what was once great as the non-apologetic in your face program with attitude and even though it may not exactly be like the attitude era it's most definitely getting real all thanks to him.

Let me ask you this question to you wrestling fans out there, how many of you respect Punk even more as he is giving a voice to the voiceless? I can honestly say I am one of the many who respect him even more as he is personally leading the charge for change and fortunately it's happening for the better. Unfortunately, the one who hasn't changed is John Cena because his character hasn't evolved whereas characters like Orton, Undertaker, Stone Cold, Triple H, and Punk himself have evolved their personas switching from heel to face. Thinking about it, Punk and the millions of fans who are possibly thinking the same thing would love nothing more than to have Cena turn heel instead of staying a face whereby much respect would be given but if that happens his female, as well as young fans would end up crying.

In retrospect, the older fans of the WWE applaud the actions of C.M. Punk as we are sick and tired of the same ole' predictable storylines where John Cena wins the title again for the upteenth time ala Hulk Hogan. True, at one time he was liked as the Dr. of Thuganomics but after a while he grew out of it and he ultimately became the man who was ultimately shoved down our throats... but I digress. Hey, you can't deny that because of the straight edge superstar WWE has become relevant again so much so the topic of ice cream bars was trending on twitter because he wanted it back.

In the end, Punk has become the quintessential Stone Cold whose rebellious attitude toward authority i.e. Triple H or any other wrestler/superstar for that matter causes absolutely explosive results each time he is in the ring holding a pipebomb in his hand.

TO THE ENDS OF THE EARTH

September 13, 2011

Andrew Sullivan once said, ~The essence of romantic love is not the company of a lover, but the pursuit.~ Let me ask you this question to those who are and were in the dating scene, what aspect of it is considered to be such a thrilling albeit considerably interesting experience? You would most definitely be correct in saying the pursuit or chase it's also known as an aspect of the dating scene where there can oftentimes be a love/hate mentality associated with it. However, it's the possibility of establishing a potentially worthwhile relationship that makes the pursuit of romantic love an absolute challenge. For it's a challenge in which the individual in pursuit puts forth 100% effort into capturing the attention, interest, and ultimately the heart of that certain someone who caught his/her eye.

Without a doubt, women love being pursued by a guy knowing it makes them feel noticed, desired, and not to mention attractive. It's a flattering situation indeed for any woman to not only have a man's adoration and admiration directed towards her but is persistent in his efforts to not give up when previous attempts have failed. When I say persistent it's not in the same context of being annoyingly stalker-ish where the guy seemingly can't take the hint that she's not interested. You see, it relates more to putting in the work whereby showing there is genuine interest on his part and I think many women would agree that any guy who is serious, as well as patient in his romantic pursuit concerning matters of the heart shows her his intentions are to be a permanent instead of a temporary fixture in their life/

As said before, there can oftentimes be a love/hate mentality associated with the aspect of the pursuit/chase regarding the dating scene. Why? If you think about it, girls don't really enjoy being pursued by a guy who only wants to get with her rather than be with her. Trust me, there is a difference. The difference is when the gentlemen in question wants to get with her he's not paying attention to anything being said because he's solely focused on making her his next conquest whereas the guy who wants to be with her is there for her paying attention to the conversation to the point where he can repeat back parts of the conversation they shared together. So to all you ladies currently in the dating scene, who have you found yourself encountering...the get with her guy or be with her guy?

For the question can be asked to the women out there who were pursued by their significant other, what did he do right ultimately letting you know he was possibly marriage material? I think it would be safe to say no playing games, being himself and not being overly aggressive towards her to where she doesn't end up feeling threatened/scared/creeped out are just a few qualities/ characteristics on their proverbial guy list that inevitably scores points with them. Thinking about it further, respect and consideration go along way with the female species leading their insecurities to fade away essentially replacing it with a sense of comfortable security from their pursuer who knows what truly makes a woman feel absolutely special not just in the big ways but in the little ways as well.

In retrospect, the word pursuit doesn't necessarily mean the act of chasing or being chased. True, there is the physical aspect of pursuit in the attempt to make a connection that we've all been accustomed to since the dawn of time but there's also the aspect of pursuing where it involves making a connection that is spiritual, mental, and certainly emotional. Hey, it's important for a woman to have those connections because it determines whether or not a guy is worth her time. In any case, when it comes to the pursuit of true happiness it should be fun and casual for both individuals rather than have it be an uncomfortable, awkward situation. In the end, I say to any of you ladies that have an incredibly great, romantic guy in their life who hasn't stopped pursuing you, I hope he continues to do so even to the ends of the earth.

LOVE WILL KEEP US ALIVE

September 21, 2011

Jiddu Krishnamurti once said, ~To love is the greatest thing in life; it's very important to talk about love, to feel it, to nourish it, to treasure it, otherwise it will soon be dissipated, for the world is very brutal. But the moment you have in your heart this extraordinary thing called and feel the depth, the delight, the ecstasy of it, you will discover that for you the world is transformed.~ As said before, one of the aspects that is considered very important when it comes to matters of the heart is to nourish it. For a certain number of people they are lucky enough to have their heart full, in a manner of speaking, with an abundance of true happiness, whereas those who are living the single life are metaphorically hungry and want nothing more than to in all intents and purposes know what it tastes like.

Without a doubt, it's a truly satisfying experience within your own heart when you're in a significant relationship because you no longer hunger for true love. It's a comforting situation indeed to know your best friend for life will always stand by your side never leaving you feeling all alone as he/she nourishes your heart causing it to be metaphorically stuffed. Thinking about it, to have a guy/ girl who gives you the will to survive by continually nourishing your heart with trust, honor, respect, honesty, loyalty, faith, hope, understanding, caring, tenderness, intimacy, contentment, commitment, etc. would most definitely bring a smile to your face. Let me tell you something, to have that type of worthwhile relationship where you don't ever hear the growling sound of your own empty heart is what every person wants.

If you think about it, there are those living the single life who are unfortunately hearing the sound of their own heart growling because of how empty it is. It's a sad state of affairs when a person has been for quite some time considerably malnourished due to the lack of feelings and emotions not being shared or given for that matter. Essentially, it's an unfortunate situation that hasn't changed for some people to the point where the emptiness felt within their heart is a representation of disappointment, frustration, confusion, anger, sadness, bitterness, heartbreak, doubt, loneliness, hopelessness, etc. You see, it's the emptiness one feels that can in some ways be like an uncomfortable case of heartburn so absolutely bothersome and irritating not even pepto bismol will be able to alleviate the pain you're feeling in your chest.

Let me ask you this question to those who are in significant relationships, has he/she so thoroughly enriched your life the physical, spiritual, emotional, and mental hunger felt within your heart before meeting him/her is gone? I think it would be safe to say when you have someone who doesn't cause you to worry, prays for/with you in regards to God's guidance, will give one's own life up for you, goes above and beyond what he/she is capable of concerning every aspect of the shared relationship inevitably casting your doubts aside, etc. you can certainly breathe out a sigh of contended relief. Hey, be proud of yourself in knowing you have a guy/girl in your life who is constantly feeding your heart with so much positivity instead of negativity you just want to puke...in a good way of course.

In retrospect, every person has a limit when filling their stomach but not when it involves their own heart. True, there can be times where one can become so overwhelmed with emotion one thinks to himself/herself how things can possibly get any better because of all the love being given and yet they do. Oftentimes, it leads a person to experience that all-too-familiar aching feeling in the pit of their heart that usually tells them that what they're experiencing is too good to be true. However, be rest assured what one is experiencing is not indigestion but is more comforting than discomforting and to all the single people out there like myself I'm certain we will have that same aching feeling in the pit of our heart as well someday. In the end, when you do find/meet or already have met that guy/girl who nourishes your heart with as much joy/happiness you can look deep into each other's eyes and say with 100% certainty love will keep us alive, which is a song by classic rock legends The Eagles that best reflects this thought.

PERMANENT
September 25, 2011

Seven Time Tour de France winner Lance Armstrong said, ~If children have the ability to ignore all odds and percentages then maybe we can learn from them. When you think about it, what choice is there but to hope? We have two options, medically and emotionally: give up, or Fight Like Hell.~ Without a doubt, cancer is considered the second most common cause of death in the United States with heart disease being at the top. For it's truly a staggering statistic indeed when you learn that about 1,536,670 new cancer cases are expected to be diagnosed and that about 571, 950 Americans are expected to die of cancer with more than 1,500 people dying a day in 2011 alone. However, there are those who have not only continued to fight the good fight, but were able to beat the odds as well.

Let me ask you this question to those who know someone or are that someone who was diagnosed with cancer, what do you think was/is the most difficult part of the process? I think it would be safe to say looking in or being looked at in the eyes is considerably difficult to do because quite frankly it can truly be tough to put into words concerning the health and well being of a close friend/ family member. Thinking about it, what can you say to someone you love/care about that's been a part of your life for a certain number of years or since you were born except prayers will be given on their/your behalf all-the-while promising yourself/ themselves tears will not be shown. Unfortunately, that particular promise tends to be broken because of the ties that bind in regards to the personal connection one has with him/her/you.

If you think about it, when a person has cancer they go through their own personal hell before, during, and after treatments. Essentially, the treatments that are commonly used primarily consist of prescription medicine in order to fight leukemia, which also include chemotherapy, biological therapy, targeted therapy, radiation therapy, and stem cell transplants. There is no doubt the pain one goes through is incredibly excruciating so much so loves ones want nothing than to ask God to take the pain away to the point of praying to have it placed their painful burden of what their experiencing on to their own shoulders. You see, as much as it is tortuous for those with cancer to go through the treatments its absolutely tortuous for those who are unable to to do anything about it but be a strong, positive support system for him/her/you.

For the question can be asked to those who are currently fighting their own battle with cancer, have you ever thought to yourself you were all alone while going through your painfully difficult ordeal? Hey, it's considered normal to think that way as one has the mindset in which no one else understands/knows what you're/they're going though causing him/her/you to be angry? Why? If I fair to guess it would most definitely be due to the fact those close to him/her/you were trying to empathize with what one is feeling to where bottled up emotions are unleashed bringing out a certain amount of frustration, anger, stress, bitterness, etc. Let me tell you something, even though you don't want to take what's said personally you do but in spite of it you/they continue to stick by your side no matter what.

Nikolai Lenin once said. ~The most important thing in illness is never to lose heart.~ In retrospect, the resiliency of the human heart is quite remarkable when facing times of great hardships, especially when going through the treatment of cancer. True, one's immune system weakens leading to possible infections that cannot be fought off, bone weakness to where they can become fragile, physically fatigued/exhausted all the time, difficulty in eating, etc. are just a number of things a cancer patient goes through. Yet, it's all worth it when a person doesn't or refuses to give up for that matter and successfully beats it because he/she/you has that never say die cancer will not beat me I will beat it mentality. In the end, all that is associated with cancer such as pain, medication, and treatment are temporary but the love, as well as the support of family/friends are always permanent, which is a song by 2008 American Idol Season 7 Winner David Cook that best reflects this thought because he lost his brother Adam to a brain tumor.

ALWAYS

October 22, 2011

Bill Shankey once said, ~Some people think football is a matter of life and death. I assure you, it's more serious than that.~ Let me ask you this question to all college/pro football fans out there, how seriously do you actually take the hard-hitting sport, which almost didn't happen because of a lockout? In any case, it can most definitely be a mind-boggling situation indeed at the seriousness individuals take when it involves their favorite team. The dedication and all out loyalty die-hard fans express in being supportive can not only truly be seen by showing/wearing their team's colors, but in the way one vocalizes it for others to hear. Let me tell you something, if you're not a football fan you don't want to find yourself caught in the middle because you're not going to get out alive.

Without a doubt, a die-hard football fan can certainly be vocal to the point where one's emotions run rampant. I think it would be safe to say many of us have witnessed someone or are that someone who exudes a Dr. Jekyll/Mr. Hyde mentality when watching a football game. You see, a guy/girl starts out cool, calm and collected but when the action of the game picks up that's when one's love for their team is vocalized. It's the individual's Mr. Hyde type mentality kicks in to where one's actions usually consist of possibly throwing food, yelling at the television screen at a specific player or ref, and/or completely losing it when a play is made that is considered so spectacular a celebration is in order. A celebration we've all been involved in as you/we ran around the room like a crazy person either screaming our heads off, high fiving, hugging, or all of the above.

If you think about it, there comes a point where a die-hard football fan essentially becomes so involved in the game itself, he or she thinks of himself/herself an unofficial head coach. True, one doesn't have the capacity to be standing right by the coach's side helping make crucial, as well as critical play decisions but we do it anyway in either the privacy and comfort of our own home or food establishment/sports bar. It's oftentimes a humorous situation for a significant other to witness their husband or wife scream directly into/at the television screen in hopes that the head coach hears him/her because in their mind they know what pivotal call to play, or which player should be sent in to possibly win the game. Hey, as insanely crazy he/she is during football season you love him/her anyway.

For the question can be asked to all football fans, how many of you take part in fantasy football? For those who may not know what fantasy football is, it's a virtual competition pitting die-hard fans against die-hard fans, mainly guys, to where they "manage" their own fantasy team. As managers of their fantasy team, they have the authority to draft, trade, add/drop, and change their player rosters with their best buds who are playing as well. Personally speaking, I don't play but I have friends that do and trust me when I say they take it very seriously, so much so a cash prize may be won with the all-star lineup they have built for themselves. Thinking about it, as much as guys take fantasy football seriously there are many women who simply scratch their heads because they don't get it and you know what they never will.

In retrospect, you gotta love the surge of energy in the air during football season. A type of energy that just can't be described in words and you know there are entire households or quite possibly a husband/bf/wife/gf who takes sides when it pertains to their rival pro/college football team. Granted, it's a friendly rivalry at most but a rivalry, nonetheless. You have to admit, football fever is contagious causing you to use phrases such as "we won" or "we're going to the playoffs" even though we aren't directly involved in a professional capacity with the team itself. Truth be told, that can be said for every fan of all sports, not just football, don't you think? In the end, Hank Williams Jr. aka Bocephus is no longer the quintessential face of football that has basically lasted 20 years or so and even though he's gone the answer we give to the question he asks is still a definite yes...we'll always be ready for some football.

WHAT WOMEN WANT (LAST YODAISM OF 2011)

December 31, 2011

Giuseppe Mazzini once said, ~Love and respect women. Look to her not only for comfort, but for strength and inspiration, and the doubling of your intellectual and moral powers. Blot for your mind any idea of superiority; you have none.~ As a guy, being able to ascertain the right ways in treating a woman with respect can most definitely be a never-ending live and learn from your mistakes type process. For it can be a tough situation indeed to undertake because there are countless aspects and not to mention qualities that strengthen a relationship to the point where there is an absolute bond between two people. I think it would be safe to say that of the countless aspects and qualities, love and respect are considered the cornerstones of what makes matter of love/true love truly inspirational, especially for women.

As said before, being able to treat a woman with love and respect can most definitely be a never-ending live and learn from your mistakes type process. It oftentimes starts with how a guy is able to communicate with a woman knowing he could very well be at a completely different wavelength/frequency with her, so to speak. In other words, he could be saying the same thing she is but in her mind the interpretation is far different causing conflict. Thinking about it further, the tendency for any guy is to immediately deflect back anything verbal and hit his way back to her in a much harder fashion as if they're in a tennis match, which is an unfortunate mistake. What it primarily comes down to is talking to/with her calmly instead of at her emotionally frustrated to no end at the seemingly sheer difficulty of keeping a level head when involved in a heated discussion.

Without a doubt, women love it when a guy is looking in their eyes actively listening to what they are saying and not just sitting/

standing there hearing whatever is coming out of their mouth. In their minds, it shows respect revealing to them he is not pretending as he genuinely cares and is interested in that matter concerning the topic of conversation being shared with him. Unfortunately, there are some guys who are disrespectful being too preoccupied playing the game in order to quench his carnal, lustful desire that he doesn't realize or refuses to see he may possibly have a worthwhile relationship. It's a sad state of affairs when a woman suffers disappointment and/or utter heartbreak at the hands of a guy who didn't take the time to listen to anything relevant that may help get a better understanding of the female species standing/sitting before him.

Let me ask you this question to those ladies who are in a potential and/or significant other, does the guy you're with/hope to be with ere problems publicly or privately. You see, a guy who loves and respects the woman he loves will certainly keep problems on the down low to avoid drama from outside factors that aren't helping matters any and are just fueling the fire, in a manner of speaking. Hey, we've all witnessed couples or quite possibly have been that couple where the guy/girl didn't have enough respect to keep problems regarding their relationship private, causing total embarrassment on his/her part. Let me tell you something ladies, to have a guy that values the meaning of privacy concerning problematic issues in the relationship shows not only a strong sense of respect and love, but a strong bond between the two of you as well.

In retrospect, there are countless other ways to show love and respect such as saying the right things in the right way, complimenting her, and treating a woman as if she's your mother or sister. It would be safe to say every guy has heard that particular statement and for the most part there are a certain number of us who continually adhere to it whereas others tend to ignore the concept completely. True, it's those types of guys who don't have a moral compass and have this innate mindset they are vastly superior to women causing them to exude an arrogant, ladies' man mentality...but I digress. In the end, when it comes to true happiness a guy can provide trust, faith, honesty, hope, contentment, commitment, constant communication, intimacy, understanding, etc.; but first provide/show some respect and that gentlemen is what women want.

MASTERPIECE (1ST YODAISM OF 2012)

January 9, 2012

Shannon Meirers once said, ~Love is like an Etch-A-Sketch. It takes a lot of skill and patience to create something beautiful, and even one little mistake can ruin the whole picture.~ In some aspect, love is certainly like an Etch-A-Sketch and for many of us who owned one as a kid back in the day knows how something that is seemingly fun for all ages can at the same time be an absolute headache. For it truly takes matters of skill, time, and patience to create what you've imagined for quite some time to be totally worthwhile. Thinking about it, when it comes to love in regards to a person's heart you can most definitely find yourself trying to navigate the proverbial white knobs of one's own feelings and emotions in order to create a beautiful picture of true happiness.

As said before, love in regard to a person's heart can have one trying to navigate the proverbial white knobs of their own feelings and emotions like that of an Etch-A-Sketch. I think it would be fair to say we've all tried to create a picture from our imagination, but the end result didn't turn out quite as planned. Why? It may seem as an easy enough situation indeed to turn the white knobs of our feelings and emotions in the direction we want it to go but when it involves matters of the heart it becomes considerably difficult to undertake. Hey, we've all been there as we tried to figure out in the past or currently figuring out now what turns to make within our heart to the point where it has taken/is taking a toll on each one of us mentally, spiritually, physically, and emotionally.

Without a doubt, mishaps such as being bumped can occur when you play with an Etch-A-Sketch causing you the unfortunate task of starting over. How? We simply shook it, whereby getting a brand new slate to work with. How did you feel when it happened? In a sense, the same can be said for one's heart as well as the bumps of drama can ruin the whole picture leading to utter heartbreak leaving you feeling disappointed, discouraged, angry, frustrated, etc. However, even though you can shake clean an Etch-A-Sketch to start over and undo what is done you can't with your heart. Unfortunately, it's not as simple as that because no matter how hard you try to shake away, in a manner of speaking, memories/feelings of the past small remnants can still be seen/felt/linger in your heart.

Let me ask you this question to those who are in a significant relationship, how many mistakes have both you made in the process of etching out together a beautiful picture? Hey, mistakes will inevitably be made and it's just a matter of being able to use the skills the two of you have been able to learn from each other over time at your disposal. Essentially, the one big mistake someone makes in a relationship is trying to fix a problem alone and if you think about it that is how we did it as kids when someone tried to help us fix a problem when drawing a picture on the Etch-A-Sketch. What it comes down to is being able to have the humility to ask for or let your best friend for life help as you both work hard together in making the necessary corrections of what is deemed something special, absolutely spectacular.

Someone said, ~An Etch-A-Sketch and love go hand in hand. Think about it. Just as you get it figured out, someone comes by and shakes the darn thing up and makes you figure it out all over again.~ In retrospect, when it comes to the Etch-A-Sketch that is the human heart we're always going to find ourselves shaking it because of the difficulties one faces in that thing called love. Yet, when we meet that certain special someone who you can put your trust, hope, faith, commitment, understanding, etc. in to help create a picture-perfect relationship knowing you'll make a few mistakes along the way is a dream come true for everyone including myself. In the end, it's the mistakes learned in a significant relationship that help create a strong bond and it may not be perfect by any means but it's a masterpiece worthy enough to display.

GET IT RIGHT

February 8, 2012

Someone once said, ~Love will blossom again. Give it a chance. You might do much better, to find a partner who is perfect for you. The fear of heartbreak is not worth losing sleep over. The risk of a breakup will always exist, but if you are strong you will rebound. Every gaping hole can be plugged, if you try.~ Without a doubt, the pangs of continually experiencing the misfortune of utter heartbreak is something that a certain number of people are very familiar with. For it can most definitely be a tough situation indeed causing one to endure a seemingly painful torture mentally, physically, spiritually, and oftentimes emotionally as well. However, a broken heart does eventually heal but the question remains how long will it take before one finally experiences true happiness?

If you think about it, when a guy or girl finds themselves continuously putting back together the broken pieces of their heart there is the tendency to place a tremendous amount of self-doubt on himself/herself concerning whether they're worth enough to know what love or true love for that matter actually feels like. It's within that self-doubt a number of questions weigh heavily on your mind to the point where it feels like the weight of the world is on not so much your shoulders per say but mainly on your heart. Why isn't all that I do not good enough? When will my heart be able to be genuinely touched by a guy/girl without fear of once again having it break apart into a million pieces? Essentially, it's those questions and countless more that can drive or already has driven a person to the brink of insanity.

As I said before, it can most definitely be a tough situation indeed to experience the pangs of constant heartbreak causing you to endure a seemingly mental, physical, spiritual, and not to mention emotional painful torture. Thinking about it further, its a type of painful torture where you find yourself dwelling on how you had the best of intentions to keep the relationship flowing smoothly and drama free. Unfortunately, it didn't happen, or should I say pan out the way one hopefully intended leading to the end result of wanting to fix it somehow after a complete mess was made of things concerning what said and/or done of that matter. Hey, it's unavoidable where the breakup occurs and as much as you want to point the finger at whose fault it was, you just have to remind yourself there is a strength, as well as resiliency within your scarred heart as it keeps on beating.

Let me ask you this question to those who have lost count on the number of times their own heart has been broken, what has helped you get through the difficult time in your life? If you said drinking yourself into a drunken stupor with your gal pals/best buds all night long my answer is no. Granted, it may help but it doesn't solve anything. You see, whenever a breakup happens a person's faith is shaken to the core of their heart causing one to have that initial mindset, he/she won't ever fall in love ever again. True, it's quite possibly the first thing that comes to mind in one's emotionally ridden state to where you say life isn't fair but after taking some time for yourself you just have to bow your head, close your eyes and breathe. What it inevitably comes down to is that while your eyes are closed, pray to God for guidance because He ultimately knows and will direct you to who you'll fall in love with.

In retrospect, whenever a person experiences time and time again the pangs of utter heartbreak it's as if he or she is on a sinking ship about to or already has gone under. In some ways, you've been able to keep your head above water, in a manner of speaking, because you consider yourself a survivor. Yet, there comes a point where the voice in the back of your head tells you to stop and just let yourself sink into the deep dark abyss of depression. For the question to be asked, do you listen to it? In any case, when it comes to the concept of starting over again it will be hard to do, which it always is but you'll get through it wiser because of it. In the end, you'll be fine but there's always that one question that you can't help but ask...will I ever get it right?

PARTY ON

February 24, 2012

Someone once said, ~Life is like a party. You invite a lot of people, some go, some join you, some laugh with you, some didn't come. But in the end, after the fun, there would be a few who would clean up the mess with you. And most of the time, those were the uninvited ones.~ If you think about it, life can be considered a party but in order to have one you need your gal pals and best buds in attendance to most definitely make it not only a truly enjoyable experience, but quite possibly a memorable one as well. For it's your circle of compadres that essentially liven the party atmosphere of life rather than having it seem to flat line, so to speak. Hey, it all comes down to the guest list of who you certainly want to not just invite but stay and continue partying away with you for years to come.

Without a doubt, one of the things you want to hear when you are hanging amongst your friends at a party is the sound of laughter. I think it would be safe to say in the party known as life you want to have people who bring absolute amusement and not to mention enjoyment to the point where the smile on your face never goes away. The pain and tears you endure are actually a good thing because of laughing so hard. It's a comforting and fun situation indeed being able to be surrounded by a group of people who aren't considered simply guests in your life as they have gradually come to be seen as family who attain the uncanny ability to make you laugh through the difficult times in your life. Thinking about it further, nobody wants to invite someone or be that someone for that matter who is the quintessential party pooper, in a manner of speaking, leaving you with less drama or none at all to deal with.

As said before, nobody wants to invite someone or be someone for that matter who is the quintessential party pooper, in a manner of speaking, leaving you with less drama or none at all to deal with. Unfortunately, when it comes to the party known as life the one uninvited guests crasher you don't want to find yourself coming face to face with is drama. You see, nothing ever good happens when the unwelcome party crasher that is drama makes its presence known in your life causing your smile to turn upside down. The stress-free and relaxing environment you were experiencing before it made its ugly surprise appearance can cause a person to become stressed out to where he/she is unable to enjoy himself/herself. Let me tell you something, its frustrating and a sad state of affairs when drama ruins particular moments/events in life causing you to clean up the mess it left behind afterwards.

Let me ask you this question to those who have hosted parties in the past: how many of your friends willingly/voluntarily stayed to help you clean up the mess left behind? I think every person is lucky enough to have established unwavering friendships that stick with you no matter what and will not leave until all the mess is cleaned, as well as picked up. Oftentimes, the same can be said when you find yourself needing to be picked up mentally. physically, spiritually, and most assuredly emotionally as well after enduring the mess drama has made. You truly have to thank God for bringing you such an eclectic group of individuals and quite possibly that one special individual into your life who are there for you even though you didn't even ask them to be showing you there are still people who not only care, but are willing to help you get through the difficult, tough times in your life.

In retrospect, every person has an invitation to the party of life but it's how you define the word "party" that determines how you live it. True, one can party like a rockstar drinking yourself into a drunken stupor with your best bud and gal pals till the wee hours of the morning, but it can become quite tiresome once you get older. The alternative could be a celebration in which you cross things off your bucket list, whereby accomplishing the goals you set for yourself with friends in tow, which many of you may be achieving as we speak. In any case, people come and go throughout the festive celebration of our lives as we keep in touch with some while losing touch with others. Granted, that is how life is at times and yet it can be full of surprises. In the end, continue to surround yourself with awesome friends who no longer need an invite to this shindig called your life and in the immortal words of two pop culture icons from the movie Wayne's World I say to you all party on.

I GOTTA HAVE IT

March 7, 2012

The late Steve Jobs once said, ~ The overall point is that new technology will not necessarily replace old technology, but it will date it. By definition, it will replace it. But it's like people who had black and white TV's when color came out. They eventually decided whether or not the new technology was worth the investment.~ Without a doubt, we live in the technological age as the devices each one of us are so accustomed to having at our fingertips to the point where it can become impossible at times to put down. For it's a tough situation indeed to control one's self because attaining the newest form of technology can truly be addicting, especially for those individuals who have the must/need/want mentality in regard to getting the newest upgrade coming out.

If you think about it, when it comes to the technological marvel that is the cell phone it gets updated practically every other week with so many features added on. In the past, it was a fairly simple and new concept but now everyone has one in their possession. It inevitably received an upgrade with the advent of something that would most definitely change the course of how we communicate with each other. How so? Well, a conversation between family members or friends for that matter are now oftentimes done through text messages while not only in the same vicinity of one's household, but quite possibly sitting next to/across from each other as you chow down together. Hey, as funny as that sounds you know it is true because you're guilty of doing it knowing full well you can just walk over/look up and talk to the person.

As said before, the cell phone is certainly a technological marvel leading it to seemingly be updated every other week with new features. I think it would be safe to say when the powers that be were able to somehow feature internet capabilities with the use of your cell phone, it was brought to a whole new level. The information superhighway becoming portable and instead of going to your nearest library in order to use the internet to look up information, calling your best buds/gal pals to get the 411, or whatever the case may be you instantly had it at your disposal. Hey, it's a considerable time saver for any individual who needs a piece of information in a pinch, especially if a debate needs to be settled concerning a particular random topic being discussed.

Let me ask you this question, back in the day would you ever in your wildest dreams thought you could actually watch television or even movies on your cell phone? My answer is no because we all had that initial mindset of the television watch ala The Jetsons. Fortunately, it has happened causing you to become one very happy camper who is unable to be at home because they're stuck at the office, in traffic, jury duty, a boring class, etc. Ultimately, one's entertainment value fits in the palm of your hand, can practically be taken anywhere, and when done it just fits in your pocket. Thinking about it further, for any guys who are die-hard sports fans and hate to leave in the middle of watching an intense football game to go to dinner they can watch it on their phone, which may not sit well with their wife/ girlfriend if they find out. Proceed with caution fellas.

In retrospect, technology will always get updated and devices such as a laptop computer, video game system, flat screen television, Kindles, Tablets, etc. are going to continue to be in demand. The consumer has an insatiable appetite involving the newest technological device that far surpasses its previous predecessor. You have to be truly amazed at what the powers that be are capable of when creating the next big thing in cell phones and with such creations as the video phone, voice recognition where it can actually talk back to you, and so much more the possibilities are endless. In the end, I know every person has that same thought whenever a commercial pops up involving a new Apple iPhone, Motorola Droid, LG Smartphone, Nexus S4G causing them to stand in line for hours on end...I gotta have it.

HOLE IN ONE
March 11, 2012

Arthur Daly once said, ~Golf is a love affair. If you don't take it seriously, it's no fun, if you do take it seriously, it breaks your heart.~ In some aspect, love or true love for that matter is like the game of golf as a person can most definitely find himself/herself trying to reach the proverbial 18th hole of true happiness, especially those who are living the single life like myself. Unfortunately, it can truly be a tough and not to mention difficult situation indeed to undertake as one metaphorically plays through within the so-called hazardous areas of the golf course that is the human heart. For it takes a tremendous amount of skill and strategy to have the golf ball of our own feelings, as well as emotions land in a specific location of a guy/girl's heart, which tends to not always work out as planned.

Let me ask you this question to those who not only watched the sport but play it as well, what is the primary objective of the game? If you answered hit the golf ball up the fairway and get it into the 18 individual cups then you would be absolutely right. Thinking about it, the 18 individual cups located within the golf course of each of our hearts are considered a representation of trust, faith, hope, respect, honesty, contentment, commitment, understanding, intimacy, communication, caring, tenderness, compassion, etc. Women, more so than guys, want to be able to sink with ease the golf ball of their own feelings and emotions into each cup regarding a potential/significant other without enduring the harsh hazards causing mental, spiritual, and certainly emotional pain. Yet, love/true love wouldn't be considered such a challenge now would it.

Without a doubt, matters of the heart in regard to true happiness is deemed a considerable challenge to the point where you deal or quite possibly have dealt with unfortunate, painful lows of the hazards of utter heartbreak. If you think about it, every experienced golfer has found himself/herself in a sand trap and it can be very difficult to get out of it to where it can leave you feeling frustrated, angry, confused, disappointed, doubtful, fearful, etc. Essentially, those exact same feelings are felt when you end up finding yourself in the sand trap known as drama. You see, the more "swings" you take at trying to get yourself out of the drama-filled bunker and miss the deeper your heart sinks leading you to unable to be properly focused. Let me tell you something, its a sad state of affairs when a guy/girl is left stuck in the hazardous sand trap called drama so much so he/she just wants to give up completely.

For those question can be asked to those golf enthusiasts who watch the sport on television, when you watch a golfers such as "The Golden Bear" Jack Nicklaus, The Great Arnold Palmer, Phil Mickelson, "The Shark" Greg Norman, Tiger Woods, Nancy Lopez, and rising stars like Rory McIlroy, as well as Michelle Wie who do they consult with? If you said their personal caddie, you're correct because they help advise them on what possible golf club to use or whatever the case may be. Oftentimes, when advice is needed concerning a love relationship such as marriage it should be sought from our own personal spiritual caddie...God. Hey, God's advice is never wrong as you use His main golf club that is the bible where you'll be able to properly ascertain the proper way in handling situations involving potential and/or significant relationships through serious prayer and the reading of His word.

In retrospect, we all hold a metaphorical scorecard in our hand showing the shots each of us made concerning a past or even a current relationship. True, it's those particular shots made whether they were par for the course or unfortunate bogeys that brought you to the brink of insanity were considered experiences for you to learn from. Granted, there were probably/have been times where you just wanted to either throw/break your golf club away because the situation wasn't going your way, which is basically most of the time. If you took it seriously, got your heart broken, and inevitably learned from your mistakes then I tip my hat to you and give a celebratory golf clap on your behalf but if not keep practicing. Ultimately, when it comes to the golf course that is our own heart, it's a tricky course to master, in a manner of speaking, but don't give up. In the end, to those who were able to master it and now wear the coveted green jacket known as the wedding ring continue to hopefully sink an eagle or should I say hole in one in your relationship for years to come.

HOW I SEE IT

March 16, 2012

Someone once said, ~Falling in love is one of the most exhilarating and life altering experiences. It can change your entire perspective.~ If you think about it, every person has their own unique perspective when it concerns falling in love to the point where it can most definitely change one's view on finally experiencing true happiness, especially for those who are living the single life. For it's an interesting situation indeed being a single guy who is able to consistently give a fresh and not to mention creative take on love or true love for that matter even though I have never had the fortunate privilege of experiencing it myself. In any case, matters of the heart give individuals such as myself the opportunity to share their own views/insights, whereby giving you the reader not only a whole new perspective, but quite possibly hope as well.

As I said before, every person has their own unique perspective in regard to that thing called love. To those individuals like myself who take a step back, so to speak, in order to mentally break down the mindset, as well as actions of what guys and girls say/go through in a potential/significant loving relationship. True, you may not have agreed at times with what I've written in the past, but it truly touches the cockles of my heart when deeply personal stories are shared so much so, that he or she seeks my advice on how a particular situation should be handled. Let me tell you something, I tip my hat to all of you peeps who shared your deeply personal and touching stories with me and I hope I was able to answer the questions you had that have mentally weighed on your mind.

Without a doubt, a person can certainly have an emotional perspective concerning falling in love, but unfortunately the focus doesn't necessarily leave him or her with that quintessential warm, fuzzy feeling inside. You see, for a certain number of people the emotional connection to love has left more of a cold, empty feeling inside causing it to be viewed with considerable harshness because of constantly experiencing utter heartbreak. It's a sad state of affairs for those who aren't able or refuse to change their perspective about love due to getting their heart broken leaving them cynical, bitter, angry, frustrated, disappointed, etc. Hey, it's those individuals who essentially embrace the emotional dark side that inevitably hold, in a manner of speaking, the pain suffered like a shield, so they won't be able to get hurt again, which doesn't always happen.

Solomon 8:6 says ~Set me as a seal upon thine heart, as a seal upon thine arm: for love is strong as death; jealousy is cruel as the grave; the coals thereof are coals of fire, which hath a most vehement flame.~ Let me ask you this question to those who are not only in love but falling in love as well, when it comes to your own perspective do you believe love/true love in purest form cannot die or be destroyed? Here's another question. Will it continue to burn like a blazing fire that is unable to be extinguished? My answer is yes, and countless marriages continue to hold strong in the warmth of each other's embrace. Hey, it's through God's divine grace as you both pray to Him all-the-while reading the scriptures of His word that will strengthen the bond of a loving relationship involving marriage.

In retrospect, a person's perspective on love/true love can change if there is a reason that gives him or her the other side of things. Granted, whether or not being given a whole new view may change one's mindset or heart for that matter but at least he or she was open to listen with open ears. What it primarily comes down to is being able to not just express your own opinion on the subject of true happiness, but willing to let others express theirs as well without being overly objective at how they see things. Thinking about it, we're not always going to see eye to eye on subjects such as looking to God for guidance in a marriage relationship, but we can hopefully discuss it like mature, grown adults. Ultimately, it's all a matter of perspective and I say to those who I have possibly enlightened over the years concerning my never-ending view on love/true love because in the end that's how I see it.

SOMETHING

March 19, 2012

Paul Geraldy once said, ~What we call love is the desire to awake and keep awake in another's body, heart, and mind the responsibility of flattering, in our place, the self of which we are not very certain.~ Without a doubt, every person desires to awaken and keep awake a potential/significant other's body, heart, and mind till they draw their very last breath on earth. For a lucky number of couples that desire continues to be fulfilled as they experience tremendous amounts of true happiness together. A type of true happiness in which the seemingly enthusiastic love shared between each other is not considered boring to others to the point where they end up yawning and inevitably fall asleep. Hey, it's what those individuals living the single life like myself not only hope and pray to God to have in our life one day, but exude that exact same enthusiasm as well.

Without a doubt, love or true love for that matter most definitely has that innate ability to awaken one's enthusiasm in not only your heart, but the heart of a potential/significant other. I think it would be safe to say it's certainly an absolutely indescribable feeling indeed for two people in a strong, loving relationship and share that enthusiasm for/with each other, as well as those around them. Essentially, it can truly be seen by the bright smiles as they look at one another face to face, the sound of their voices when having a conversation together, and not to mention the public display of affection exchanged. True, it can be considerably annoying for many of us who aren't in relationships but truth be told you're happy for the both of them to where you wish/pray for continual, enthusiasm, joy and happiness in their relationship.

If you think about it, not everyone desires to be in an enthusiastic relationship because of experiencing unfortunate past heartbreaks.

Oftentimes, the main cause of it is the lack of love from either the guy or girl. Thinking about it further, it's a sad state of affairs when there is absolutely no enthusiasm whatsoever shown by a husband/boyfriend/wife/girlfriend leading him or her to simply go through the motions of just being in a relationship. Let me tell you something, couples in Hollywood who were once married are a perfect example as bonds of holy matrimony last for a brief moment in times such as basketball star Kris Humphries and reality superstar Kim Kardashian whose marriage lasted only a whopping 72 days. True, the enthusiasm was quite possibly there in the beginning but as time/reality set in the relationship itself began to fade and crumble, which everyone knew it would.

Let me ask you this question to those couples who have been married for a number of years, do the two of you continue to feel the enthusiastic desire of unwavering love within each other's heart? Here's another question. Are the two of you as much more in love now in the latter years of your life than back in your younger days but with a greater amount of enthusiasm than ever before? Unfortunately, that isn't the case these days as some people may currently be in a situation where he/she so wants to experience a much-needed change for himself/herself in order to know what the feeling of excitement actually is. You see, what it primarily comes down to is not being in a casual going nowhere relationship but a close, committed relationship with two people who consider each other their best friend for life and are working hard to bring about absolute longevity to their worthwhile relationship.

In retrospect, the desire to awaken a person's body, heart, and mind in regard to matters of love/true love is considerably easy. Granted, if it were on an individual basis, it would be a simple enough task to undertake but to be able to awaken all three at once and keep them awake without losing enthusiasm within the relationship itself that's the true challenge there my friend. You can help but wonder how many couples out there today still have the desire or should I say never-ending zeal for one another that doesn't just involve physical carnal lust. Ultimately, it's the little things in a relationship that can be taken for granted at times are what bring about absolute excitement not only make a big difference but are absolutely unforgettable. In the end, I say to those couples out there who still have the enthusiastic desire for each other I hope it never fades away as both of you continue to see, hear, and feel that certain something keeping the spark alive after all these years, which is a song that reflects this thought by the iconic group from across the pond The Beatles.

GAME-SET-MATCH
March 22, 2012

Someone once said. ~Life is like a game of tennis; the player who serves well seldom loses.~ As said before, life is like a game of tennis as each of us on a daily basis step on the proverbial tennis court of life facing one of the or should I say THE toughest opponent one will ever face...life itself. In a sense, we all are in the zone and match ready with our metaphorical tennis racket in hand as we try to hit the tennis ball known as our goals/ hopes/dreams we set for ourselves but in order to achieve them one must get it past the obstacle(s) that are across the net, so to speak, ready to return what you served. For it's considered a tough situation indeed for any person to face an opponent such as life when it comes to matters of importance such as friendships, work, and most definitely love/true love.

Without a doubt, every person has "battled" their friends on the so-called tennis court of life and whether it be verbal or physical it can certainly test how hard a "hit" we can not only take but give as well as we "hit" back. Hey, that's what gal pals/best buds say/do to each other having that back-and-forth relationship as we oftentimes serve up stinging insults, the cold hard truth, some much needed advice when they need to hear it, or whatever the case may be. Thinking about it further, it's our friends who have our back no matter what and even though it may seem we're facing them as an opponent they're merely pushing us to become a much better player. Why? You see, in their eyes each one is destined for greatness and now we have that never quit never say die mentality similar to tennis legend Jimmy Connors.

If you think about it, our professional career is a considerably tough opponent as well as we try to achieve objectives like working hard to get a promotion. In other words, getting to the next level on the quintessential ladder of success and for a certain number of people they've been able to hit several aces and/or winning break points concerning their career goals. However, that wouldn't be the case without experiencing lousy/missed calls, faults, double faults, defaults, forced errors and at times countless never-ending deuce situations hindering one's victory to the point where you wanted to throw or ended up throwing an all-out tantrum ala John McEnroe. Let me tell you something, every individual works hard as we dig deep within ourselves and in some aspect, seemingly running every which way so as to not let the ball representing our future to either get past us or end up landing/dropping where it's impossible for us to reach.

Let me ask you this question to those who are not just fans of the sport of tennis but actually watch it live in person, who oversees the match between the two players? If you said the umpire who sits down in an umpire's chair above the tennis court closely observing play, then you're correct. Essentially, the spiritual umpire that is God watches over us in His umpire's chair/thrown in regard to our potential/significant relationship or lack thereof and intervenes in His own way to where a challenge is called causing a disagreement. I think it's safe to say we've all had a spiritual tennis battle with God going on with our own heart as the tennis ball and even though we so selfishly want true happiness, He absolutely knows who our Steffi Graph to our Andre Agassi or vice versa is going to be. What it primarily comes down to is a matter of absolute patience as you continue to pray to Him and read His word for guidance.

Someone said, ~Life is like a tennis game. It can serve the ball to you as hard as it wants and you'd never know what direction it was going in.~ In retrospect, that's how seemingly it as we find ourselves trying to mentally figure out/anticipate what and where life is going to serve us knowing full well it's not going to make it easy as it serves up a hard, cross court, slicing smash like Ivo Karlovic, who coincidentally holds the record for fastest tennis serve of 156 mph. In any case, we all strive in hopes to get to our own Wimbledon and whatever it may be for you, don't let things like the noise of drama, self-doubt, fear, etc. psyche you out because it will completely throw you off your game. In the end, if and when you achieve or already have achieved your own personal, as well as professional grand slam titles and continue to work hard with absolute determination for more I say to you game-set-match.

FUNNY BONE
April 11, 2012

Comedian Lenny Bruce once said, ~ Today's comedian has a cross to bear that he built himself. A comedian of the older generation did an "act" and he told the audience "This is my act." Today's comic is not doing an act. The audience assumes he's telling the truth. What is truth today may be a damn lie next week.~ Without a doubt, laughter is considered the best medicine, and you most definitely have a deep appreciation for people who make you laugh, especially those who do it for a living. Yet, you truly have an even deeper appreciation for a comedian who has that innate ability to completely avoid using profanity in their act just to get a teary eyed, gut-wrenching, side-splitting laugh like the following three individuals: Sinbad, Tim Conway, and Bob Hope.

Let me ask you this question to those who have watched on Comedy Central or quite possibly live in person Sinbad's stand-up routine, did you enjoy not only listening to him but watching him too knowing his performances are 100% clean? I think many would agree the man who once starred in A Different World can make any subject matter absolutely hilarious and to do it without spewing profanity is considered an impressive situation indeed. When it comes to his performances, he talks about experiences that each one of us can relate to from growing up as a kid and getting spanked to dealing with the pangs of getting older. Let me tell you something, he is very versatile but a highly underrated comedian who deserves much bigger props don't you think?

If you think about it, the days of a classic comedian have unfortunately fallen by the wayside as it has been replaced by vulgar content filled with profanity and sexual innuendo...but I digress. Essentially, when I mention classic comedians I'm referring to the likes of a comedy legend such as Tim Conway who could make you laugh without uttering a single word. What ultimately makes him funny without the use of curse words in his act is not only his comedic timing but his old-fashioned sense of wit that just brings a smile to your face, especially when teamed up with his comedic partner in crime Harvey Korman. Thinking about it, of the many hilarious comedy sketches he's been a part of on The Carol Burnett Show the one known as The Dentist is by far the best of them all.

For the question can be asked to those who actually know who Bob Hope is, do you think he is considered the king of clean comedy? If you said yes I would agree with you because you were fortunate enough to listen and/or watch his specials on tv back in the day. you know how much of a treat it was to be witnessing greatness right before our eyes. For it's true that you didn't have to worry about any profanity coming out of his mouth. Instead, what came out of it was pure comedy cold as he expressed funny satire oftentimes political ones at that. Hey, he is and will always be deemed a true comedic entertainer who appeared, as well as hosted 199 known USO shows to the point where in 1996 U.S. Congress honored him by declaring him the "first and only honorary veteran of the U.S. armed forces."

In retrospect, there are countless comedians who have a clean act and have not sold out by adding profanity into their act in order to get more fans or exposure for that matter. Comedy greats like Jerry Seinfeld, Billy Crystal, and Bill Cosby continue to have flourishing careers without the use of any profanity whatsoever in their performances. Granted, comedians such as Katt Williams, Dave Chappelle, Chris Rock, Daniel Tosh, etc. use it and have had not only very lucrative careers but huge fan bases also. What it primarily comes down to is that what may be funny to some may not be funny to others type mentality. In the end, the old school comics are and will always be the best because they didn't have to curse or use the "N" word in their act and knew how to tickle our funny bone the right way.

MORE THAN ENOUGH

March 21, 2012

Jonathan Lockwood Huie once said, ~Real love is never a selfish emotion. If you want something from someone - especially if that something is sex - what you are feeling is not true love. True love is about wanting happiness for the person you love - and not about seeking happiness for yourself. Fortunately, in most cases our own loving presence is the greatest gift we can give to a person we love. Nonetheless, the litmus test of love is knowing we would choose never to see that person again if we believed that distance would bring them greater happiness.~ Let me ask this question to you ladies out there who were or are currently in a potential and/or significant relationships, is/was there a selfish bone in the guy you are/thought you were in love with to where you have questioned/are questioning the love he has for you?

As a guy, you oftentimes hear about how a girl's relationship with a guy didn't last or is suffering because he treated/is treating her wrong and how absolutely selfish he was. True, it would have been the best time to say I told you so, but we didn't...but I digress. For it's an unfortunate situation indeed to those women who in their minds not only don't feel appreciated, but seemingly don't see themselves as attractive enough for their man that she loves with all her heart. Hey ladies, let me share with you four words that I hope will set you mentally and emotionally at ease... it's not your fault. Essentially, you've done nothing wrong as the fault lies with the guy in question who wants more than he already has causing him to be seen as selfish and not to mention greedy in regard to his own needs/wants knowing true happiness is standing right in front of him.

Without a doubt, we've all heard the saying why buy the cow

when you can get the milk for free, which relates to a guy's selfishness when it involves the lack of love and respect for the women he supposedly loves. You see, there are a certain number of guys who, even though they seem to be in strong, happy relationships, they want more to the point they seek out other women in order to fulfill their lustful desire for the physical relationship. In other words, it is basically a slap in the face to those women who don't deserve to be treated that way. Thinking about it further, it's "gentlemen" like these who treat them with disrespect and yet you can't help but fathom why these same women continue to stay by their side knowing they are far more deserving of a guy who they'll experience/share a love or a true love for that matter that is most definitely genuinely real.

If you think about it, it's considerably rare these days for any woman to meet a guy who doesn't have any ulterior motives or a selfish bone in their body when it pertains to being in a loving, committed relationship. I think it would be safe to say it's an absolute dream come true for many women to meet/be with a guy who loves them so much he's willing to set aside his own happiness to make their happiness not only memorable, but certainly worthwhile as well. A type of guy who will be there for you at 3.am. in order to be a sounding board or a shoulder to cry on knowing full well he didn't have to be there, but he is anyway as a friend. What it primarily comes down to is sacrifice and any guy who unselfishly puts himself second in order to make sure there's always a smile on the face of the woman he loves is worthy of her love.

In retrospect, it's a sad state of affairs when there are countless women who even though they are in a potential and/or significant relationship they feel neglected. Let me tell you something to the guys who are doing the neglecting, you had better watch out. Why? If you continue to ignore her there are guys like myself who are giving her attention. There are problems that arise that you cause, a guy like myself is listening to them. When you say you're too busy for her, guys like me make time for her. She's crying because of something you said or did, a guy like me will say or do something to make her smile. If you decide she's not worth your time, a guy like me knows she is. In the end, I say to those women who end up having that unfortunate mindset that you're not enough, don't think that because to some guy like myself you are more than enough.

NEVERMORE

April 30, 2012

Edgar Allen Poe once said, ~I was never really insane except where my heart is touched.~ If you think about it, when it comes to matters of the heart concerning falling in love, being in love, and not to mention utter heartbreak it can oftentimes feel as if or should I say compared to the well-known poem The Raven by Edgar Allen Poe. Essentially, the feelings, memories, and emotions one tries to deal with in their heart/head don't necessarily have that warm, butterflies in the pit of your stomach experience. You see, there are times where it can quite possibly be a midnight dreary of an existence within, leaving you weak and weary physically, mentally, spiritually, as well as emotionally to the point where it pushes you to the brink of absolute insanity.

Without a doubt, it can most definitely be a tough situation indeed as you endure the consistent tapping, so to speak, on the metaphorical chamber door of your own heart when love or the lack thereof causes you unfortunate and unbearable pain. It's within the chamber door of a person's heart where true happiness or the painful sorrow of a guy/girl who is known as their own personal Lenore. Thinking about it further, the thoughts and memories of him/her are thrilling and terrifying at the same time as the sound of continuous knocking is heard on the metaphorical door of one's own heart. A knock that can certainly resonate/echo within so much so to where it raises so many questions that it haunts not just every chamber of your heart but mind as well

As I said before, the sound of a continuous metaphorical knock on the chamber door of one's heart can raise so many questions that inevitably haunt your heart and mind. I think it would be safe to say we've all answered the door to our own heart countless times only to find there are no answers to speak of. It's an annoying and seemingly frustrating state of affairs to find yourself in as you stand there at the doorway of your own heart not only deeply staring into the darkness searching for any presence of the answer, but intently listening for it also. However, what all you get before you is instead dead silence. Let me tell you something, its the haunting and terror filled silence in your heart/head that leaves you wanting to rip your own hair out as it whispers his/her name leading you to gradually slip into absolute madness.

Let me ask you this question to those who are in love/falling in love and suffered an unfortunate heartbreak, were you able to calm your heart/mind giving you the time/opportunity to continue exploring/searching for the answers you've been seeking for that are deemed a mystery to you? If you said no you're right. There comes a point while attempting to get those particular answers you've been driven to the brink of insanity for someone or something comes along, swoops in and perches on the chamber door of your heart uttering not a single word, which is a representation of a stately raven. Hey, every person is currently in or has been in that type of situation where the answers we so want are perched on our heart/mind staring each one of us in the face torturing us with deafening silence. Yet, the question remains: have those questions been answered for you?

In retrospect, when the raven of unanswered question perches on your heart and mind, you can't help experiencing a stirring restlessness that can be described as nagging torture. For a certain number of people portray an outward calm but on the inside their screaming at the top of their lungs at the raven of unanswered questions wanting badly to be given the answers they've been seeking for quite some time. Unfortunately, some never receive those answers and find themselves being silently taunted by their own metaphorical dark, ominous metaphorical bird while others were able to figure it out on their own. In the end, I say to those who are continually being taunted by the raven of unanswered questions to true happiness, you will someday be given those answers and the silent, tortuous pain you've been experiencing will no longer be felt Quoth the Yoda Guru "Nevermore."

NEVER LOSE FAITH

May 22, 2012

Eric Fromm once said, ~Love is an act of faith, and whoever is of little faith is also of little love.~ If you think about it, love and faith are synonymous with each other as one doesn't work without the other. For its an unfortunate situation indeed to those who are in potential and/or significant relationships as he or she found/ is currently finding one's self losing/lost their faith in matters of the heart concerning love/true love. Hey, it can most definitely be difficult to keep the faith when it comes to your own heart, but don't ever give up hope on someday experiencing it. Essentially, what it primarily comes down to is the right choice in the guy/ girl that ultimately determines whether you'll be constantly experiencing the pangs of utter heartbreak many times over or end up finding absolute true happiness in that one person who makes you a better person.

Without a doubt, to place not only your heart but your unwavering faith in someone else's hands, so to speak, is considered one of the greatest risks anyone can put themselves through. So the question is why do it? Thinking about it, that is what makes falling in love such an unknown. To put yourself out there without any walls built up in front of you whatsoever leaving you to become vulnerable or should I say exposed to feeling the pain of getting mentally, as well as emotionally hurt. In other words, just being you. True, there is the innate fear of having your feelings, thoughts, and emotions be stomped on/toyed with/thrown back at you, which is understandable. However, in order to be in a place of peaceful contentment you have to be able to have faith in what truly scares you will hopefully bring a smile on not only your lips, but within your heart as well.

As said before, whoever is of little faith is also of little love. It's a sad state of affairs for those who have been hurt many times over in the past to the point where their faith in falling in love again for real with their best friend for life has been considerably shaken to its core. Granted, it's these particular number of people who even though may be in a worthwhile loving relationship with a great guy/girl but their faith in it to possibly go the distance tends to be lackluster to say the least, so much so they find any reason to break up. I think it's safe to say we know someone like this or are that someone whose scars of bad past relationships led him/her to bail out because they're basically scared to actually fall for someone who is actually being treated with the respect they deserve. A surprising and not to mention a frightening concept to even fathom, especially for women.

Mark 11:22-24 says, ~And Jesus answering saith unto them, Have faith in God. For verily I say unto you, That whosoever shall say unto this mountain, Be thou removed, and be thou cast into the sea; and shall not doubt in his heart, but shall believe that those things which he saith shall come to pass; he shall have whatsoever he saith. Therefore I say unto you, What things soever ye desire, when ye pray, believe that ye receive them, and ye shall have them.~ Let me ask you this question to those who are in potential and/or significant relationships, how many of you have put your unwavering faith in God as both of you continually prayer to him for spiritual guidance involving your relationship? You see, the love you have for Him will strengthen the love for each other through the tough times whereby strengthening the faith of fully believing the strong bond shared will certainly last a lifetime.

In retrospect, it's considerably hard these days to put 100% faith in love/true love when you're constantly hearing/showing the lack of loving faithfulness leading you to become a sarcastic cynic. Of course, you can't let that become a mental obstacle to where you consistently over analyze or second guess yourself and if one does you miss out on something potentially worthwhile. Oftentimes, the lack of faith within your heart will hopefully be restored by a certain special guy or girl who will give you the courage to open yourself up, leading you to do something that you haven't been able to do for quite some time...trust. In the end, to those who are struggling in their belief/faith in the actual existence of love/true love because of enduring past painful heartbreak I say keep praying to God, read His word for guidance, and never lose faith that your someday will eventually happen.

TO BE A KID AGAIN

June 18, 2012

Louis de Bernieros once said, ~ Did you know that childhood is the only time in our lives when insanity is not permitted to us but expected.~ Without a doubt, being a kid of the 70's, 80's, and early part of the 90's was/still is considered tremendously awesome to be a part of unlike the childhood of kids today. For it was a thrilling and not to mention interesting situation indeed for those of us who grew up/survived/made it out alive doing activities that were deemed absolutely fun and creative, but at the same time were seen as insanely crazy. Hey, it was most definitely a different time back in our day when cell phones, laptops, Facebook, Myspace, Twitter, etc. didn't exist and each one of us had to create our own form of entertainment considered to be absolutely priceless...our imagination.

Let me ask you this question to all you MacGyvers out there, when it comes to your imagination what type of insanity could you put together with the following items: your bike, a large piece of plywood, and several bricks or whatever was laying around. Now, put it all together and what do you have? If you said you're very own Evil Knievel start up stunt show, then you would be right. I think it's safe to say every boy and girl as well growing up created their own makeshift ramp to jump over and even though it didn't look impressive it served its purpose in being a form of entertainment lasting for hours on end. Unfortunately, there were drawbacks such as landing wrong causing considerable pain, especially for a guy if you know what I mean.

If you think about it, building forts made of wood in your backyard or in a secret place in the woods the way you wanted it was a way to use one's imagination. As a kid, it's fun but now as an adult you would be seen as insane for even playing in one let alone building one. However, if you still have your inner child building a fort within the confines of your own house using the "tools" like blankets, pillows, couch cushions, and the couch itself are necessary to create your so-called fortress of solitude. How many of us remember spending hours on end having an awesome time spent with your siblings, friends, and maybe even your parents just bonding, as well as talking with each other? Let me tell you something, as an adult building a fort with your couch is something that doesn't sound insane at all to the point where I would actually find myself doing it knowing I turn 35 in two months.

For the question can be asked to those who used their imagination when it involves a red wagon, a very steep hill in your neighborhood, and friends who you trusted to be lookouts? We've all at some point back in the day nearly killed ourselves as kids doing our own version of Cool Runnings. Thinking about it, we held on for dear life using not only the handle to attempt to steer but our own feet as the brake pedal, which worked 99.9% of the time. Oftentimes, we knew it was a bad idea but the thrill of hurtling down the hill at a great amount of speed superseded common sense during that particular time. Thankfully, many of us survived practically unscathed to where we almost got hit by passing cars because our friends were too pumped to notice cars were coming so much so, that we all ended up saying these 4 words...let's do it again!

In retrospect, there are so many things we did that were considered insanely crazy when we put our imagination to good use. For instance, pretending to be Spider-Man climbing the side of our bedroom door and if we fell...you know we all did... we endured a possible concussion afterwards. In addition, we jumped from couch to couch pretending that the floor was made out of lava or anything fire related. You see, the power of our imagination is a truly powerful weapon that I'm sad to say isn't being utilized by today's generation of ankle biters. In any case, for each one of us we've all suffered the battle wounds of our childhood essentially considered badges of honors using our imagination. In the end, when you think back and reminisce with your friends concerning the all out insanity you think to yourself or say out loud ah...to be a kid again.

MY BLOOD

July 1, 2012

Erica E. Goode once said, ~Sibling relationships - and 80 percent of Americans have at least one - outlast marriage, survive the death of parents, resurface after quarrels that would sink any friendship. They flourish in a thousand incarnations of closeness and distance, warmth, loyalty, and distrust.~ Let me ask you this question to those who have a sibling or a number of siblings, how close are you to him, her, and/or them? Essentially, the dichotomy of the relationship involving brothers and sisters can most definitely not only be considered interesting, but oftentimes complex as well. For it's a humorous situation indeed at times to stand back and simply observe the interaction between siblings whether they be an all-male, all female, or a mixture of both to where it's to say the least an absolute learning experience.

As I said before, the sibling relationship is not only considered interesting but complex as well. How so you may be asking yourself? You see, siblings, as they often do go through their fair share of physical and verbal altercations to the point where he, she, or they had to be separated from each other in order to cool off. It's during the swinging fists, tackles, wrestling takedowns, pulling of hair on the ground, etc. that verbal insults are thrown at one another in the heat of the moment causing both to become angry and quite possibly emotionally hurt at the same time. Hey, that's what brothers and sisters do as siblings certainly get on each other's nerves. Yet, it's our siblings we physically fight and verbally insult that we instantly come to their defense because you're the only one who is allowed to call him/her/them names, as well as fight with other individuals attempting to do so.

Without a doubt, there can be strong connections when it pertains to the ties that bind us to our siblings. Unfortunately, for a certain number of people there hasn't been or no longer is a strong connection between a particular brother or sister to where words have not been spoken to each other for quite some time. In addition, you may have to not have seen him, her, or them either causing an estranged sibling relationship. Words exchanged, specific action in the past deemed unforgivable, or whatever the case may be are examples may be a reason for the rift that once established an inseparable bond growing up in the past. So, do any of you have a brother or sister you haven't talked to/seen in a while because of something that happened in the past? If so, are you willing to make the first move to make contact in order to have a relationship once again?

Personally speaking, the relationship between my brother and I is considered close. He is 3 years younger than I am but he is taller so it even out in the whole scheme of things. Granted, we've had our fair share of physical fights when we were younger but now that we're older and in our 30's we just verbally insult each other to no end. I'm proud of him for the man, the husband, and father he's become to the point where I hope to be in the position, he is one day when it comes to having a family of my own someday. Thinking about it, my mom gave me the following words of wisdom that I'll share with you which are: ~No matter where you are or the distance that separates the two of us, always keep in contact with each other. You two will always be brothers and that's never going to change.~ It's a piece of valuable advice that I will keep in my mind and heart forever.

In retrospect, there is always going to be that love/dislike/hate relationship between siblings. The younger siblings will seemingly get away with anything if they are in trouble, but they should always listen to their older counterparts. They are truly looking out for you even if it doesn't seem like it. To the middle child/children of the family who have developed a Peter and Jan Bray inferiority complex, I'm just going to say your siblings for the most part care about you too. What it comes down to is showing it in their own strange and unique way. Finally, to those kids who were an only child. Well, nobody cares about you because you turned out to be spoiled brats. Just kidding. In the end, you know you can be proud of your siblings when you talk about them with a smile on your face to other people saying to him/her/them that's my best friend, my partner in crime, my familia; but most of all...my blood.

A SIGHT TO BEHOLD

July 5, 2012

Jeph Jacques once said, ~A good relationship is like fireworks: loud, explosive, and liable to maim you if you hold on too long.~ In some aspect, matters of the heart in regard to a loving/true love relationship are like spectacular fireworks display but never ends. For its an amazing situation indeed to be a part of something absolutely special and yet it can all be over within the blink of an eye. In a sense, that's how true happiness can most definitely be perceived as at times as a person's heart strings are metaphorically lit when a guy or girl potentially falls in love. However, it's the so-called explosive material within an individual's heart that determines whether the fireworks of a possibly flourishing relationship will either be a complete dud or shoot straight up and go off with a bang, in a good way of course.

Without a doubt, you get more bang for your buck...pun intended...when experiencing not just the amazing visual effects/ display but hearing how much of a huge impact it can be on a deeply personal level. Thinking about it, the same sensory experience can also certainly be felt and in some ways seen within one's own heart to the point where the explosive material within represents our feelings and emotions being set off either one by one or all at once. Every person has been in the past or currently is in a type of situation where there was/is a grand light show of explosions going on inside his/her heart because of a guy or girl that essentially lit the fuse, so to speak. Let me tell you something, the success of a relationship shooting up towards the stars depends on the genuine purity of the initial spark for that special someone.

If you think about it, like fireworks, relationships to a certain degree can be considered explosive if handled in the correct way.

I think I can safely say we all know someone or quite possibly are someone who handled a relationship incorrectly. You see, it started off in the beginning stages of a seemingly wondrous and awe-inspiring extravaganza of love where the explosiveness between the two of you was too hot to handle. However, it's during their dance across the metaphorical night sky that is the human heart, negative factors such as jealousy, anger, dishonesty, disrespect, mistrust, doubt, fear, etc. caused an explosive and not to mention volatile relationship. It's a sad state of affairs when you, him/her, or both of you end up getting maimed or burned, in a manner of speaking, to where a scar has been left on your/their heart as an unfortunate reminder.

Let me ask you this question to those who have witnessed in person or on tv a fireworks show, what part of it do you look forward to the most? If you said the finale, you would be correct because you want to view an awesome instead of disappointing ending leaving you with a smile on your face rather than a frown. In a way, each of us wants to experience that one-of-a-kind memorable finale but with one difference, which is it's a never-ending light show filled with joy, happiness, contentment, honesty, trust, faith, hope, communication, etc. Fortunately, for a certain number of people they're currently experiencing it right now as we speak and it's awesome so much so that you can't help but smile for them. Hey, there is no end in sight for those you know that their relationships will last forever as it's a continual grand finale after grand finale for the both of them.

In retrospect, fireworks can oftentimes be taken for granted and the same can be said for a loving relationship too. Essentially, a person can go through the motions, or should I say the oohs and aahs when it pertains to the colorful bursts/picture of a new relationship. The unfortunate tendency is to burn or explode brighter than the other and that is the mistake right there my friend. Unfortunately, they tend to forget what the true meaning is all about and that is the special moments, big or small, are shared together to make an even tremendous portrait for others to see. What it primarily comes down to is not using up all the fireworks because every once in a while, he'll/she'll/you'll shoot up a few surprises for him/her/you. In the end, I say to those who continue to have a flourishing loving relationship that dances across the night sky of each other's heart I hope it never ends because for people like me it's truly a sight to behold.

HEART KNOCK LIFE
July 9, 2012

Cherie Carter-Scott once said, ~Remember, there are no mistakes, only lessons. Love yourself, trust your choices, and everything is possible.~ Without a doubt, the mistakes made inevitably become life lessons to learn, especially when it pertains to matters of the heart. Thinking about it, the easy way isn't always the proverbial route taken to learn the unfortunate lesson after experiencing times of utter heartbreak. For it's a tough and oftentimes frustrating situation indeed learning the hard way the choices made concerning your own heart were in hindsight not healthy whatsoever personally, mentally, spiritually, and most definitely emotionally. However, the past is past and hopefully one's sad, painful lessons of love have led or are leading you to absolute true happiness.

If you think about it. one of the lessons you try to learn after being the dumpee whereby suffering a mixture of emotions is staying true to who you are once you get back into the dating scene. Women, more often than not, tend to do the self-evaluation checklist in which they go over qualities that in their minds are apparently lacking leading them to believe something is totally wrong causing a warped mindset to set in all thanks to a past relationship. Unfortunately, while breaking themselves personally and mentally, there can certainly be a so-called storm of emotional turmoil within their own heart as they figure out whether to stay true to their unique individuality or be similar to every other woman out there. Let me tell you something ladies, just be you and nobody else because the unique, attractive qualities that make you who you are will shine forth for the right guy to take notice.

As a guy, there is a tendency to go with and trust the choices we make regarding the pursuit of the female species to the point where the following lesson is learned: what we think will happen to what actually happens. You see, when a particular female of interest is in our crosshairs, in a manner of speaking, we will automatically act on our basic, primal hunting, gut instincts, which ends 99.9% being a big mistake as we say or do something absolutely foolish. Hey, every guy including myself has been there but fortunately it's a live and learn process where we take the lessons learned from past mistakes to eventually correctly handle a possible heart to heart connection by doing the total opposite of what we're planning to do/say. Essentially, the wisdom gained determines whether we receive an affectionate rather than a harsh blank stare in return.

Luke 18:26 says, ~And he said, The things which are impossible with men are possible with God.~ Let me ask you this question to those who learned the lesson that love/true is possible if you just put your faith and trust in the hands of God? True, there are times where our faith and trust in Him are lacking causing one to believe their happily ever after is a mere fairy tale; but you got to remember nothing is impossible when He is in control. It's a sad state of affairs for those who are unable to grasp that concept and rely on themselves rather than on high. What it primarily comes down to is fervently praying to the Lord Jesus Christ for spiritual guidance, having a deeper understanding when reading His biblical principles, and finally putting the love you have for the Lord first will show you how all things are possible when it involves the happiness you deserve for your own heart.

In retrospect, love always teaches us something new and even though it may be a harsh pill to swallow sometimes, the key lessons we take from it turn each one of us into better people because of it. Granted, one may not realize it because of the mixed combo of thoughts, feelings and emotions swirling around within not only your heart, but mind as well. The human heart is quite fascinating as it is considered a resilient muscle taking a tremendous beating, in a manner of speaking, time after time enduring all sorts of trauma such as being stabbed, knocked around, stomped on, etc. Ultimately, it keeps on beating despite all that it has been through emotionally. In the end, if I may tweak the title to one of Jay Z's popular songs when I say that we've all at some point or are experiencing right now a heart knock life; but with our family, best buds, gal pals, and God at our side we'll be just fine.

ALL THE RIGHT MOVES
August 6, 2012

Someone once said, ~Love is like a game of chess: One false move and you're mated.~As mentioned before, love is like a game of chess and it most definitely takes strategy when it comes to making certain moves on the metaphorical chess board that is a person's heart. For its a matter of playing correctly, so to speak, as each chess piece is a representation of our own feelings, thoughts, and not to mention emotions concerning a special someone of interest. Thinking about it, if you're living the single life the moves made in regard to the proverbial chess board of one's heart to another are considered important to where they can certainly range from simple to absolutely critical. Hey, when it comes to the possibility of true happiness you don't want to make any crucial mistakes whatsoever.

If you think about it, chess is more of a mental game than anything else with one's feelings, thoughts, and emotions not being involved. However, that isn't the case regarding the chess game known as love/true love. It can be a tough, frustrating, and stressful situation indeed when not just the mental aspect plays a pivotal role but the emotional, spiritual, as well as physical roles too. You see, all four are essentially connected to the individual chess pieces representing far more than you think. Trust, honesty, loyalty, faith, hope, commitment, respect, etc. are a number of genuine qualities being shown within each move for the guy/girl in question to see on the board, in a manner of speaking. Let me tell you something, it's better to take your time than making a rash decision whereby not letting your emotions take control causes you to find/put yourself in an unfortunate check situation.

Without a doubt, there comes a point that while playing chess you may possibly second guess yourself when making a potential move. Oftentimes, having second thoughts in making a particular move can lead to doubt and fear setting in thus causing you to question whether the strategy one's taking will in all intents and purposes pay off, especially in matters of the heart. Truth be told, you can't know for sure so much so one word tends to stick within your mind...maybe. Maybe I'm being foolish. Maybe I'm just kidding myself. Maybe I'm not that person's type. Maybe I should quit before I completely embarrass myself. True, the word maybe can certainly mess with your head; but you have to block it out to where you think to yourself, maybe I should stop over thinking/analyzing it and simply play smart from your heart all-the-while controlling every aspect of your emotions/thoughts/feelings in the process.

Let me ask this question to those who know and play the game of chess, do you use a chess clock in order to give yourself a fixed period of time and keep track of the total amount of time one takes for his or her own move? To be perfectly honest, I wouldn't want to use a chess clock because even though it makes the game quicker it leaves you vulnerable to making an unfortunate mistake. In a sense, you wouldn't want to rush a worthwhile relationship by making moves that don't make sense or end up costing you the close friendship you already established with him/her right? Unfortunately, it's a sad state of affairs for those individuals who did just that and found themselves in checkmate due to their own stupidity. So, the question remains to the so-called chess players out there: are you making each move within your heart count or are you just rushing through it without even thinking about the consequences?

In retrospect, if you're living the single life, we're all, in some aspect, searching for our own Bobby Fischer. In other words, we all want to meet/find our very own special chess prodigy who will be able to match up with us not only move for move, but in playing style as well. A type of person who you don't want to find out too late you were simply a pawn in his/her twisted game. Granted, for some people they've played countless chess matches until they were able to finally meet the Queen to their King or vice versa. On the other hand, it took only one game for you to match up and through time, along with patience, inevitably became quintessential grandmasters together. In the end, I say to those who are currently taking their time on the metaphorical chess board that is someone's heart, I hope you make all the right moves towards a potentially worthwhile relationship.

THANKS FOR THE MEMORIES

August 19, 2012

William Rudolph once said, ~ Winning is great, sure, but if you are really going to do something in life, the secret is knowing how to lose. Nobody goes undefeated all the time. If you can pick yourself up after a crushing defeat, and go on to win again, you are going to be a champion someday.~ Without a doubt, the above mentioned quote relates to everybody in regards to playing sports, but it relates more to those individuals who competed in the 2012 London Olympics for the past 2 weeks who had one goal in mind...winning gold. For its truly a memorable and not to mention awe inspiring situation indeed for those of us who watched on tv but even more so for the athletes themselves proudly representing their country, especially those who were either there for the very first time or their last making it quite literally one for the record books.

Let me ask you this question to those of us who watched the 2012 London Olympics, who inspired you to the point where you thought to yourself if that person can do it why can't I? I think it's safe to say we all were or should I say still are inspired by the story of 25-year-old South African track runner Oscar "Blade Runner" Pistorious who is a double amputee. For Pistorious, just being at the Olympics was considered a victory in itself even though there were critics who believed he shouldn't be there because his prosthetic legs would give him an unfair advantage but that wasn't the case. In any case, whether he won or lost he most definitely won the hearts and support of millions of people around the world, inevitably inspiring us to where he spread the message of strength, determination, resiliency, and nothing is impossible if you want to go for/live out your dream.

If you think about it, when it comes to the Olympics we have certainly seen a number of familiar faces such as the charismatic Usain Bolt, Ryan Lochte, Michael Phelps, Pro NBA stars for Team USA, May and Walsh, etc.; but it's the fresh, new faces that have graced our presence who have made a significant/lasting impression on each one of us. 5 time medalists/ swimmer Missy Franklin and 5 Gymnasts simply known as The Fierce Five (Gabby Douglass, Aly Raisman, McKayla Maroney, Jordan Weiber, and Kyla Ross) have essentially become America's golden girls capturing not only our attention but hearts as well. True, they maybe first time newbies to the Olympics but they will ultimately carry the torch inevitably passed down by the old guard, so to speak, who made their final...considerably bittersweet for us...decision to retire from their event they so dominated

As I said before, the fresh-faced Olympians will surely carry the torch passed down by the quintessential "old guard" like 3 Time Olympic Medalist in Beach Volleyball Misty May-Treanor and a man who is considered to be both a legend with 22 medals, as well as arguably THE greatest of all time Michael Phelps. Misty May parts ways with her long-time beach volleyball partner Kerri Walsh-Jennings but their friendship continues on and even though Walsh will have a new partner at the 2016 Olympics in Rio it won't be the same seeing those two together dominating the sand they unofficially deemed their kingdom. When it comes to Phelps, he leaves behind a legacy that every future Olympic swimmer strives to attain and hopefully there will possibly be one guy or girl who will one day surpass the 22 medals set by a man who had an absolutely remarkable career.

In retrospect, the 2012 London Olympics optimized world unity by showing the thrill of victory and the agony of defeat but doing it with as much restraint as they possibly can. Granted, there were a few unfortunate losing tantrums by way of USA's Morgan Uceny who tripped for the second time involving the women's 1500 final and South Korea's Shin A-Lam who refused to leave the stage after suffering a loss to her German opponent. Of course, the lows of the games didn't dampen the all-out highs in regard to Team USA kicking butt and taking names in the medal department....in your face France! I digress. In the end, 2016 in Rio is 4 years away and we were surely seeing the likes of Missy Franklin, Usain Bolt, Rebecca Soni, Team USA Basketball/VolleyBall, etc. winning medals once again, but to Michael Phelps and Misty May-Treanor we Americans say to you both thanks for the memories.

EXPECT THE UNEXPECTED
August 25, 2012

Someone once said, ~Teaching children responsibility requires wisdom and perseverance. Styles of leadership are as different as each child. Parenting kids starts with simple life lessons and short time frames. There will probably be fear, complaining, and a lack of effort. As kids mature, they take on expanded assignments and handle increased accountability and interaction with others. Eventually, children learn to exercise self motivation as they see the needs around them. Embracing challenges and problems is a start towards taking o n the role of a leader. Thoughtful and persistent involvement is needed to encourage children along the path. Without a doubt, working with kids/youth is most definitely a challenge and I should know as I've spent a better part of 12 years in the childcare profession.

As I said before, I've spent a better part of 12 years working with kids and whether you're a teacher or work in the childcare profession I can safely say they can truly be unpredictable, which is an assessment many of you quite possibly agree with. For it can certainly be an interesting and not to mention oftentimes bizarre situation indeed concerning the things said and done by kids to the point where you have to do an all out double take just to know what one witnessed or heard actually happened. It just befuddles the mind the seemingly bold/fearless actions and the words coming out of a kid's mouths today that if we said or did it back in the day in front of/to any adult our parents would beat the living snot out of each one of us for being totally disrespectful.

If you think about it, today's generation of kids are considered more outspoken, so much so they speak their minds no matter the consequences causing you to wonder if they talk like that to their own parents? Yet, it's not so much the how but rather the way you're being spoken to inevitably leading you or more importantly me with the kids I work with now to do the following 4 things: Raise my eyebrows, step back, stare them down, and firmly state as calm as can be the words excuse me. The eye/neck roll, non-caring shoulder shrug combined with the lip smack are so annoying and irritating to me every time I ask "my kids"...mainly the girls...why they are in trouble. Let me tell you something, I know one day they are going to do it to the wrong person and they're either going to end up beat down, shot, stabbed, or far worse...dead.

Let me ask this question to those who are teachers and/or work in the childcare profession, what is the most memorable thing a child has done that you're simply speechless and shaking your head in absolute disbelief? Truth be told, you can't just name one specific situation in the past or recently mind you, but they can be ranked from "standing there hanging your head in embarrassment" to the "see I told you so" moments. Personally speaking, I've had more of the hanging head because of embarrassing moments in the past 4 months because when it comes to "my kids" they will cross the line and don't even care that they do. Hey, they may be frustrating to no end making what hair I have left go entirely gray, but I know they will eventually smarten up if because the real world is more cruel and meaner than I am.

A friend once asked me if you complain about "your kids" constantly not listening and disrespecting you then why do you keep going back to work? My usual go to answer would always be because I'm crazy and I'm a glutton for mental punishment. However, I would quickly follow it up with it because I enjoy the challenge it involves and the added benefit to it is I get to see many of them grow up into fine young men/women who I consider to be a quintessentially big brother too. Thinking about it, those same kids I continue to keep in contact with and are friends of mine on Facebook. Ultimately, you're rewarded with a long-lasting friendship and that my friend is worthwhile. Granted, "my kids" now are wild bulls that are gradually being tamed and it will take vast amounts of time and patience but in the end, all I got to say is when you're around them expect the unexpected.

DEAD AND GONE
August 30, 2012

Someone once said, ~Hiding your feelings isn't the easy way out, but sometimes its the only thing you can do.~ If you think about it, matters of the heart concerning our own feelings for a certain guy or girl can most definitely lead you to experience a mixture of emotions. Frustration, confusion, and anger are just a number of emotions causing you to lose focus to the point where it may push you to the brink of mental insanity. To be perfectly honest, it's a sad state of affairs for any person to live that way but it's a choice an individual makes. You see, for some people they have dealt with it by opening up to the cause of their emotional torture face to face, inevitably freeing themselves of the weight/ burden they've been holding on to/suppressing deep down inside for quite some time. Yet, for others keeping their feelings hidden is all that they've ever really known and been familiar with, whereby making life a bit more complicated than easy.

Without a doubt, to continually keep your feelings for a guy or girl on the down low is never an experience you don't want to put yourself through. In other words, it's a fate worse than death. As said before, it can be a frustrating and not to mention confusing situation indeed as a hurricane of emotions stir within; but you have to understand the circumstances behind it in locking down what each one of us deem in our mind fearful to reveal. Why? Thinking about it, you don't want to lose the friendship already established with him/her and there is a point of no return you can never really go back from. For the most part, it may not be as it once was, knowing the friend zone was attempted to be crossed and it didn't end up turning out the way you thought it would. Hey, we've all been through it in the past and those who continue to live an unbearable life of constantly being emotionally constipated they've been able to manage just fine.

Oftentimes, having feelings for someone is at times more trouble than they're worth because it causes you to become unfocused. The guy/girl did nothing wrong whatsoever just to be clear. I think many who have or are experiencing it right now agree you aren't yourself and the people around may keenly notice the change in demeanor/behavior/attitude. Of course, if you have the ability to show that absolutely nothing is wrong with your emotional instability then you are not only a pro at this but deserving of an Oscar for best actor/actress as well my friend. In any case, what it comes down to is having an outlet to drain, in a manner of speaking, the feeling/thoughts/emotions you're in a sense drowning in. Let me tell you something, whether it be creative or not, the way you maturely handle your hidden emotions will gradually, even if its merely on a temporary basis, help bring back one's level of sanity until another issue rises to the surface.

Personally speaking, I have never been the guy who has been able to verbally express my feelings when it comes to making a heart-to-heart connection, especially now with a particular female of interest in the proverbial picture. You see, that's not me and unfortunate past experiences have gradually turned me in all intents and purposes emotionally constipated but have given form to what I do best. Essentially, when it comes to searching my feelings in regard to this certain female is that she is beautiful both inside and out bringing a smile to my face. She intrigues me. Her tenacity, strength, the drive/determination in setting out for her goals, and selflessness in caring for others make her a truly remarkable, as well as special woman in my eyes. My focus has become compromised. Is this love? My answer is no. However, the feelings I have are stirring within and they're absolutely genuine. Unfortunately, she will hear only silence because I would rather keep silent than to find myself in another embarrassing, awkward situation, whereby turning me into more of a cynical, sarcastic individual than I already am.

In retrospect, there is a flip side to this in which you should tell someone how you feel because opportunities are lost within the blink of an eye and regret can last a lifetime. I wholeheartedly agree with the sentiment but again you have to go back to a person's past circumstances that have caused people such as myself to be tight lipped about sharing their feelings to someone they genuinely like and want to get to know on a more personal level. When it comes to my emotional outlet, I fall back on writing it down in a notebook then transferring it from the page to my blog and it's at that point all the weight/burden I've been experiencing during that particular moment/day/week has dissipated. As long as I am able to have a mechanical pencil, notebook in hand, and my blog, my thoughts/feelings/emotions will always have a way to express how/the way I feel in my own heart. In the end, the choice to hide your feelings is solely your own decision so despite suppressing/pushing them aside they're never dead and gone giving you the opportunity to act if it's not too late.

HEART OF THE STORM

September 1, 2012

Someone once said, ~Love is like a hurricane. There is no stopping it. You can't control when or where it hits. It comes and stirs up your whole life. Then it's so beautiful that you can't get enough of it. Then it starts getting rocky again. Afterwards, it leaves your whole world in pieces. It's how you rebuild your world that brings that "perfect storm". Without a doubt, just like a hurricane the force of nature known as love can most definitely wreak havoc on people's lives to the point where it ends up leaving a path of destruction in its wake. Yet, the path of destruction, in a manner of speaking, may either be something so absolutely beautiful you're at a loss for words or a completely horrific nightmare to where you're left speechless for an entirely different reason.

Let me ask you this question to those who have been through a hurricane or several for that matter, what do you do to prepare for the approaching storm? If your answer is putting up a protective wooden barrier around your house, then you would be correct. In a sense, that's how it is when the destructive hurricane force of possible true happiness approaches a protective wall/ barrier that is metaphorically built/put up around your heart to keep the proverbial flood of thoughts/feeling/emotions from damaging/destroying all you hold truly valuable within. Hey, it can certainly be a tough situation indeed to try to mentally and emotionally hold back what can at times be immensely overpowering; unless you have experienced it so many times over in the past so much so you've grown into an incredibly strong person in every sense of the word.

If you think about it, with every hurricane there is always an eye of the storm in which you'll find yourself in a momentary state of calm until the chaos resumes once again. I think I can safely say each one of us has been or are currently in the momentary calming eye of their own personal hurricane in regard to a potential relationship. Essentially, you're able to take a step back from within yourself as the stormy winds/rain of your own thoughts/feelings/emotions briefly stopped swirling or should I say thrashing around your mind, as well as heart. For it primarily gives you, along with your best buds/gal pals by your side, the opportunity to in all intents and purposes assess the damage, if any, it has caused you. Let me tell you something, you receive much better clarity concerning yourself once the utter whirlwind of chaos that is over analyzing/thinking settles down whereby you're given 3 options: run, hunker down within yourself, or move forward facing it head on.

Isaiah 25:4 says, ~For thou hast been a strength to the poor, a strength to the needy in his distress, a refuge from the storm, a shadow from the heart, when the blast of the terrible ones is as a storm against the wall.~ Thinking about it, don't rely on yourself to get through the difficulties of the hurricane of all that is weighing/burdening your mind and heart because you'll end up driving yourself absolutely insane. For the most part, you can constantly ask the same questions over and over before realizing you're at a dead end. In that moment, give the questions to God involving matters of the heart for they will be answered in His time and while you wait for them to come to fruition open the word of the Lord. What it comes down to is deeply meditating in the Lamb's Book of Life all the while fervently praying to Him to safely spiritually guide you through the chaotic madness.

In retrospect, we've all heard or have been told to hope for the best but prepare for the worst and it pertains to the hurricane such as love. It's a sad state of affairs for those individuals who have the mindset of being 100% prepared if they do find themselves falling in love and nothing worse could ever go wrong. True, they may quite possibly be fully prepared but what they end up not knowing is how massive it is thinking it's going to be just a tropical storm/category 1 type conditions but it's really a category 5 monster. In other words, never underestimate its power or you'll find yourself suddenly sucked up without anything to grab on to and before you know it your heart winds up needing National Guard/Red Cross assistance. In the end, I say to those who are at/in the heart of the storm when it comes to a potential or even significant relationship, I hope the worst is over for you as you finally experience some much needed peace.

PATH OF LOVE

September 9, 2012

Mary Miyavi posed this question, ~ Is it better to be in love and feel vulnerable or to be loved and feel safe?~ Essentially, that is considered to be the 100 million dollar question my friend. You see, an individual may not always be able to distinguish between the two because quite frankly the powerful force known as true happiness can certainly be overpowering to the point where the emotional, as well as mental lines are blurred. It's a sad state of affairs when a person doesn't have any idea as they've become impaired mentally and emotionally, so much so they can't answer the question or in some cases refuses to answer it. For it's a tough situation indeed for any person to try to figure it out for themselves all the while knowing it's not going to be an easy task whatsoever to undertake while traveling the quintessential path to the promised land.

If you think about it, to be loved and feel safe is a situation where a certain number of people find one's self to be in. True, being in a significant relationship has been established and feeling that sense of safety due to their presences is there but it doesn't necessarily mean its the better path to take, so to speak. Oftentimes, when a person is in this type of relationship, he/she quite possibly has this innate feeling as if something is missing. Thinking about it further, it's that particular something, whatever it may be, in which a guy/girl will not do anything about it and continue to ignore it for that matter. Why? Truth be told, one would rather be comfortable instead of dealing with issues of the heart whereby leading to a stronger, deeper connection sorely needed to build up a lasting worthwhile partnership.

Without a doubt, being in what I refer to as "A Roommate Relationship" there is more of an internal distance going within a person's heart/mind even though it may seem a happy couple altogether on the outside. As it has been said many times before, looks can most definitely be deceiving. For the most part, these types of couples who despite showering each other with love and affection there is a considerable disconnect when it comes to connecting to a deeply personal, as well as emotional level. In other words, they feel so comfortable going through the motions of a relationship to where they do their best to avoid any kind of conflict. Hey, I think we all know a couple or may in fact be the other half of a couple who just feels absolutely disconnected and missing something in their relationship even though you/he/she is feeling the love and safety with a certain someone.

Let me ask this question to those who are in potential and/or significant relationships, which type of relationship are you or would you want to be in? To be perfectly honest, I would choose the path of being in a relationship where I'm in love and feel truly vulnerable rather than to be in love and feel safe. Unfortunately, it's a rarity these days to experience because of how much utter heartbreak and trust issues there are leading to so many people choosing the path that doesn't hurt so much. Ultimately, what one does is simply settling for comfort instead of what one is more deserving of. Granted, you may be afraid to completely open yourself up knowing he/she may end up stabbing/stomping your heart into the ground but that's the risk one takes in regard to love/true love. Let me tell you something ladies and gents, it's so worth it once you do.

In retrospect, every person will eventually walk, is walking or has walked a long, winding path within their heart and there's always going to be the proverbial fork reached. The path of putting in the hard work or the one of least resistance. The decision to go for easy or go for hard is all up to you but know this and that is love and relationship aren't easy by any means, which it generally never is. For the question can be asked, would you want a relationship where you constantly feel the butterflies in your stomach with someone special or continually have the annoying, nagging feeling of something missing within your heart. What it comes down to is being absolutely honest with yourself. In the end, I say to those who are traveling the path of love to true happiness it's going to be tough on you emotionally, mentally, personally, and spiritually so choose wisely.

YOU ARE NOT ALONE

September 16, 2012

Anais Nin once said, ~I know why families were created with their imperfections. They humanize you. They are made to make you forget yourself occasionally, so that the beautiful balance of life is not destroyed.~ As said before many Yodaisms ago, we've all felt like at some point in our lives that each of us have been adopted as we stood around our own family members wondering who these dysfunctional people are in my life. Thinking about it, being part of a family means taking the insanely weird, strange, and certainly frustratingly bad times along with the good. You see, no family is perfect and even though the situations may be different than others it's the struggle, pain, and not to mention the unwanted drama that remain the same. For it's the ups and downs of life in which you and your family experience to the point where it has either brought all of you closer together or ended up completely torn apart. Hey, its how you correctly deal with your blood that essentially determines the strength, as well as resiliency within yourself.

Without a doubt, there is always going to be the proverbial power struggle between parent and child, which has been happening since the dawn of time. For those of you who are parents, it's a tough situation indeed to continually impart safe wisdom to your offspring in order to help them mentally, emotionally, physically, and most definitely spiritually grow even when they've reached adulthood. The teachings/lessons never stop. True, there is substantial resistance on their part causing a considerable amount of rebellion but sooner or later they'll get it. I have to tip my hat to all you parents out there who have enormous amounts of time and patience all the while knowing your efforts as a parent will significantly pay off immensely to where years down the road, they will greatly appreciate everything you've done/sacrificed for them.

If you think about it, a family does humanize you, so much so that there will oftentimes be a quintessential role reversal in behavior/attitude where the parent(s) act like kids and the kids themselves take more of a parental role. I think it would be safe to say every person knows someone who is that someone who had to grow up fast for the sake of their family whereby the weight of more responsibility is placed on their/your own shoulders. He/she/you stepped up into the parent role because your mom and/or dad is acting more like a selfish teenager fulfilling their own personal needs than to their family. This also applies in a professional capacity as well...but I digress. Let me tell you something, it can take an emotional and mental toll on you or any person for that matter leading to a breakdown in which tears are possibly shed; but through times of sadness comes strength.

Philippians 2:1-3 says ~If there be therefore any consolation in Christ, if any comfort of love, if any fellowship of the Spirit, if any bowels and mercies. Fulfill ye my joy, that ye be like minded, having the same love, being of one accord, of one mind. Let nothing be done through strife or vainglory; but in lowliness of mind, let each esteem others better than himself~ Let me ask you this question to you, despite the dysfunctional drama within your crew of embarrassingly insane mental patients do you still love them, nonetheless? Oftentimes, the love we have for God should be the same for the individuals in our family. It's hard, I know at times. Yet, it's a sad state of affairs when one experiences disappointment after disappointment from a certain family member, inevitably putting strain on the relationship. However, you don't give up on them and continue to pray To Him they'll make the right decisions because that's what family does for each other right?

In retrospect, we all got to deal with the cards dealt to us when it comes to the family we grew with. As the saying goes, friends come and go but family is forever. Granted, you may cringe at that particular saying after thinking about a particular family member but at the same time you can't help but laugh or smile for that matter. Why? As much as you want to secretly swap/ trade in your mom/dad/brother/sister you know they make your life that much interesting. Of course, they'll test your patience and everything else in between but that's what a family does as we drive each other to the brink of insanity. Personally speaking, I love my abnormally crazy family and wouldn't want to be part of anyone else's. In the end, I say to those who think they have no idea what one is going through in regard to family, you're not alone, because someone out there is wondering/thinking/saying the exact same thing.

OVERRATED
September 22, 2012

Two time Oscar winning actress Jodie Foster once said, ~Normal is not something to aspire to, it's something to get away from.~ Are you normal? Essentially, it's a question every person has been asked once or quite possibly many times before. Thinking about it, you aren't easily offended by being asked that particular question because to be perfectly honest nobody in this world is considered 100% normal. For it's an interesting and not to mention humorous situation indeed as countless people practically go against the norm in order to show/express their own unique individuality. You see, each one of us aren't normal by any stretch of the imagination and we tend to show our friends, family, co-workers, etc. in the following three ways: think, act, and most definitely dress.

Without a doubt, actions speak louder than words and it truly rings true concerning anyone who does things so out of the ordinary you wonder if they're in the right mindset. Hey, every person does or has done something so out of character on any given day but it's how high on the abnormal scale inevitably determines whether you're deemed weird/strange or need to be sent to a mental institution for psychiatric help. A perfect example is a celebrity with an ego maniacal, narcissistic personality whose actions of the past have been questionable to downright unbelievable, especially with the leaked Scientology interview he did that put him in a whole new light. True, on a professional level Tom Cruise is mostly golden in the box office but when it comes to him personally, he's a complete and utter whack job who is living in his own distorted world.

Let me ask you this question to those who have their own style of clothing: in your mind how normal is it to wear something you believe makes you stand out a bit from the crowd. Granted, each of us does from time-to-time follow fashion trends that are style one minute and then are out the next. It's pretty much the norm not just in the United States but all over the world. Now, would you ever consider going completely out of the norm and wear something like countless amounts of meat in order to make a fashion statement? My answer is no and hopefully yours too. Fortunately, one such individual is bold enough to redefine what isn't normal when it involves fashion and has become the quintessential poster child for wearing outlandish stuff so much so you're no longer surprised at what Lady GaGa is wearing to where you think she can't top herself. Could she?

In retrospect, being normal takes a lot of hard work to pull off but pulling off not being normal is easier than you think. Oftentimes, being you all the while showing how real you are, weird tendencies/quirks and all, is much better than trying to pull off something you know you aren't. Let me tell you something, I know it's not considered normal by society standards to dress up in costume when movies such as Star Trek, Star Wars, etc. play; but when you're a die-hard fan you don't care what society thinks because you enjoy it. Ultimately, you have to be comfortable within yourself to express your inner nerd/dork/geekiness and still be you without selling out, whereby showing how abnormally cool you are. In the end, who really wants to be normal in this crazy mixed up world we live in because I don't and besides, it's highly overrated if you ask me.

I WON'T GIVE UP
September 26, 2012

Someone once said, ~Being single isn't bad. What is bad is giving up hope in finding that special someone.~ Without a doubt, for those who are living the single life like myself we hope to one day stand right there in front of looking into the eyes of who we're going to spend the rest of our lives with. It's his/her eyes in which they quite possibly hold so much behind/within them to where they're considered an old soul in a fairly young body. However, there comes a point where each of us ends up struggling with that sense of hoping to inevitably meet the guy/girl essentially representing true happiness. For it can most definitely be a tough and not to mention frustrating situation indeed so much so you've contemplated giving up and abandoning any or all hope in every truly experiencing love/true love. So, the question remains to those who are in fact single, have you given up hope?

As I said before, it certainly can be tough and frustrating for any individual struggling to keep hope alive within one's heart. Thinking about it further, even though we might be in serious contemplation about giving up the idea of finally falling in love, you don't necessarily set it aside completely in never happening either. Hey, you know with 100% assurance the special qualities and moral character traits making you who you are will eventually be noticed by a guy/girl, whoever he/she is, mirroring maybe the same special qualities and moral character traits as well. Granted, the mere thought of it puts a smile on any single person's face but at the same time leaves you with ample amount of time to mentally/personally/spiritually/emotionally navigate your heart/mind, which isn't always a good thing.

If you think about it, when you're left navigating your own heart/mind you contend with that proverbial inner voice concerning where and when one will meet your best friend for life. A definite test in every sense of the word for many single people who are going through and trying not to listen to it as we speak. You see, it's during those moments you suddenly realize you're simply wasting your time in trying to question/control your own love life to where you just let go of the control whereby putting it in the hands of God. Let me tell you something, its always going to be a live and learn process that I'm personally trying to adhere to knowing how much I over-think/analyze matters of my own heart. In other words, when I relinquished control of my heart and continually pray to Him, it will be so worth it when I eventually meet the woman of my dreams who I'll give all my love to and have waited patiently for/

Let me ask this question to my fellow single peeps out there, are you the type of person who gives up and easily walks away in regard to the scary possibility of getting hurt or stands your ground in hopes that a heart-to-heart connection may come to fruition? Oftentimes, it's our utter heartbreaks of the past are, in some ways, gifts used as teaching tools helping us to understand ourselves better and show us how strong and wise for that matter each of us has become. Of course, the similarities shared help lay the groundwork, in a manner of speaking, but it's in the differences we find in that certain special someone can lead to a much deeper relationship. What it primarily comes down to is not negatively stripping away who you are just to be in a significant relationship with him/her as it is about positively adding more to be the awesome person you are because of him/her and vice versa.

In retrospect, the single life isn't as terrible as it seems as mentioned in the above quote. We all have our support system of gal pals/best buds to hang with and are given when we need an abundance of laughs to keep us from thinking about how we're constantly reminded of how we lack a significant other on a seemingly semi-daily basis....but I digress. In any case, it's God who knows how emotionally, personally, mentally, and spiritually tough we are as we individually go about our lives all the while unknowingly or knowingly making a difference in the lives of others. We never stop learning when it comes to our own heart and when things look bleak or depressing just look up, get on your knees, and pray. Trust me it works. In the end, it's a sad state of affairs when people give up entirely having lost all hope pertaining to their own heart; but as for myself and my fellow single peeps out there who still strongly believe with continued hope in our heart we firmly say together as one I won't give up, which is a song by 2 Time Grammy winner Jason Mraz.

HAVEN'T MET YOU YET

September 29, 2012

Karen Saunders once said, ~Right now, someone you haven't met
is out there wondering what it would be like to meet someone
like you.~ If you think about it, for those living the single life
like myself has wondered or is wondering where and when we're
going to meet that special someone we've been dreaming of for
quite some time. You can't help but think about it from time
to time so much so it can most definitely lead you to the brink
of insanity. For it's a tough situation indeed to keep yourself
mentally, as well as emotionally stable and not completely focus
on the arrival/appearance of our heart's innermost desire. Yet,
you know he/she is out there to the point where you wonder
if that guy/girl is absolutely everything you've possibly ever
imagined to be.

As I said before, it's a tough situation for any person to keep
himself/herself mentally and emotionally stable and not focus
on the arrival/appearance of our heart's innermost desire. I
think its safe to say single people tend to have a continual verbal/
nonverbal discussion or should I say pep talk with themselves
concerning our time of true happiness will inevitably come to
absolute fruition. Thinking about it further, there are moments
where while in deep contemplation you try not to drive yourself
insane, make excuses on why you're not deserving of love/true
love, and every other possibility conjured up not only within your
mind, but heart as well. Hey, no one is immune to a seemingly
powerful force and at times those same doubts/fears/worries will
undoubtedly be erased when one's best friend for life finally steps
into the picture

Without a doubt, being patient is considered a virtuous trait
to have and even though one has experienced/is experiencing

times of frustration, disappointment, confusion, heartbreak, etc. they'll never give up hope or faith for that matter. You see, when the time of one's heart to heart connection with whoever you meet and meant to be with happens you know with 100% surety, you'll work hard to make the established relationship long lasting and totally worthwhile. Essentially, it's a promise a number of people firmly stand by and continue to do so. However, it's a sad state of affairs when the promise made is broken leaving one unfortunately feeling betrayed, confused, heartbroken, not being able to trust again, etc. Let me tell you something, as a single guy who has been waiting to meet my special someone for what seems like forever, trust me when I say it's a definite promise I intend to keep.

Let me ask you this question to those who were once single and are now in a significant relationship with the guy/girl of their dreams, was it timing or just pure luck in meeting your lifetime partner? In my honest opinion, it primarily comes down to 3 parts rather than 2 for couples who have met and continue to experience a flourishing relationship...timing, luck, and faith in God. True, a sense of good timing and pure luck play an essential part but having a strong faith in God's divine power plays an immensely pivotal part in the meeting process. What it basically comes down to is fervently praying to Him while reading key scriptures in order to guide your own personal matters of the heart in the right direction, which more than anything helps in one's spiritual growth each day.

In retrospect, the one key aspect for any single person in eventually meeting the proverbial one who will complete one's heart is not pushing or fighting to make it happen. Granted, there is a part of you that wants to try to somehow speed things along but a person can make matters worse than better. Ultimately, you just have to trust God that He will unite you with the love of your life in due time and by His timing only. Of course, once you do the meeting you have with the proverbial one you've been patiently waiting for, perhaps popping up out of nowhere will turn out to be a truly amazing experience one will never be able to forget as long as you live. Personally speaking, I say to the unknown woman out there who God has planned for me that even though I haven't met you yet I know my life will be forever changed allowing me endless amounts of possibilities of a bright future shared together with you, which is a song by 3 time Grammy and multiple Juno Award winner Michael Buble.

THE 12TH ROUND
October 1, 2012

Sly Stallone's iconic character Rocky Balboa once said, ~...It ain't about how hard ya hit. It's about how hard you can get hit and keep moving forward. How much you can take and keep moving forward. That's how winning is done. Now, if you know what you're worth then go out and get what you're worth. But you gotta be willing to take the hits...~ In some aspect, when you're living the single life it seems as if you're in a metaphorical box ring facing what is considered to be a tough or should I say THE toughest opponent one will ever face...love/true love. For its most definitely a tough and not to mention scary situation indeed to be up against such a formidable, as well as experienced "fighter" whose win/loss record far surpasses any professional boxing heavyweight champion fighting today.

Without a doubt, any single person including myself is considered in some ways amateur pugilists in the proverbial ring located within our own heart. However, it's not body parts such as one's head, face, stomach, or ribs for that matter taking the brunt of the punishment but rather our heart. You see, countless individuals have in all intents and purposes had their hearts cut up, battered, bruised, and certainly been broken by the sheer Mike Tyson back in his hay day like power punches leaving each one of us to protect ourselves as best we can from getting utterly demoralized by a much stronger force than ourselves. Thinking about it further, you can tightly bandage up the physical wounds suffered from taking a beating but it's difficult to do so with our own heart knowing it will take a tremendous amount of time to let not only the emotional but mental wounds heal as well.

If you think about it, brawn over brains tends to get wins in the boxing ring but not when it comes to matters of the heart.

Oftentimes, making smart choices and being able to relax/slow down helps give a guy/girl the chance to think clearly so as to make the right moves instead of making costly mistakes whereby backing you up against the ropes or dropping you to the mat. True, one may/will inevitably find himself/herself trying to get out from being up against the ropes/in the corner essentially representing our own frustration, disappointment, anger, confusion, doubt, worry, fear, etc. Yet, if one doesn't mentally/emotionally panic, cover up, and patiently wait for a key opportunity to open itself up then my friend you'll be able to pull off a rope a dope the Great Muhammad Ali would definitely be proud of to where the possibility of true happiness will turn in your favor.

Let me ask you this question to those who have watched the movie Rocky, what is the name of the elderly tough, gritty, no nonsense corner man who trained The Italian Stallion? If you answered Mickey Goldmill played brilliantly by accomplished actor Burgess Meredith then you are correct. Let me tell you something, each one of us has our own personal cornerman training us by giving us words of divine inspiration, encouragement, and keeps us motivated to keep fighting knowing how mentally, physically, emotionally, as well as spiritually fatigued we are. Granted, his name isn't Mickey, but His name is God our Lord and Savior Jesus Christ. Although the Lord may not be physically present with us, His spiritual presence will forever be felt to where you know He will always be in our corner guiding us every step of the way through prayer and daily devotional bible reading.

In retrospect, boxing and love/true love parallel each other in the sense they share a cruel sense of sheer brutality. Of course, blood is spilled in one whereas tears in the other. Both are the end result of either a triumphant victory or the agony of a loss. Listen, if you want a strong, long-lasting, worthwhile relationship then fight till you hear the sound of the bell. If you don't hear it then continue to work hard for it to the point where win or lose you can look back with a smile on your face and be proud of how you were able to get to a place of comforting contentment. Unfortunately, its a sad state of affairs when a person decides to take a dive, in a manner of speaking, in order to have the big payoff, which is the easy way out if you ask me. In other words, one is simply settling for a mediocre relationship and deserves far better for himself/herself. In the end, I say to my fellow single peeps out there I hope you keep fighting, take the hits, don't back down, keep moving forward and continue well past the 12th round to where two hearts will be raised while yelling out together the following words: Yo, we did it!

WHAT'S YOUR STORY
October 14, 2012

Robert Frost once said, ~Never be bullied into silence. Never allow yourself to be made a victim. Accept no one's definition of your life; Define yourself.~ Without a doubt, bullying is considered to be a hot button topic as of late that personally affects everyone, and it most definitely doesn't discriminate either. For it's a tough and not to mention heartbreaking situation indeed to see, hear, and/or read stories concerning the actions of a bully, especially when it pertains to children. In any case, a bully can certainly have cruel intentions both in a verbal and physical way but now in the age where social media is part of the social interaction dynamic, he/she has the ability to anonymously hide behind a computer screen/keyboard. However, every person has the power to stop bullying by simply taking a stand and it takes just one person to step up, whereby leading others to follow.

Let me ask you this question, have you or someone you know in a situation past, or present have ever been bullied? According to www.kidsandmedia.co.uk, the tell-tale signs of someone who is being bullied are the look of distress or anxiousness, unexplained cuts/bruises, changes in mood/behavior, lack of self-confidence/self esteem, etc. It's certainly a sad state of affairs when one finds himself/herself an unexpected target of a bully. True, the method usually chosen to inflict harm is usually physical along with the verbal aspect of it added to it causing considerable amount of pain to the point where a person's/child's health and well-being take a brutal beating, so to speak. Yes, the physical wound will heal but when it comes to the emotional and mental wounds, they tend to take more time depending on how severe it truly is.

As I said before, in the technological age where Facebook,

189

Twitter, Blogs, etc., are the norm in today's society, we are in an era where bullying can be done without coming face to face or actually speaking to another individual. I think we've all seen/ watched the video where the female Wisconsin news anchor Jennifer Livingston took a stand against a "gentlemen" who blasted her weight via an email he sent her How she responded was in a very articulate and classy way to where she earned the respect of not only myself but many others across the nation maybe even around the world as well. Granted, critics have deemed her way of standing up to her bullying a method of bullying being that she used the power of the media in order to possibly humiliate him. So, the question remains, did Jennifer Livingston do the right thing by standing up for herself by using the power of the airwaves as a platform to express a heartfelt response all-the-while staying professional on the air

Personally speaking, I've worked with kids for 12 years and continue to work in the childcare profession, which I thoroughly enjoy. Of course, I've gradually become insanely crazy in a good way mind you...but I digress. Hey, what I'm trying to get at is I've witnessed and heard plenty of kids bullying each other by way of fighting or verbal smackdowns. The way I've handled it in the past and continue to handle it is by telling "my kids" to walk away and ignore what he/she is saying knowing full well it's not true. Unfortunately, it doesn't work half the time causing enormous amounts of conflict because he/she can't let it go. Let me tell you something, I've broken up more physical and verbal fights involving a child bullying another where I work than I did at my last job. However, it's a challenge in trying to get through to them knowing I can make a difference and I'm not giving up by any means whatsoever.

October is anti-bullying month and each of us has the opportunity to be a shining example to not let ourselves or others become unfortunate victims. You see, there are bullies out there of every sort who dislike you sometimes for no reason at all and they do it because it's simply entertaining for them, or they're bored. If you think about it, you have to develop an incredibly impenetrable thick skin in this world or you won't be able to survive. Hey, we've all learned to ignore it knowing words can't hurt us unless we allow them to and I know I've been called plenty of things and experienced being bullied in the past. Fortunately, I was/still am surrounded by exceptional, positive friends who accept me for the short, uniquely weird and insanely crazy individual I am. In the end, every one of us has a personal account concerning bullying so I ask you and don't be afraid to share it...what's your story?

IN THE ZONE

October 20, 2012

Mimi Pari once said, ~Life is a lot like bowling. You're playing
your own game and only you can determine how well you do.
Sometimes, you play the game alone and sometimes, you play it as
a part of a team. But its still on your game that you have control
over - you don't have any control over anyone else's game.~ If
you think about it, we're in some aspect individually standing in
the bowling lane of life ready to throw or should I say setting our
sights on knocking down every pin standing. For it's those pins
that metaphorically represent one's hopes, dreams, and not to
mention dreams we attempt to hit at all once but at the same time
trying not to end up in the gutter, so to speak. Unfortunately, it
doesn't end up happening that way at times, whereby giving us
the opportunity for a second chance when we're unable to achieve
success the first time around.

Without a doubt, bowling is most definitely considered a metaphor
for life as the bowling ball held in our hand is a representation of our
strength and determination in getting continuous strikes in regard
to personal, as well as professional achievements set for ourselves.
Yet, it's how we in all intents and purposes throw the ball down
the lane that determines whether or not we accurately hit the
pins or miss them completely. You see, there are some people who
strategize specifically targeting the location of where to hit the pin
whereas others simply go after it with reckless abandon. In other
words, people tend to have life planned out when it involves their
own future but not so much for those who don't as they go a you live
only once mentality experiencing the unexpected surprises of what
life brings on. So, how do you live life?

As I said before, each bowling pin is a representation of our hopes,
goals, and dreams we attempt to hit all at once hoping to not end

up in the gutter. In a sense, when we throw the proverbial bowling ball of success representing our strength and determination, we basically try our very best to not end up in the gutter. What I'm saying is, aspects of life such as work, family, friends, spiritual walk with God, as well as potential/significant relationships are things we strive to continually roll strike after strike for, in a manner of speaking. True, if we're unable to keep the ball on the lane we at least try our best to get the all-purpose spare or second chance that we so want to achieve in life. What it primarily comes down to is not giving up in one's pursuit of climbing or in this particular case stepping forward each time to rear back and fire the ball down the bowling lane of success to the top.

Let me ask you this question to those who are avid bowlers or just play every once in a while, for fun, what is one aspect of the game you never want to find yourself facing? If you answered the dreaded 7/10 split, then you're correct. A catch 22 if you will. You see, we've all been in a situation where we take the risk of turning the impossible into a possible, especially when it pertains to matters of the heart regarding love/true love. Hey, every person has been strategizing within their heart/mind concerning a special someone to the point where he/she/you end up throwing caution to the wind in hopes a possible heart to heart connection happens. Thinking about it further, there's always going to be a 50/50 chance in love where you either hang your head in disappointment because all the body language in the world couldn't help you achieve the so-called perfect game of true happiness or raise your heart in victory knowing you at least gave it a shot.

In retrospect, life and the game of bowling are truly synonymous with each other in certain ways. Above all else, before ever throwing the ball down the lane we take a moment to prepare ourselves for getting the right stance or feel mind you to achieve total dominance in what we're striving for. Of course, this means taking a moment to breathe and pray to God when eventually taking a step forward in one's personal and professional life so much so that once you rear back, you're not going to be able to stop. Granted, you'll experience initial fear and doubt but that's when you know you'll have the support of your fellow teammates/friends and family backing you up all the way giving/cheering you on with encouraging/inspiring words. Ultimately, in the bowling game of life, keep your prayer life/focus on God because quite frankly it's primarily His alley to begin and in the end with Him as your teammate you'll always be in the zone.

THE RUNDOWN

November 4, 2012

Joy Maniscalo once said. ~It's funny, when you first start dating someone you go over the checklist that you have in your head, the criteria that you think will embody your "perfect mate." The thing is someone can sound amazing on paper, they can look the part but it doesn't necessarily mean they're supposed to be your leading man.~ Without a doubt, when it comes to a potential and/or significant relationship a person can most definitely define the guy/girl as a simple checklist. A checklist in which the guy/girl will at times unintentionally view the individual in question as what he/she likes, dislikes, favorite hobbies, and/or smalls, etc. For its a sad state of affairs indeed when a relationship is primarily built on a mental list within your mind rather than one coming from your heart.

If you think about it, for those who are currently in the dating scene they have their own personal and possibly professional standards in regard to potentially meeting their best friend for life. A written or unwritten list of what attracts or even repels him/her involving the opposite sex, which are in all intents and purposes known as deal breakers. Women, more so than guys, are notorious for a long laundry list of seemingly high expectations concerning the man of their dreams, which is totally mind blowing. Unfortunately, it's quite difficult to live up to those high expectations listed by a certain number of women who adhere to it as if it's their bible, so to speak. Yet, as a guy you're thankful when a woman is willing to give a guy a chance even though he doesn't necessarily meet her criteria and vice versa.

As I said before, it's a sad state of affairs when a relationship is primarily built on a mental list within one's mind rather than an emotional one in their heart. Thinking about it, if you're truly in

195

a loving, worthwhile, long-lasting relationship you don't have to constantly stop and think what your bf/gr/husband/wife likes, dislikes, her favorite song, etc. because you automatically know the answer in your heart. You see, a strong relationship established by the bonds of not only love/true love but utmost respect for him/her doesn't need a list to help remind you what or why he/she makes you happy. What it basically comes down to is keenly paying attention and not just nonchalantly observing to the point where it's listed in your memory backs either. Essentially, if done correctly, it leaves a lasting impression within the memory of his/her heart.

Let me ask you this question to you ladies who are in the dating scene, how many of you see guys merely as a checklist and if he doesn't measure up at all to your standards, he's considered to be a waste of your time? True, there are some women out there who are absolutely shallow and stick to a checklist that mainly has the following criteria: Excellent well-paying job, physically fit, muscular is a plus, and is very attractive to the eyes. The trifecta if you will. On the other hand, there are women out there who also have a list but focus more on what really matters such as spirituality, faith in God, family, etc. As a guy, who has been keenly observing relationships for the past 12 years, I've been fortunate enough to have female friends share their list with me. Let's just say, some are still single but as for others they are the lucky few who have met and married their so-called man of their dreams.

In retrospect, matters of the heart regarding true happiness aren't listed that you can simply cross off or put a check mark by ladies and gentlemen. The list of qualities we all seek in a wife/ husband like honesty, patience, trust, faith, Godly, commitment, communication, understanding, respect, etc. all have substance. They're not just words written down on a piece of paper to list down off the top of your head. Far from it. For a guy like myself who is living the single life, the qualities I'm looking for in a wife hold not only value but meaning as well, which is what you should strive for too. In the end, to my fellow single peeps out there don't let who you're wanting to be spend the rest of your life with be a checklist where you'll continually be mentally giving the rundown of what's wrong or right about this person; instead, I say throw away the list and go with the flow.

HEART OF A WARRIOR

November 11, 2012

Dan Millman once said, ~You haven't yet opened your heart fully, to life, to each moment. The peaceful warrior's way is not about invulnerability, but absolute vulnerability - to the world, to life, and to the presence you felt. All along I've shown you by example that a warrior's life is not about imagined imperfection or victory; it is about love. Love is a warrior's sword; wherever it cuts, it gives life; not death.~ In some aspect, the dating scene can most definitely be considered the quintessential field of battle for those who are living the single life such as myself. For it's a tough, disappointing, and oftentimes tiring situation indeed to continually step on the so-called field of battle in regards to putting yourself out there because you never know if you're coming back alive, so to speak.

If you think about it, when we step on the proverbial battlefield that is the dating world each of us are equipped with the necessary armor to protect ourselves from being hurt in every sense of the word. Of course, I'm not referring to it in the literal sense but a metaphorical one. Yet, it doesn't necessarily mean it will keep us from suffering the painful injuries of being physically, mentally, emotionally, and not to mention spiritually hurt. The helmet of knowledge, an impenetrable shield, the breastplate of protection, footwear of dependability, etc. are what each one of us unknowingly possesses. Unfortunately, they're not always used to the point where you mentally kick yourself for knowing better as you endured the pain, you're unable to deflect, felt the impact of sadness/heartbreak trying to protect your fragile heart, and retreated rather than stood your ground in times of utter defeat.

Without a doubt, every person has past battle scars when it comes to matters of the heart in regard to love/true love. It's those battle scars that, as previously mentioned, physically, mentally, emotionally, and spiritually hurt, so much so they're constant reminders of the wars you've been through, in a manner of speaking. You see, each individual relationship scar tells a story and depending on the level of pain one feels when touching or should I say talking about it to where a mixture of emotions is expressed. Thinking about it further, it's a sad state of affairs when a guy or girl holds onto those scares inevitably using the anger, frustration, disappointment, etc. as a strength and not letting go of it all to truly move forward in his/her love life or lack thereof. So, are you still holding on to your past scars?

Let me ask you this question to those warriors who are still on the battlefield known as the dating world, how strong and durable is your armor? As I said before, it's the armor we may be unknowingly wearing that doesn't necessarily keep us from harm's way when it comes to a potential relationship. True, you have to play it smart and know when not to go too fast when meeting someone new, but mistakes can be made with one's heart and not with their head. Hey, when you're in the middle of the battle the one thing you have to protect other than your heart is your head. Why? What it primarily comes down to is we all tend to in all intents and purposes lose our heads when the possibility of true happiness enters our lives. Granted, we can't help it and at the same time we must keep focused because at any moment someone or something could very well come up in any direction causing our heads to roll both figuratively, as well as literally.

In retrospect, there comes a point where you second guess yourself as to whether or not it's all worth it to step day in and day out on the battlefield of love/true love. As a warrior, you've been fighting so long that you don't have any idea what you're fighting for anymore that you end up wanting to give up allowing yourself to be killed. Let me tell you something, we've all felt that way including myself and it's just a matter of keeping the fire of determination and strength to keep pressing on despite the odds stacked against you. In other words, you go down fighting not only with honor, but with the dignity you have for yourself knowing you fought, and you fought by being yourself. In the end, I say to those who are still out there fighting and suffering or are suffering battle scars don't for one second raise your sword/heart to surrender because it's too hard; however, like me, I know you have the heart of a warrior as well.

IMAGINE THAT

November 24, 2012

James Hillman once said, ~For a relationship to stay alive, love alone is not enough. Without imagination, love stales into sentiment, duty, boredom. Relationships fail not because we have stopped loving but because we failed to imagine.~ Without a doubt, when it comes to matters of the heart in regard to the pursuit of love/true love a key aspect is keeping that sense of mystery alive, whereby allowing yourself to utilize your imagination, in a good way of course. Thinking about it further, it's an unfortunate situation indeed when guys, as well as girls tend to only be visually stimulated and therefore lack the internal imagination to properly gauge a potential relationship that may possibly not only be truly informative, but absolutely worthwhile as well.

If you think about it, imagination and love are synonymous with each other as both bring to reality what's hidden not only in your heart but that certain special someone's heart as well. In other words, having the capacity to see in the non-visual sense and to mention recognizing the best qualities of a person on the inside. You see, being able to keenly be aware of and notice important elements about someone you're interested in or quite possibly in love with concerning what he/she has to offer show's your most definitely paying attention to where your imagination runs wild. However, when I say run wild, I don't mean in a negative, lustful, disrespectful context but rather in a positive, genuinely interested/ in love, respectful way where one imagines a long-lasting relationship instead of just a hookup.

As I said before, a key aspect of matters of the heart in regard to the pursuit of love/true love is keeping that sense of mystery alive to the point where it allows you to utilize your imagination. Essentially, what you've totally imagined him/her to be on the outside is also who she/she is on the inside. A double whammy of true happiness. Hey, if you're lucky enough and have the courage to share what you see within them that they themselves are capable of seeing then don't miss the opportunity to take it. Unfortunately, it's a sad state of affairs when a person musses their shot causing the proverbial window of opportunity to close, so much so that all the things they've imagined within their heart/mind slips through their fingers, in a manner of speaking.

Let me ask you this question to those living the single life such as yours truly, how many of you continue to imagine what it will be like to finally fall in love and have your dreams of spending the rest of your life with your best friend be fulfilled? Truth be told, I think it would be safe to say every single person hopes what they've imagined for quite some time in their heart and mind comes to fruition soon or in the near future. True, patience is a virtue but it's certainly hard to wait knowing how those around you are living the reality of what they've imagined for himself/herself with a permanent smile on one's face. Ultimately, it all boils down to putting your faith and trust in God as He will direct you to the one you're supposed to be with because it's all in His time of course.

Actor/Comedian/Best Selling Author/Talk Show Host Steve Harvey said, ~Let a man see what he can get, but let him imagine what he can have.~ In retrospect, every woman should take heed to this particular quote because the fact of the matter is every guy is still a guy. As a guy, I can personally say my eyes have spotted a lot of women but only a few have truly captured my imagination, attention, and heart. Granted, it may not have turned out the way I wanted to go in my head but at least I gave it a shot. In any case, for a lady to truly capture a guy's imagination, attention, and heart is by showing you are women but at the same time not reveal too much. In the end, for a guy like myself when I finally do meet the woman God is directing me towards, I can say out loud to myself with a smile on my face the following two words... imagine that.

FEATURE PRESENTATION
December 2, 2012

Someone once said, ~Life is like going to a movie. You paid the money, get your snacks, choose your seats, and wait with absolute anticipation for the movie to begin. If you end up sleeping through it, you possibly miss out on the good parts; but do you really care if you do?~ If you think about it, life is in some aspect like going to a movie because each morning we wake up our quintessential movie ticket of life is already waiting for us to use and it's free no less. For its a ticket that provides each one of us access to a cinematic extravaganza, so to speak, that most definitely has a beginning and ending, but when it comes to the scenes in between it practically changes. Essentially, it's the unpredictability of life of an oftentimes unforeseen twists and turns making our own lives so compelling up on the so-called big screen of life.

Without a doubt, what any person sometimes looks forward to other than watching an awesome movie is being able to eat at an assortment of snacks provided on display inevitably located at the front snack counter. Thinking about it further, you practically have the choice to purchase anything you want that is displayed either in the glass case or advertised on the board. In a sense, when we step into the movie theater of life, we're given the choice to not only meet an assorted number of people displayed out in the world and be friends with them; but make the conscious decision to quite possibly form a lasting relationship as well. Hey, we all have different tastes in regard to the type of people we want to associate with to where we don't want to end up wanting a refund, in a manner of speaking, concerning a regrettably, costly mistake in picking him/her as a friend.

As said before in the above-mentioned quote, one of the things about having a pleasurable experience at a movie is getting the right seat, which truly makes all the difference. You see, it can either be a considerably easy or tough situation indeed depending how early or late you get there. I think it's safe to say we've all had that unfortunate experience of trying to evolve into a higher being, locating a seat within the darkness of a movie theater. In the same context, it's that way with one's professional life as we strive to maneuver around in our very own perpetual darkness of the unknown future of locating what career that best suits us long term. True, there are some people who have been able to find their place in the working world and yet there are others who unfortunately continue to stand at the bottom of the stairs looking up or stumbling within the darkness finding an open seat.

Let me ask you this question to those who are avid movie goers, no matter what movie you go to, are you the type of person who has the tendency to fall asleep thus missing out on the important and pivotal moments of a movie scene? In life, there are certain moments we ultimately miss out on because we were in all intents and purposes asleep at the wheel, especially when it pertains to matters of the heart. It's a sad state of affairs when you find yourself "waking up" during a moment of a potentially worthwhile relationship where you realize love/true love is/has been standing right in front of you. Unfortunately, one was too late in making that realization causing you to have that inner or outer scream session while watching the metaphorical credits of your love life sadly rolling down the movie screen of life. However, it doesn't have to be that way because it's your love story and you have the ability to have it end with true happiness.

In retrospect, the matinee that is our life is primarily viewed by everyone to see and vice versa. Of course, there are going to be those individuals who will annoy you to no end by either having a conversation with someone or talking on their cell phone knowing full well they're causing you to have an enjoyable movie going experience. In other words, those particular people are the ones who live for drama and have nothing better to do than disturb the pure enjoyment you're having with a certain someone of interest, family, co-workers, and or friends. Granted, you'll want you to shush them but it just provokes them even more. What it primarily comes down to is ignoring them and the annoying noise of drama will hopefully stop. In the end, I say to you I hope the feature presentation of your life playing before your eyes as you wake up each day is worthy at the end of day of a thumbs up instead of a thumbs down.

TELL ME...
December 8, 2012

Oscar Wilde once said, ~Fashion is what one wears oneself. What is unfashionable is what other people wear.~ Without a doubt, the fashion choices each one of us make on a daily basis is most definitely the style we're accustomed to wearing within reason mind you. You see, what may be the trend for others isn't necessarily getting others to follow suit because quite frankly what people choose to wear out in public can certainly leave you absolutely speechless, in a bad way of course. For it's a mind-boggling situation indeed to witness the horrifying and at the same time humorous display of public fashion that is considered not only an oddity, but a truly bizarre phenomenon in which you can't help shaking your head in disbelief at.

If you think about it, we've all at some point regretted the style choices of the past as we took a look back at past photos of ourselves back in the day and thought what in the world was I wearing when it came to dressing for school. Essentially, its that particular cool mindset in regard to school fashion that has inevitably become astonishingly embarrassing evidence to share with the younger generation, especially for those who are in our early to late 30's and older. Thinking about it further, you have to have a sense of humor concerning the clothes we wore back then knowing full well the ridiculousness of it all to the point of wondering why our parents didn't stop us from leaving the house dressed like that. Hey, it was our own skewed vision of what seemingly worked that unfortunately became a lesson learned in what not to wear in the future.

As I said before, we've all at some point witnessed the mind boggling, horrifying and not to mention humorous display of public fashion that's not only an oddity but a truly bizarre phenomenon in which you can't help but shake your head at in disbelief. I think it would be safe to say every person would gladly have the capability of making a phone call and have the individual(s) in question who are boldly making an unfortunate fashion statement or lack thereof disappear. Granted, it involves contacting men in black suits and wearing dark sunglasses snatching up people who broke the laws of fashion instead of being an alien. which is a initiative many would gladly get behind if it were legal, that is. Let me tell you something, these unfortunate crimes of fashion can oftentimes be found practically everywhere but none more so that one place...Wal-Mart.

Let me ask you this question to those who are avid shoppers at Wallyworld, what is the most outrageous outfit you've seen there that you had to take a picture of him or her? Oftentimes, you certainly can't help but stare as if it's like a car crash and as much as you want to look away, you're unable to because of how awesomely tragic it is. In other words, it's a crime against humanity and I'm 100% sure it also can cause a person to go to therapy because as hard as you try what is seen can't be unseen. True, you have the tendency to just stop what you're shopping for or aimlessly walking around because you're bored so much so you not only quite possibly call a friend but send him/her a picture/ vid of the individual as well. Fortunately, many of these pics the spectacle that is the complete train-wreck for you along with the rest of the world, can view them on the following website: peopleofwalmart.com.

In retrospect, the conscious choice one makes to boldly wear something or the lack thereof out in public is their own right. Yet, what they lack in self-respect and tackiness they gain in being the butt of jokes for those around the world to view in regard to the aforementioned website above. Personally speaking, I saw a mother and a daughter at the post office just a couple of days ago wearing the exact same thing...jean short-shorts and black tank top, which is just totally wrong. It's a sad state of affairs when you have people who don't care what they're dressed in or the amusing/horrified stares people give towards him/her knowing full well they're getting the attention they secretly want to receive. In the end, there comes a moment when you witness something so unbelievable in regard to outlandish fashion you end up stopping in tracks, let the image sink in your mind, and say out loud to yourself or those around you tell me I did not just see that.

THE VILLAGE IDIOT

December 11, 2012

Someone once said, ~In this world full of hurt and pain, I need someone who would help me through the rain. To comfort me when I'm sad, doing everything just to make me glad. In this world I need a brave knight, who would never give up any fight.~ Let me ask you this question to all the fair single ladies/maidens/ damsels out there, how many of you are patiently waiting for your proverbial knight in shining armor to arrive? For its most definitely a tough question to answer knowing full well there are possibly a number of women who feel as if their happiness has been cursed by Morgana Lefay to be metaphorically forever locked away in a castle tower unable to be freed. Essentially, it can certainly be a frustrating situation indeed for any female to keep hope alive within their heart but know one's curse of utter heartbreak will be broken someday.

As I mentioned before, there are possibly a number of women who feel as if their happiness has been cursed to be metaphorically forever locked away in a castle tower unable to be freed. Thinking about it further, a woman's feelings, thoughts, and emotions concerning the pangs of love/true love can be locked within the castle tower representing their own heart. A truly impenetrable heart has the capability to not only keep anyone from getting in, but not letting anything out as well. It's a sad state of affairs when a fair damsel is in distress personally, mentally, physically, spiritually, and emotionally whereby using the unfortunate pain as a force field the likes of Merlin would likely cast for their own protection. However, it takes a brave knight with purely, genuine intentions who can magically break the spell freeing her from the bonds of sorrow for quite some time.

Without a doubt, when it comes to matters of the heart women oftentimes find themselves dealing with or facing the fire breathing dragon known as drama. True, there are many lucky women who are fortunate to have a man who continues to put up a valiant effort in defending them from the scorching attacks of unwanted drama. Unfortunately, for others they're alone in defending themselves to where they've suffered scars from being burned in the past. You see, that behemoth of a monster leaves a path of fiery destruction either by the hands of those who wish to see all that you so want/deserve burn to ashes or by your own. Let me tell you something ladies, it's sometimes better to ignore the flames of negativity to where the scorching words don't affect you whatsoever, allowing you to focus on one day finally removing Excalibur from your heart.

If you think about it, the story of Excalibur and true happiness are synonymous with each other. In Arthurian romance, King Arthur obtained the throne by pulling the sword from a stone. The act could not be performed except by "the true king," meaning the divinely appointing king or true heir of Uther Pendragon. In a sense, every single woman is hoping to meet that special guy who is their true love and is able to rightly pull, in a manner of speaking, the quintessential sword of true happiness from their heart. Of course, many have attempted to try but to no avail and as much as it's disappointing to experience you're not giving up the faith any time soon. What it primarily comes down to is keeping Excalibur in the protective hands of the lady of the lake until a rightful heir presents himself, which in this particular case is God Almighty.

In retrospect, hurt and pain are inevitable in regard to falling/ being in love, as well as heartbreak. I think many women would agree that when a heartbreak happens it takes time to heal and recover, so much so they want to disappear into their very own island of Arthurian legend Avalon. While recuperating they know they'll return stronger than ever personally, mentally, physically, spiritually, and emotionally. Hey, it's nice to know that during your time away from the dating scene you have your ladies of the round table by your side supporting you all the way. In the end, I say this to every fair damsel who is single waiting for their knight and shining armor; trust me he'll show up as long you don't keep betraying yourself to the Sir Lancelots of the world otherwise known as the village idiot.

WELCOME HOME

December 14, 2012

Robert Brault once said, ~Senseless tragedy remains forever tragic, but its up to us whether it remains forever senseless.~ Without a doubt, it's impossible to understand why senseless tragedies happen, especially when it involves innocent kids who did absolutely nothing wrong. For its a difficult and sad situation indeed to be sitting, as well as watching the events unfold on television. Yet, not so much for the parents who are living a nightmare as they lost their child/children due to a cowardly act of senseless brutality by a man who doesn't deserve the spotlight. Essentially, there is quite possibly a roller coaster of emotions each one of us are experiencing because of how it has immensely affected us even though we don't know them on a personal level.

If you think about it, you have to be amazed at how a nation comes together when a horrific tragedy such as this occurs. You see, it doesn't matter what race, religion, color, creed, political affiliation, etc. you are as long as we become one in regard to the cause of coming together in supporting the families of Newton, Connecticut. Thinking about it further, there should not be anything politically attached to this unfortunate situation as it most definitely turns the attention away from what really matters... the loss of innocent loves both young and adult. Granted, the topic of gun control will be discussed but where the focus should be is on the support of the families who lost what is most valuable and not to mention priceless in this world that can never be replaced.

As I said before, there is quite possibly a roller coaster of emotions each one of us are experiencing because of how it has immensely affected us even though we don't know them on a personal level. Of course, as a parent you can't help but be personally and emotionally invested in this knowing it could have been your own child, which is truly unimaginable. The lives of 6 adults and 20 children will no longer be able to spend Christmas with their loved ones and what about the presents meant for them under the Christmas tree> True, it's going to greatly affect the parents/families not just emotionally but mentally, personally, and spiritually. However, the thoughts and prayers of complete strangers are being sent from all around the world hoping they are heard loud and clear in Newton, CT.

Revelations 2:4 says, ~And God shall wipe away all tears from their eyes; and there shall be no more death, neither sorrow, not crying, neither shall there be any more pain: for the former things are passed away.~ Let me ask you this question as it pertains to the senseless tragedy at Sandy Hook Elementary School, has this situation caused you to not only cherish what is most important, but thanking God for having him/her/them in your life? Hey, it's a sad state of affairs when a painful event such as this brings to reality and puts into perspective what's been totally lacking these days. Tears will be shed, anger will be felt, questions will be constantly asked as to why this happened but ultimately what needs to happen is for everyone to turn their eyes upon The Lord Jesus Christ more than ever.

In retrospect, there comes a point where we as individuals want to help in any way possible like giving donations to help the victims of the families. The possibilities are endless when we open our hearts for a cause that brings anyone to tears. Personally speaking, I took what happened in Newton as deeply personal because for 12 years or so I worked with kids and though I don't know them I can't help being emotionally invested. Unfortunately, we may never know the sick and twisted reasons why those 20 kids and 6 adults were brutally murdered. Only God knows. The dastardly and despicable actions of that who shall not be named will answer to The Lord Almighty. In the end, even though it's a time of sadness we know they are all in Heaven with God who stood at the pearly gates saying with a smile on His face the following two words...welcome home.

FALL

December 24, 2012

William Shakespeare once said, ~Love asks me no questions, and gives me endless support.~ If you think about it, one of the most important aspects to have for those in a potential and/or significant relationship is their support. Essentially, having the unwavering support of someone you truly love means so much and vice versa to where it gives one that much needed sense of security, especially for women. Hey, it's just one of the many aspects in a relationship both the male and female species are looking for, which has been found by a lucky number of people. For it's a comforting situation indeed to have a certain special someone who most definitely has your back through not only the good times, but the tough/bad/difficult times as well.

Without a doubt, a potential and/or significant other knows with absolute certainty how bad of day you've had despite flashing a smile towards you/him/her. True, the guy/girl/you could quite possibly take their word concerning the answer of "I'm Fine" after being asked if they're doing okay but he/she/you know better if you're paying close attention. You see, one has to be keenly observant in the sound of their voice, facial expressions, and not to mention body language. Its all three combined in which you witness the one you love/care about to their very best to keep it together and at the same time knowing full well at any moment they'll emotionally, mentally, and physically crumble in front of you. Fortunately, you're there to catch him/her when it happens.

As I said before, having the unwavering support of someone you truly love means so much and vice versa to where it gives one that much needed sense of security, especially for women. Thinking about it further, any woman absolutely appreciates a guy who is supportive in every sense of the word to the point where if things in life go horribly wrong he's consistently right there by your side every step of the way. Yet, it's a sad state of affairs when a guy who one thinks will help pick up the broken/shattered pieces has completely disappeared out of sight. Unfortunately, it may possibly lead to her breaking down mentally, physically, spiritually, as well as emotionally. Let me tell you something ladies, not all guys are like this because they weren't taught the time-honored tradition of being respectful and considerate to a lady.

Let me ask you this question to you ladies who are in a potential/ significant relationship, when life beats you down do you share all the worries, fears, and tears showing you have 100% trust in your best friend for life in not ever dropping them, so to speak? I think it's safe to say, a woman is undoubtedly touched within her heart to have a man who is able to have her forget about the stresses of the world felt by the embrace of his warm embrace. What it primarily comes down to is him being there for her even when tears are being shed and oftentimes no words need to be spoken because their mere presence is all that is oftentimes needed. In other words, a shoulder to cry on gives her the comfort and satisfaction that even though she's vulnerable he's not going to take advantage of her whatsoever. Of course, it's rare to experience but it is a reality.

In retrospect, there comes a point in life when the weight of the world is a heavy burden on each of us so much so you want someone to either take some or all of it off our weary shoulders. As an individual who is living the single life, you can't help but be somewhat envious, jealous, and/or have considerable admiration to those fortunate people who don't question the unwavering support of their potential/significant other. The decision made in life, though it may be risky in his/her/your eyes, will wholeheartedly be supported by one who brings you true happiness within your heart. In the end, I say to those who are continuing to patiently wait for the one who gives you endless support for the rest of your days, I hope you'll meet the guy/girl who'll catch you every time you fall, which is a song by country recording artist Clay Walker performed by recent X-Factor winner Tate Stevens.

THE NEXT LEVEL
December 28, 2012

Someone once said, ~Life is like Tetris. Things just keep coming one by one, and you can't stop it all.~ In some aspect, life is indeed like the game for the Nintendo Gameboy Tetris, which I own. Thinking about it, the game many of us like myself grew up playing as a kid is not only about strategy but racking up major points in the process as well. In a sense, that is how life is as it pertains to making moves/strategizing to the point where each of us are metaphorically racking up major life points, so to speak, in certain areas of one's daily living. Of course, we can't restart the game of life when things don't necessarily go our way and you end up just having to continue playing until you reach the point where you see the following two words pop up, in a manner of speaking, on screen: game over.

Let me ask you this question to those who have mastered the game of Tetris such as myself: were you the type of person who waits and builds up the blocks in order to eventually get a high score or goes for the points immediately upon seeing an open opportunity? Personally speaking, I was the type of guy who waited and built up the blocks so I would be able to pick up big numbers on the points scale. Hey, in my opinion, it's a sound/reasonable strategy and like life we're given the choice to either wait patiently for or go after with reckless abandon the big build ups in regard to friendships, our professional career, and/or matters of the heart concerning love/true love. So the question remains, do you live by the credo good things come to those who wait?

Without a doubt, each of us is in control of the decision of where we want to be in life because every move, whether it be big or small, is considered absolutely critical. In other words, it's the risks we take on a semi daily basis that determines if we made a truly great accomplishment in which our friends, family, and/or peers can be proud of or a grave mistake causing disappointment/disbelief to be seen on the faces we love/care about. Let me tell you something, it can most definitely be tricky and not to mention a difficult situation to maneuver where you want to be in life. However, it can be achieved by not giving up any unwanted blocks or should I say obstacles that you find standing in your way, which can be frustrating to experience. Yet, it is possible to turn those negatives into positives.

For the question can be asked once again to those who are experts on the game of Tetris, what is the one thing you found challenging and to be perfectly honest didn't look forward to while playing? If you answered the level of play becoming increasingly faster leaving to make a quick second decision in where to put the blocks you would be correct. You see, in the similar context things in life can seem as if they're moving towards you at such great speed, you don't have time to think. Oftentimes, it feels like they're all coming at you at once to where you have the tendency to freak out as it involves maybe finances/bills, a rocky relationship/friendship/marriage, a job, drama, etc. True, it can be certainly overwhelming but if you take a moment to breathe, close your eyes, and pray to God knowing full well He is ultimately in control of your life.

In retrospect, it would be a whole lot easier and simpler mind you if life were in fact the game of Tetris. The important decisions would literally be made at the press of an A or B button along with moving left and/or right on the directional keypad. Unfortunately, it's not how life is and previously mentioned in the beginning you can't start over by just turning off the system because if it were that easy all of us would continually do it. Granted, it would be interesting to experience blasting off in a rocket ship once you've reached over 100,000 points as a reward for achieving personal or professional goals...but I digress. In any case, nobody should be satisfied staying on the same level when it comes to living comfortably because it gets quite boring. In the end, always strive to get to/go for the next level in the game of life and if you do, you'll find yourself surpassing your very own high score every time.

A NEW CHAPTER (LAST YODAISM OF 2012)

December 31, 2012

Liss Mariyama once said, ~If a relationship is to evolve, it must go through a series of endings.~ Without a doubt, one of the or quite possibly THE toughest things in regard to establishing a potential/ and or significant relationship is being able to move on from a past one. For it can most definitely be a considerably easy situation indeed for some but unfortunately there are a number of men/ women who are unable to let go of the past in order to have a fresh start with a certain special someone. Thinking about it, a truly worthwhile relationship won't be able to ever experience longevity if he/she is constantly looking over their shoulder so much, so it is literally holding him/her back from moving on not only with the present, but the future as well.

If you think about it, it's a true statement to adhere to concerning that for a relationship to evolve it must go through a series of endings. Essentially, one of those endings is eliminating the hypocrite you have within you when it pertains to taking back a promise you made for yourself involving a recent past relationship ending in utter heartbreak. In other words, practice what you preach for your own heart knowing full well your family and friends will be shaking their heads in disbelief, as well as disappointment for the mistakes in the decisions made you know deep down in the pit of your gut are/were absolutely wrong. Hey, we're all human but for the sake of love/true love and not to mention emotional/mental sanity you have to stick to your word or once again face dire consequences.

As said before, there are a number of people who are unable to let go of the past in order to have a fresh start with a certain special someone. In that instance, you have to re-evaluate being the supposed victim because in all honesty it was much more your fault than it is his/hers. What do I mean? As harsh as it may sound, there are those who really need to hear the cold, hard truth. It's a sad state of affairs for any guy/girl who simply finds themselves going back to the person that hurt him/her the most thinking it will be different this time and things will change for the better. However, the unfortunate reality of it all is that it's neither different nor has it changed causing the same feelings, thoughts, and emotions to rise up. So, does this sound familiar to anyone reading this?

Let me ask you this question to those who are living the single life who have the tendency to continually look back instead of looking forward, what is the one thing you have to concentrate on ending in the so-called battlefield of love? If you answered feeling as if you're always a casualty of love, so to speak, then you're correct. You see, what it primarily comes down to is having the common sense to know you were in an extremely toxic relationship, especially for women. Granted, it's difficult to move forward but it can be done by doing what Dr. Phil calls a relationship autopsy but in my version you simply break down the pros and cons instead of making a timeline of the relationship itself. Let me tell you something, if the cons outweigh the pros then you're smart enough to know ladies you deserve far better for yourself.

In retrospect, the year 2012 is coming to an end and 2013 begins at the stroke of midnight giving each one of us the opportunity for a fresh start. Of course, for those who are hoping to meet someone, fall in love, and potentially be in a worthwhile, long term significant relationship then I wish you luck. Yet, when it comes to matters of the heart just be patient, take your time and don't rush into a relationship too quickly. Ultimately, every marriage starts off as a friend and it inevitably builds up from there, which is the best way to go. Granted, there may not be chemistry there to begin with, but time will tell in the long run. In the end, the possibility of true happiness awaits us in a new chapter that is 2013 peeps; but in the meantime, live life, focus on you, have fun with family/friends, and make the most of it.

THE BEST POLICY (FIRST YODAISM OF 2013)
January 4, 2013

Kari Torkalson once said, ~Loving honesty builds on up, bitter honesty makes one strong, whereas secrets, even those with good intent, are death to the fragile flower of trust.~ If you think about it, one of the most important aspects when it comes to being a loving, worthwhile relationship is honesty. For it seems these days it's a rarity to meet a guy/girl who has the proverbial moral compass to be totally honest with someone they either love/care about or just met in regard to the dating scene. It's most definitely a tough and frustrating situation indeed for any person when dealing with dishonesty, especially when it happens on a consistent basis to the point where faith is lost in possibly meeting that certain special someone.

As I said before, it seems as if it's a rarity these days to meet a guy/girl who has the proverbial moral compass to be totally honest with someone they either love/care about or just met in regard to the dating scene. Women, more so than men, feel there is a lack of honesty from the entire male species causing them to not only be cautious, but not trust anything a guy says as absolute truth. True, there are a number of "gentlemen" out there who will say anything a woman wants to hear knowing full well they're lying through their teeth in order to in every sense of the word get in. However, not all guys are like this ladies as guys like myself are openly genuine, honest, and up front without a hidden agenda whatsoever. Hey, as shocking as that sounds it's the God's honest truth.

Without a doubt, to be honest and trustworthy are two essential qualities many women want/looking for in a potential best friend for life. Of course, it doesn't necessarily work out that way to where an unfortunate utter heartbreak occurs leaving one personally, mentally, physically, spiritually, and not to mention emotionally hurt in the past or recently. Thinking about it further, it's a sad state of affairs when the guy who blatantly lied to them is someone they've known for quite some time whereby the betrayal is much more painful to bear. I think it's safe to say a plethora of women know all too well the experience of having the shared trust in a potential/significant relationship be broken from being lied to and having those lies covered up with more lies, which ends up blowing up in their face by their own outright stupidity.

Let me ask this question to you ladies out there who are sick and tired of being lied to, have you sworn off guys completely or just temporarily in order to focus on you for the time being? Oftentimes, swearing off guys on a temporary basis is great for the heart and soul because it gives a woman the opportunity to focus on themselves while living life to the fullest with their gal pals by her side. You see, while she's on a dating sabbatical she doesn't have to deal with the nonsense of dishonesty and untrustworthiness of certain guys who led her to the point she loses complete faith in love/true love. What it primarily comes down to is having patience and not rushing into a relationship just because you're in a mindset where you're simply lonely or you miss your ex. Ultimately, you deserve to experience true honesty in matters of the heart.

In retrospect, honesty and trust along with love is truly a powerful combination if you ask me. Yet, when combined with other potent qualities such as respect, honor, communication, understanding, faith, hope, integrity, etc. and shared with someone who makes you smile inward, as well as outward you've truly met/found "the one". Granted, women can be dishonest as well when it comes to the dating/potential/dating relationships as well...but I digress. Essentially, you have to give it to God for giving you the patience as He guides you to the guy, you're going to spend the rest of your days with who will speak the truth from his own heart instead of his buttocks region. In the end, I say to you ladies who are living the single life it's absolutely the best policy when you finally have the sweet smell, so to speak, of honesty within true happiness.

NO GUARANTEES

January 8, 2013

Someone once said. ~Love without trust is like a car with no engine. You can push, but won't get very far.~ In some aspect, love is like a car and when it comes to our own heart it can most definitely be a representation of an engine, battery, odometer, etc. I think it's safe to say in matters of the heart in regard to love/true love each one of us certainly want a relationship that is absolutely reliable, can go the distance, and won't ever give up on you when you truly need it the most. Women, more often than not, are much more prone to doing their homework for a great deal, so to speak, as they take into account a list of expectations to fulfill their so-called transportation needs towards the possibility of absolute true happiness.

Let me ask you this question ladies concerning choosing what you believe is compatible for your own heart, would you rather have quality or quantity involving that certain special someone? In other words, are you basing your heart's decision on all the features, in manner of speaking, to where you're not only mentally but visually stimulated as well? For it's an unfortunate situation indeed for any woman who may have the mindset that by having all the proverbial bells and whistles pertaining to their relationship list it will be a dream come true. Granted, it may bring you happiness and satisfaction but like a fully equipped car there are going to be more repairs required whereby causes you more grief, headache, frustration, etc.

As I said before, our own heart can most definitely be a representation of an engine, battery, odometer, etc. Thinking about it further, one's heart surely represents an odometer more than anything else because it, in a sense, tracks the number of "miles" your heart has traveled/been up and down on relationship road. It's a sad state of affairs for those unfortunate number of people who have wasted miles upon miles within their heart due to going in the wrong direction or nowhere, for that matter knowing full well he/she will never get it back ever again. However, what one loses in wasted mileage in the form of tears one fortunately/ hopefully gains in learning experience to the point where you know where you want to be and being absolutely deserving of it with all the miles you've traveled to get there.

For the question can be asked to those who have found themselves with a dead car battery, what is the one thing you hope to get from a friend or complete stranger? Of course, the answer is a jump start in order to temporarily rejuvenate the engine because without it you're not going anywhere. You see, when suffering utter heartbreak, the battery of one's heart tends to metaphorically die. Even though it may not be a complete stranger per say, you're thankful you have your best buds/gal pals to help jump start your heart in getting you in all intents and purposes slowly back on the road of life. Let me tell you something, to have that kind of unwavering support when dealing with personal, physical, mental, spiritual, and not to mention emotional turmoil gives you that much needed spark to gradually come alive.

Oron D said, ~Falling in love is like buying a car. Nothing to compare and it is sure much more than that. One can buy many brand new cars but never experience the excitement and the thrill of falling in real true love.~ In retrospect, nobody knows the blue book value of a potential significant other. What it primarily comes down to is research. True, your eyes may attract you to the flashy, superficial outside but what you end up getting yourself into without even thinking is countless drama and high maintenance. In the end, there are no guarantees in a lasting worthwhile relationship unless you take a good, hard look under the hood, kick the tires, take it for a spin, and familiarize yourself with who you have in front of you.

NATURE OF THE BEAST

January 14, 2013

Albert Einstein once said, ~The important thing is not to stop questioning. Curiosity has its own reason for existing.~ As said before, it is important to never stop asking questions because quite frankly the answers one seeks out of vapid curiosity can most definitely broaden each of us spiritually, emotionally, and not to mention mentally. The knowledge we individually seek and may gain in order to answer life's not only interesting and thought provoking, but difficult questions as well is considered a never-ending journey. For it's a journey within one's own mind in which a person receives a possibly better understanding of what oftentimes does not make any kind of sense whatsoever, which can be truly a struggle to comprehend.

What is the meaning of life? Essentially, it's a question that has existed since the dawn of time to the point where so many people including myself have thought about answering. Thinking about it, the question itself remains the same but the answers are completely different for a number of individuals who sat and thought about it to where they inevitably delved deep into their brain may even from dusk till dawn. The question of why and for what purpose are we put on this Earth is something we ask ourselves on a seemingly daily basis. Fortunately, for simple people they know their calling while others are still in search of the answer. True, it can certainly be a frustrating situation indeed but if you don't stop continually asking them then the spark of curiosity will surely never burn out.

When will I find love/true love? Without a doubt, true happiness is an absolute big question mark for those living the single life. We all know it can be attainable evident by the happy couples around us. You see, it's when you question the arrival of your best friend for life more questions lie within causing the curiosity within your heart to be peaked. Of course, one can become deeply analytically minded so much so a self-evaluation is done whereby leading to the breakdown of what is personally working and not working for him/her in the dating scene. Granted, it can be a positive or negative depending on the type of person one is in either knowing they're accepting the honest truth instead of accepting the lie. What it primarily comes down to is realizing the questions being sought after are easy and it only becomes complicated by the answers one gives.

Why does God let bad things happen? Ecclesiastes 7:25 says. ~I applied mine heart to know and to search, and to seek out wisdom, and the reason of things, and to know the wickedness of folly, even of foolishness and madness: Unfortunately, it's hard to fully make sense of horrific tragedies that have occurred none more recently than the events of December 14, 2012 at around 9:30 a.m. in Sandy Hook Elementary School in Newtown, CT. The simple question is why? Endless questions of why and wherein turning to the morbid curiosity of what would make any person take the life of 20 innocent children who had their whole lives ahead of them. Sadly, there is sometimes no rhyme or reason, but we take comfort in knowing the 27 victims are in the comforting arms of our Lord Jesus Christ in heaven.

In retrospect, there will always be something that will leave each and every one of us intrigued. In that instance, our immense curiosity will take over causing us to question the who, what, when, where, why, and how of it all. In a way, it's like following the white rabbit of Wonderland down the proverbial rabbit hole. If you think about it, once you make the conscious decision to ask the question then you must follow it down further within the recesses of your mind. Hey, that's who we are and always will be. To seek out the unanswered questions. In the end, each one of us may never know what we may come up with once one emerges from the other side; but as long as there are questions the determination to gain those answers will be there because we're really never satisfied and that my friend is the nature of the beast.

50/50

January 16, 2013

Someone once said, ~Life is like a box of cracker jacks. Rip it open. Determine to work hard in order to get the prize inside. You know it's there.~ If you think about it, life can most definitely be like a box of cracker jacks because we're all given the opportunity to rip open each day what it offers within when we wake up in the morning. Of course, there may not even be any prize in store whatsoever to begin with but it's how life is at times as we go about our daily lives with either a pessimistic or optimistic attitude. Granted, one may not know what the proverbial prize inside whatever it may be and that is what makes it so interesting because it can certainly be a complete surprise indeed for any one of us each time our eyes open.

Let me ask you this question to those who have eaten a box of cracker jacks, what was your favorite flavor? Personally speaking, I still enjoy the original caramel coated popcorn and peanuts, which is possibly what everyone else enjoys as well. True, there are other flavors also such as marshmallow crunch, cheddar bbq, salted caramel, peanut butter and chocolate, etc. Thinking about it further, when it comes to the different flavors of cracker jacks to choose from, we're also given the choice in the friends we hang out with who are of every different flavor, so to speak. Hey, what it primarily comes down to is a matter of taste as what we enjoy about our friends may in all intents and purposes end up leaving a bad taste in the mouth of others.

As I said before, there may be times when opening a box of cracker jacks you find yourself coming up empty handed in the prize department. How would/did you feel not finding a prize inside? I think it would be safe to say we all would feel/have felt jipped and disappointed fully expecting to not only hold it in our hands but partake in the cheaply manufactured prize held within. In a sense, it's that same feeling of being jipped and utter disappointment can very well crossover to one's professional career too. In other words, working hard to climb the quintessential ladder of success and striving to attain the prize of a much-deserved raise or promotion. Unfortunately, one comes empty handed causing you to experience the bittersweet aftertaste so much so it sticks with you for quite some time.

For the question can be asked for any of you who grew up eating cracker jacks as a snack back in the day or still do, what was the one prize you hoped to get when you ripped open the box? If you said a one-time cheapo now collectable ring that's worth a lot of money on Ebay, you're correct. You see, the hope of getting a collectable ring in a small cardboard box worth money on a bidding website is similar to the hopes of many single women who anticipate one day being shown a named brand jewelry box with an expensive engagement/wedding ring. For it's the ring of the non-plastic variety that comes from the guy of their dreams as he gets down on bended knee to propose. Essentially, the woman ultimately becomes the richest prize of a lifetime for a guy who is truly the luckiest man in the world.

In retrospect, the "win some-you lose some" mentality can be applied in this particular case because you never really know what you'll find or should I say come across on any given day. However, that's half the fun of it as each one of us has the capacity to view life as either a box full or broken dreams or one of endless possibilities. For the most part, one just has to tap into their inner child and let the grown adult take a back seat in order to regain the child-like viewpoint of the world each of us had growing up...but I digress. In the end, on a seemingly daily basis life is pretty much a 50/50 gamble when we open the cracker jack box of life so have fun, make the most of it with what you have, and try not to take it too seriously.

HOW DO YOU KNOW

January 18, 2013

Dr. Suess once said, ~You know you're in love when you don't want to fall asleep because reality is finally better than your dreams.~ Without a doubt, each one of us has questioned or is questioning the proverbial tell tale signs of falling in love. For it's most definitely a frustrating and confusing situation indeed for any individual as one attempts to navigate or should I say figure out if their own thoughts, feelings, as well as emotions concerning the guy/girl is truly legitimate. Thinking about it, there are so many things a person goes through whether it be personally, mentally, emotionally, and not to mention spiritually he/she can certainly find himself/herself in absolute disbelief to the point where they're being pushed to the brink of insanity.

If you think about it, a person may not necessarily know if they're in love or merely attracted to him/her by way of the physical sense. You see, the line can be blurred, so much so that it's difficult to ascertain the difference. Essentially, what one views as simply falling in love could be lustful desire for another. As said before, there lies the confusion as it plays a practical role in determining which side of the line you're standing on. The complexities of love or list pertaining to the heart versus the eyes may very well come down to asking one question involving the guy/girl in question. Do you want a worthwhile, romantic relationship built on a strong friendship or one where your desire to just hook up is the only mindset established?

Oftentimes, just being yourself is considered to be one of the most powerful ways to attract the opposite sex. A woman, more often than not, knows with 100% surety as to how genuinely real and comfortable a man is when he's around her than when hanging with his friends. True, a seemingly peaceful calm tends to happen to where the enjoyment of her company leaves the guy to express a smile never before experienced. Granted, it may be a smile in which those around him not only keenly notice but are aware of his demeanor showing he's much more of an open, relaxed body language instead of being quietly closed off in every sense of the word. Let me tell you something, as a guy, to have that sense of comforting calmness both mentally and emotionally in regard to my future best friend for life is a dream come true

Let me ask you this question to those who absolutely know what it's like to fall in love, were there ever any tests given to pass so as to reveal his/her capacity of how far/much the individual will gain in true happiness? I think it would be safe to say doing something such as testing a man/woman's dedication shows a total lack of appreciation, admiration, and respect for him/her/you. It's a sad and disappointing state of affairs for those who try to manipulate a potential/significant other's thoughts, feelings, and/or emotions in matters pertaining to their relationship. However, you can't but root for those who fall in love the right way letting nature take its course without any ulterior motives or hidden agendas whatsoever on one another's part, which is rare to experience these days.

In retrospect, there are so many ways a person may possibly know they're falling in love. Of course, it may be a feeling like a knife stabbing you in the heart in a good way mind you. Hey, to have wonderful images of true happiness carved within your heart and soul instead of past scars of utter heartbreak is a feeling you would want to last a lifetime don't you think? In any case, other examples are difficulty in breathing, the quintessential butterflies in the stomach that never go away, the inability to fall asleep causing sleepless nights, saying anything to him/her to where he/she doesn't laugh at you, the small things become a last memory, etc. Frankly, it's just the tip of the iceberg my friends. In the end, so-called experts think they know the signs of falling in love; but really, I ask each and every one of you how do you know?

THE WAY

January 21, 2013

Mahatma Gandhi once said, ~In the attitude of silence the soul finds the path in a clearer light, and what is elusive and deceptive resolves itself into the crystal clearness. Our life is a long and arduous quest after truth.~ In some aspect, love can most definitely silently sneak up on you like a stealthy ninja or otherwise known as a shinobi. Essentially, like love a ninja has the innate ability to not only be elusive, but its presence can certainly be felt despite not being able to see it. For the ninja that's love it's easily deceptive by the mental, physical, spiritual, and not to mention emotional tactics used, which are considered absolute distractions. Hey, when it comes to the experienced silent assassin its skills are unmatched, so much so no one has ever been able to know/see when it approaches.

Without a doubt, a ninja has the ability to approach its so-called victims with an incredible amount of stealth without alerting anyone of its presence. In a sense, that is how love is as it approaches in silence, armed and ready to take down, so to speak, the unsuspecting victim's heart. Thinking about it further, the weapons of choice aren't necessarily throwing stars, daggers, smoke bombs, and/or a sword for that matter; but an arsenal so deadly it causes one's knees to shake, pulse race, heart skip a beat, etc. A soft smile, a unique laugh, alluring eyes, a big heart, faith in God or whatever the case may be are in all intents and purposes an assortment of "weapons" that stroke deep into a person's heart to the point where he/she falls either gradually or instantly.

If you think about it, one of the many aspects a trained ninja has in their skill set is being able to stay hidden within plain sight. Oftentimes, love/true love is standing right in front of you staring back at you in the face and sometimes don't even realize it. For it's a sad state of affairs for those who are too late in finally opening their eyes only to find themselves falling to their knees in utter disappointment or heartbreak. It's a tough and frustrating situation indeed to experience because quite frankly an individual doesn't have any idea, he/she is there because they're either not paying attention or too focused on someone else. Let me tell you something, it happens to the best of us who tend to have this mindset in which we're keenly aware of our surroundings in regard to true happiness and yet are taken completely by surprise.

Let me ask you this question to those who have watched movies or read books about ninjas, what ability do they have that they do extremely well? The answer would be staying and being concealed within the shadows. I think it would be safe to say we've all at some point felt as if someone was behind us causing us to turn around but nobody was there. In a way, love is exactly similar as you can feel its presence, in a manner of speaking, within your heart but when you look within nothing can be see/found...at first. Of course, the elusive deceptiveness that is matters of the heart is shrouded in mystery, deadly by reputation, successful in its mission and it will appear by its own accord when you least expect it in complete and utter silence.

Someone said, ~True happiness is a sneaky and elusive creature. Very few can find it, but to those who have are truly lucky to have it.~ In retrospect, you can never really be fully prepared to defend yourself when love/true love strikes. You see, one pretty much does their best in trying to not make a fool of themselves in going for the offensive. In other words, doing or saying something so stupid you end up wanting to perform hari kari on yourself in order to hopefully die an honorable death. What it primarily comes down to is instilling self discipline, trusting your instincts, and having the support of your clan of gal pals/best buds. Ultimately, never look for love/true love because you won't find it no matter how hard you search. In the end, the truth is it's when you stop looking it will strike your heart out of nowhere because that is the way of a shinobi.

THE INSIDE TRACK
February 1, 2013

Someone once said, ~A guy and girl can be just friends, but at one point or another one of them will fall for the other; maybe temporarily...maybe at the wrong time...maybe too late or maybe, just maybe...forever.~ Without a doubt, there lies what is considered to be the million dollar question concerning men and women, which is can they have a purely platonic relationship? For it's most definitely a debatable topic indeed knowing there are countless arguments stating they can't because it's impossible whereas others believe it is a possible situation to have a non-romantic relationship with the opposite sex. Essentially, it is possible if one knows the ground rules and doesn't overstep or cross boundary lines to where the friendship either becomes awkward or broken afterwards.

Let me ask you this question to those of you who have a best/close friend of the opposite sex, whether he/she is single or otherwise taken at any point have you had any thoughts of pursuing something more due to your overwhelming feelings? Let me tell you something ladies, if you say none of your guy friends have ever had any feelings or thoughts about you as more than a friend, they are flat out lying because they have. As a guy friend, one knows full well how attractive, fun, smart, quirky, weird, strange, etc. you are, being that we've spent time in your company witnessing when you're at your best, worst and everything in between. You see, we think about going for it to the point where we take into account a plethora of criteria stirring within the back of our minds.

As I said before, guys like myself certainly take into account a criteria of thoughts stirring within the back of our minds in regard to the possibility of going for true happiness. In other words, before we pass the proverbial point of no return, we have a mental debate to where we prepare ourselves for either a yes or no. Yet, several things can come into play pertaining to the female friend in question causing our heart to skip a beat such as: way of life like being known for always being a flirt, incredibly high standards, continuous mistakes in the guys dated, committed relationship/marriage to a great guy, and/or the close family brother-sister relationship established if any. True, all 5 will play a pivotal role in whether a guy risks it all for matters of the heart but if he doesn't step over any boundaries it's because he cares/loves/respects her that much.

For the question can be asked to you ladies out there, how many of you actually believe guys aren't capable of sharing a platonic, non-sexual relationship with a woman? Hey, as crazy as this sounds, there are guys who have the capability of knowing the difference between being in love and just loving their female friend. Unfortunately, the lines can be blurred so much so, one experiences confusion in every sense of the words. What it primarily comes down to is romantic chemistry. If you think about it, if a guy and girl hit it off and they find they genuinely share common interests but there isn't a spark between them then it's just a friendship nothing more nothing less. Granted, its an incredibly rare friendship these days to have but to have one nonetheless is absolutely priceless, special, and not to mention very informative.

In retrospect, for men and women to be just friends is a dynamic that a number of people don't necessarily put stock in. Why? Thinking about it further, one or the other will have feelings and it's how one deals with them that determines if they're either handled the right or wrong way. It's a sad state of affairs when close guy-girl relationships turn messy when emotions and thoughts within a person's feelings lead him/her/both to part ways. Of course, the flip-side to this is that single/married women have at their disposal the guy's perspective from their male friends and the same can be said for men with their female friend's perspective as well. In the end, I honestly believe men and women can be just friends and having the inside track from either side on marriage or dating does have its advantages.

RIPPLE EFFECT

February 4, 2013

Someone once said, ~If you cast a small pebble on to the surface of a glassy, calm pond, ripples form and move outwards across the water. Each ripple causes another and another and so on. A very small act can make a significant difference. Make a ripple- Make a difference.~ If you think about it, you never truly know the effect you have on someone until you hear about or speak with, for that matter, with him/her sharing not only how much of an encouragement one is, but a positive influence as well. For it can most definitely be considered a humbling situation indeed as he/she is thankful for being a major influence in regard to their personal and/or professional lives even though you may think you're playing a minor part in it.

Without a doubt, a small act certainly does make a seemingly tremendous impact like a stone hitting the surface of the water. You see, unbeknownst to the individual doing the smallest of good deeds whatever it may be, the man/woman/young person is absolutely appreciative to the point where it touches the bottom of their heart, leaves a smile on his/her face, brings tears to one's eyes, etc. Paying for another customers meal/coffee, leaving bags of groceries for a person/family indeed on their doorstep, helping/volunteering to help in any way involving a fallen community when disaster strikes, etc. are acts of kind done because you want to instead of needing to in order to get recognition, which is a totally wrong mindset to go by.

Oftentimes, simple acts are done without even thinking about it to where it inevitably turns into a pay it forward moment. As said before, just like a stone tossed into the still water ripples form and move outwards essentially affecting its surroundings. Thinking about it further, doing something such as helping someone across the street, picking up trash off the ground, opening the door for a complete stranger or whatever the case may be all in front of the viewing public can very well be influential to others to do so too. Of course, it may not bring those around you to jump in immediately into action, but you've basically led by example as the mental seeds, in a manner of speaking, have been planted in their minds of what they've witnessed whereby giving them the opportunity to act in the near future.

Personally speaking, working with kids I have had the opportunity to metaphorically cast so many stones into their so-called watery lives and possibly have made positive ripples. Granted, for the past 12+ years and counting, I've been fortunate enough to meet/talk with/get to know/become friends with countless kids who have grown up before my very eyes. Yet the question remains, have any of these kids have become better kids turned adults because I significantly impacted their lives in some way, share or form. My honest answer is I don't know because who's to say if I did or didn't. What it primarily comes down to is the answers can only come from my former kids who I taught giving words of advice and wisdom. Hey, if I played a small part in them spreading what they learned from me then I'm humbled and honored.

In retrospect, doing a good deed whether we know it or not brings you a sense of fulfillment. True, we live in a cynical and not to mention dangerous world but every once in a while, we tend to hear about or witness for ourselves the side of humanity that tends to be rarely seen these days. Unfortunately, It's a sad state of affairs when newspapers and news stations focus solely on the bad with selfishness, violence, war, death, etc. leaving you doubtful as to the future of America. However, there is hope and it all begins with just one person doing something that may seem insignificant that it becomes absolutely significant so much so it touches someone else. In the end, I challenge you to throw a metaphorical stone to someone you know or a complete stranger causing a ripple effect and see the positive results that hopefully occur.

PLAY NICE

February 8, 2013

Someone once said, ~Life is a lot like legos. It is important to have
a fun life: try to have it as you build your life.~ In some aspect,
life is a lot like legos in the sense that every person tries to build
or should I say create a better life with their own two hands.
Unfortunately, it doesn't necessarily turn out the way we want it
to be as there are pieces broken, missing/lost, don't fit, are in the
possession of others, etc. For it can most definitely be a tough but
worthwhile situation indeed for any person in putting together
a life one has imagined all-the-while working with the assorted
pieces we have in front of us. Hey, it's just a matter of having the
drive and determination to keep building instead of simply giving
up when it gets too difficult.

Without a doubt, legos come in all colors, sizes, and shapes
to the point where building something is considered loads of
because there are endless possibilities when it comes to our own
imagination. Thinking about it further, there is an absolute
similarity when it comes to friendships as well in regard to
building strong bonds with one's gal pals/best buds who are not
only of different colors, sizes, and shapes but ethnicities, faiths,
genders, religion, as well as, political affiliations. True, there may
possibly be differences in opinion concerning hot button topics and
yet you've established a cohesive connection between you along
with your circle of friends. It's that tight connection in which no
matter how many attempts there are to break the friendship apart
you'll always stay together through thick and thin.

If you think about it, we've all at some point as young kids
fought over legos because of childish thinking such as he/she has
the piece/pieces we wanted. In a sense, when it comes to our
professional lives, we all intents and purposes fight for the lego

pieces representing a promotion, a big pay raise, the corner office on the top floor, our own parking space, etc. In other words, "fighting" for a quality of life means facing not just others, but ourselves regarding the proverbial ladder of success. Granted, it's not going to be easy by any stretch of the imagination leading one to experience times of frustration; but you know full well going to take tremendous amounts of time, effort, and not to mention patience building piece by piece what you are working so hard for.

Let me ask you this question for the lego enthusiasts who still play every now and then: what is the most annoying part about playing with legos other than trying to take certain ones apart causing considerable pain to your fingers? If you answered stepping on them leaving you to suffer the painful physical aftermath on your feet then you're correct. Essentially, that same pain can also be felt when it comes to matters of the heart involving a potential and/ or significant relationship with a difference of course. I think it's safe to say guys/girls have experienced times where they've said/ done something totally regrettable to someone they love/care about leading one to suffer mental and emotional pain rather than physical. So, how long did the pain within your heart last for you?

Someone said, ~A box of legos are like life. Sometimes they get stuck together. Sometimes they get chewed on. Sometimes they get lost; but in the end, they always seem to somehow fit together.~ In retrospect, life can turn out either two ways...easy or complex. What it primarily comes down to is how each of us make it to be knowing that every lego piece of life isn't going to fit where we want to go. Sadly, far too many people are continuing to put the wrong lego pieces together whether it be friends, a relationship, and/or job causing strife amongst friends/family. Fortunately, for others they for the most part know where the right pieces fit whereby stress/strain isn't there involving the friend/family dynamic. In the end, remember to have fun in this serious, albeit crazy life each of us have and oh one more thing...play nice.

HIGHLY ILLOGICAL
February 13, 2013

Someone once said, ~A love that defies all logic is something the most logical thing in the world.~ Love vs. logic. Essentially, the two have battled each other, so to speak, since the dawn of time. For it's the actions done and words said pertaining to matters of the heart in regard to a potential and/or significant relationship cause us to lose our sense of reasoning. It's an absolutely bewildering situation indeed for guys, as well as girls who oftentimes lose their minds because their heart and mind are metaphorically locked in a war with each other when it comes to the possibility of true happiness. True, decisions are going to be/ have been made where there is a conflict involving one's heart and mind, but you hopefully have truly valid reasons as to why the relationship works between the two of you.

If you think about it, love or true love for that matter does in fact defy all logic because quite frankly it doesn't make any sense whatsoever the things we do or say in pursuit of it. As said before, the actions done, and words said pertaining to matters of the heart for potential and/or significant relationships can very well cause us to lose our sense of reasoning. Thinking about it further, it's oftentimes unexplainable as to why we make complete fools of ourselves concerning someone we're in or not even in a relationship with. Granted, in your head you keep telling yourself to keep it together, but that particular logic is thrown out the window, in a manner of speaking, when you're in and/or around their presence. Hey, it can most definitely push any fairly normal person with their head on straight to the brink of insanity.

Without a doubt, love/true love can certainly be considered blinding, especially if you know someone or are in fact that someone who is in a considerably toxic relationship. Women, more often that note, have this delusional sense of logic in which there is this belief they can change the man they love who is the quintessential bad boy. The same man who doesn't have any respect for her to the point where she not only makes excuses for his attitude/behavior, but her self-esteem gradually degrades the longer she's with him. Unfortunately, it's a sad state of affairs when a woman becomes highly illogical and has this skewed view of what love is in the form of a guy who she believes makes her happy. However, in reality there is a tremendous amount of emotional turmoil behind the smile given.

Let me ask this question to those who were in an utterly bad past relationship: how many of you refused to hear the logic of those around you who clearly warned you about the guy/girl in question until it was too late? Of course, all the warning signs were there plain as day but your happiness for a better future superseded the stone cold facts that would turn your dream come true into a harsh, nightmarish reality? There is a saying that goes, relationships come and go but your gal pals/best buds will always be there no matter what. In other words, the bonds of friendship may take a hit from time to time because he or she didn't want to listen because their logical mind was completely closed off to what was believed to be the unreasonable truth whereas their heart was fully open for reasonable love.

Valentine's Day is almost upon once again giving way to seemingly reasonable, as well as expensive logic for corporate commercialism aimed at men to bring joy and happiness to the woman they love happily. As a single guy, the sarcastic cynic in me would rather not be in a relationship because in my view their logic is utterly flawed and totally unreasonable. Yet, if I were ever in a relationship the part of me that is romantic wherever it is would totally get the logical reasoning behind it. In the end, love makes sense to those who are genuinely experiencing it whereas for others trying to make sense of it all it can cause each one of us to channel our inner Spock from the original Star Trek series uttering 2 words...highly illogical.

LOCKED OUT OF HEAVEN
February 18, 2013

Lord Byron once said, ~Yes, love indeed is light from heaven; A spark of that immortal fire with angels shared by God given to life from earth our low desire.~ Let me ask you this question to those who are in a truly significant relationship, how many of you feel as if you're such a heavenly place sharing a life together? For it's a comforting and not to mention peaceful situation indeed to experience a type of love where the warmth of their light continually brightens your heart, as well as soul each and every day instead of leaving you feeling not only cold, but alone as well. Essentially, it's considerably rare these days to find/meet someone who is more into the joyous prosperity of a guy/girl considered to be heaven sent rather than the sinful pleasures it brings into their lives.

Without a doubt, you're truly lucky if you find true happiness with a special someone who in your eyes is a considerably angelic individual. A person you know has been quintessentially sent down from the heavens and has most definitely made your life brighter than you could ever possibly imagine. Thinking about it further, it's when you finally come face to face with your best friend for life, it's as if the trumpets sound within your heart and quite possibly his/hers as well. True, there is immense joy and excitement with an added mixture of disbelief when your prayers have been answered by God. What it primarily comes down to is having unwavering patience knowing full well you'll be tested mentally, emotionally, and spiritually, which for a number of people it's like being in hell.

If you think about it, not all significant relationships stand the test of time as one falls from grace to the point where faith is lost in ever experiencing love/true love ever again. As said before, unwavering patience is needed as you'll be tested mentally, emotionally, and spiritually, which for a number of people is like being in hell. Oftentimes, relationships falter to where you become a fallen angel enduring the seemingly fiery hellish nightmare of trying to ascend back up into the kingdom of absolute true happiness. In other words, the dating scene where it's as if one's faith can gradually be lost meeting more demonic-like male/female species than potential angels in hopes to someday metaphorically walk the streets of gold located not only in your heart, but his/her heart too.

For the question can be asked to those who are in all intents and purposes fallen angels, how long have you been standing on earth's mortal plain looking up towards the heavens above, imagine the day of stepping through the proverbial pearly gates of love/ true love. You see, depending on the length of time one has been without their wings, in a manner of speaking, it can certainly be difficult to wait for one's own ascension in regard to a worthwhile relationship. Granted, a person can become desperate finding a way to get back in so much so he or she will make an unfortunate deal with the devil to do so. Hey, to the fortunate souls who didn't make the deal signing their name with their own blood you've absolutely earned your wings.

Walter Scott said, ~True love's the gift which God hath given, to man alone beneath the heaven. The silver link, the silver tie, which heart to heart, and mind to mind, in body and in soul can bind.~ In retrospect, heaven is what every person wants to experience concerning matters of the heart and not ending up getting burned by the fires of hell. Of course, by that I mean the pain, suffering, and utter turmoil of feeling earth's impact as you fell from high amongst the clouds. Let me tell you something, the brokenhearted definitely want to seek redemption when love is lost but not too quickly though. In the end, I say to all the fallen angels who feel they've been locked out of heaven trust me when I say you'll enter in once again when you least expect it.

TRUE LOVE'S SOUL
February 21, 2013

Tupac Shakur once said, ~Death is not the greatest loss in life. The greatest loss is what dies inside while still alive. Never surrender.~ In some aspect, when true love dies in a person's heart, the soul within is carried off to the great beyond, somewhat similar to the movie The Crow starring the late Brandon Lee. In any case, one can experience a truly tremendous heartbreak to the point where the individual's soul suffers absolute restlessness so much so it's unable to properly rest. For it's a tortuous situation indeed for any guy/girl who has gone or is going through a terrible sadness whereby the crow representing one's thoughts, feelings, and emotions can most definitely be considered not only a weakness, but a strength as well.

If you think about it, even though you're alive you feel this sense of a numbing type of death after suffering a breakup of a long-standing relationship. In other words, the physical pain may not be felt but when it involves feeling any sort of pain emotionally, as well as mentally, it certainly has the propensity to bring you down to your knees hence the weakness as previously mentioned. Thinking about it further, it's at that point the tortured soul with a broken heart tries to find their way back in order to smile once again. Unfortunately, the journey back is quite difficult before it gets much easier. What it primarily comes down to is having the inner strength to face and take care of one's own personal issues like Eric Draven did with Tin Tin, Funboy, Skank, and T-Bird.

Without a doubt, you're never really alone in your "fight" against personal issues within your own heart. You see, as Eric Draven had Sarah and Albrecht supporting him, you have the support of gal pals and best buds helping you cope by having your back every step of the way. Granted, they're not the unlikely duo of a tough, skateboarding young girl and a veteran cop; but it's your eclectic group of friends who do their best to help take the bullets, in a manner of speaking, for you when the mass emotional and/ or mental hysteria/inner chaos ensue. Hey, to have that type of strength in the bonds of friendship in the midst of dealing with unwanted pain and strife shows how much you're truly loved/ cared about by not just the people you know, but those you may not know also.

Let me ask you this question to those who know and have watched the cult classic movie, how did Eric Draven defeat the main villain Top Dollar? If you answered grabbing him by the head and transferring the 30 hours of pain he felt concerning Shelly's death onto him inevitably causing his ultimate demise then you're correct. Of course, if every person had that particular real life ability they would with 100%c surely transfer all the pain, sadness, disappointment, bitterness, suffering, anger, hatred. etc. towards an ex. Let me tell you something, I know a number of people who would put that ability to good use and they wouldn't hold anything back giving him/her all they've endured in the past weeks, months, and/or years.

In retrospect, each one of us who are living the single life such as myself hope to one day spend the rest of our lives with our own Shelly whereas for the females its their own Eric Draven. In the meantime, we're all to a certain extent have a crow's heart where it's teetering between the land of the living and the realm of the dead. Yet, for a lucky few they're fortunate enough to have met/fallen into an eternal true happiness that far surpasses life and death. Essentially, it's a rarity these days to have a forever love where there is no sign whatsoever of a crow appearing and carrying off the pieces of a broken relationship to the land of the dead. In the end, true love's soul can return to a person's heart and all it takes is meeting a guy/girl who can help prove to you it can come back from the dead.

THAT'S A STRETCH
February 25, 2013

Marilyn Mackenzi once said, ~Life is like a rubber band. Sometimes we're stretched to the limit and we break. Sometimes we fly hither and fro with no direction in mind, landing somewhere we never planned to be.~ If you think about it, life can oftentimes be like a rubber band as each one of us stretch ourselves in certain aspects of life. For it's most definitely a risky situation indeed to do so but one has to in order to step out of our proverbial comfort zone. Thinking about it further, you never know how far you'll be able to prove not only yourself, but others as well on how durable the rubber band of your own life is. True, there may be doubts and fear of it snapping apart causing you to experience, which is certainly to be expected in friendship, career, and matters of the heart.

Without a doubt, the sole purpose of a rubber band is to hold certain things tightly together in place. In some aspect, every person has a rubber band like tightness when it comes to establishing friendships. You see, the more friends you make the wider it expands but unlike the metaphorical rubber band wrapped around one's gal pals/best buds there is a limit in how much it can hold to the point where it snaps. It's at that point, you have to determine who is worth keeping in your tight knit inner circle and who is simply there taking up space. Essentially, you then make the decision to remove them from your life whereby making the tension on your own personal rubber band hopefully become stress or should I say absolutely drama free.

As I said before, it's most definitely a risky situation indeed to stretch yourself in certain aspects of life in order to step out of our proverbial comfort zone, especially pertaining to one's professional career. True, you can in all intents and purposes have things tightly wrapped in regard to their profession that he/she/you excels at. However, there may/will come a time when one chooses a totally different path to follow and you want to stretch yourself in every sense of the word knowing full well, you'll feel an overwhelming sense of fear and doubt. Yet, as much as there is uncertainty of the unknown regarding one new career you take your time expanding your head knowledge of the business all the while slowly attaining the experience needed to climb the quintessential ladder of success.

Let me ask you this question to those who are in a potential and/or significant relationship, do you share a love that even though the relationship has been stretched far beyond what it's capable of, does it continue to hold strong? Unfortunately, it's a sad state of affairs when relationships snap apart before they are even given time to become wrapped tightly together mentally, personally, physically, emotionally, and not to mention spiritually. Of course, when utter heartbreak occurs you truly feel the seemingly stinging harsh reality of it all snapping back at you leaving you to endure the lingering pain within your own heart. Let me tell you something, pain lingers but it will eventually go away to where you'll one day be tightly wrapped in true happiness' warm loving embrace.

In retrospect, we all have a definite purpose concerning the rubber band of life as we're individually holding our family together whereas others are possibly trying to keep a secure hold on what they have. Hey, whatever the case may be one mustn't stretch themselves too hard or too fast because if you do then you'll run the risk of your sanity flying off somewhere. Ultimately, it's a rarity these days to still keep every aspect of your life together with the original one you have. In the end, if you actually started out with the original one then I say to you that's a stretch; but if you didn't then I tip my hat to you as every broken rubber band tells a story of where you started from and where you are now.

THE CREW

February 27. 2013

Doug Coupland once said, ~I like doing radio because it's so intimate. The moment people hear your voice, you're in their heads, not only that, you're in there laying eggs.~ Without a doubt, radio has become one of the ways to occupy one's time while you're either getting ready to got to work/school and/or driving in a car towards your intended destination. For it most definitely helps wake you up in the morning to start your day knowing full well the voices behind the mic are doing their very best to get you not only motivated, but at the same time be entertaining as well. When it comes to helping an individual become motivated and entertained at the start of an early morning, none do it better than the Gulf Coast's Qtip and Blondie in the Morning from the hit station 97.5 WABD.

If you think about it, there aren't a lot of people or in this particular case listeners who consider themselves a morning person and you can certainly include myself in that category. However, Qtip and Blondie in the Morning is the exception as I and possibly many others set their alarms to be awoken by the all-to-familiar voices of Glenn "Qtip" Johnson and Rachel "Blondie" Jones along with Intern Alyssa, Nick Fox, Producer Heather, as well as Scott Adams on occasion. As a loyal listener for a number of years you truly look forward to the hi-jinks, conversations, stories, challenges, etc. that are either planned or unplanned involving the quirky personalities associated with the morning show. In other words, it's all about unpredictability Monday through Friday.

As I said before, the voices heard on the radio help wake you up in the morning to help start your day knowing full well the voices behind the mic are doing their very best to get you not only motivated but at the same time be entertaining as well. Fortunately, Qtip and Blondie are well known for that, so much so listeners such as myself expect nothing less. Of course, there are memorable moments of entertainment involving stunts from the station once known as 97.5 WABB such as Lil' Joe being dropped high in the sky from inside a car. Granted, I started listening when the voices of Wayne and Jay were behind the mics and yet the quality of laughter and all out amusement has never wavered to the point where it has, in my honest opinion, continued to rise instead of decline.

Let me ask you this question to those who are avid listeners to 97.5 WABD, how did you feel when the radio station was sold, and it was going off the air? I think it would be safe to say a mixture of sadness, shock and disbelief were experienced by every listener on the Gulf Coast. On the other hand, as the countdown to the end started, those who worked in the past for the show came to reflect by sharing their stories like Matt McCoy, Mena Anderson, Little Joe, Pablo, Cherish Lombard, and countless others. You see, it was a sad state of affairs when at the stroke of midnight WABB officially went off the air leaving a void on the radio. Let me tell you something though, the morning show returned back home full force to where it belonged but with a new name, which pleased many in the Gulf Coast.

In retrospect, you never really think about getting the chance to meet the people on your favorite radio station until the opportunity is given to you. Personally speaking, the opportunity was given to me last year during the Toys For Tots drive being held at the Wal-Mart Supercenter. One word: awesome. Blondie tackled me with a hug...best memory ever. Unfortunately, I wasn't able to meet Intern Alyssa until recently at a Pensacola Ice Flyers game along with Scott Adams. Producer Heather, a meeting will hopefully be in the works someday. In the end, the crew from 97.5 WABD/Qtip and Blondie in the Morning aren't just voices on the radio or faces on YouTube to me anymore, they've become great friends who I keep in touch with and I'm fairly positive they would say the same for me because to them I'm a local celebrity.

MAN'S BEST FRIEND

March 3, 2013

Alfred A. Montapart once said, ~Animals are reliable; many full of love, true in their affections, predictable in their actions, grateful, and loyal. Difficult standards for people to live up to.~ Let me ask you this question to those who have pets, do you consider him/her/them a part of your family? Granted, I know it's a truly ridiculous question to ask knowing full well the absolute bond shared with an animal you've grown to not only care about, but love as well. For it's a type of caring love in which one can't help but become sentimental to the point where tears are shed? Why? It's due to the strong, emotional attachment towards the lovable creature who essentially has become an important family member in your own eyes, which many pet owners would most definitely agree with.

Without a doubt, the connection between pets and their owner is deeply rooted in companionship, friendship, affection, caring, gratefulness, respect, admiration, and not to mention love. You see, depending on how long the pet-owner relationship has lasted there is certainly an unspoken bond that oftentimes can't be explained, especially to those who don't know the experience of having a sidekick of the animal variety. I wholeheartedly believe along with the pet owning community when I say you'll never know what it's like to look into the eyes of not just unwavering loyalty, but of pure innocence whereby it puts a smile on your lips and heart. Thinking about it further, the loyalty and innocence expressed from their eyes can unfortunately be lost by the owners who promised to always protect them.

As I mentioned previously, the loyalty and innocence expressed from their eyes can unfortunately be lost by the owners who promised to protect them. True, it's hard to imagine the all-out cruelty inflicted on a creature who has done nothing wrong except love you unconditionally. Sadly, it's a sad state of affairs when you read/ listen/watch stories on tv concerning animal cruelty by individuals who seemingly have no heart whatsoever to where it simply breaks your own heart just thinking about it. Hey, I challenge you to think about or look your own pet(s) in the eyes and answer the following question to yourself: Do I have the capacity to inflict harm against my friend/family member whereby the promises made are broken? Let me tell you something, if the question brings tears to your eyes then you know you're a human being and not a heartless monster.

For the question can be asked to all pet owners out there, have you ever wondered or possibly even imagined what it's like from your pet's point of view. Oftentimes, it's hard to imagine indeed the life of a pet through their own eyes, such as a cat or dog because we're so wrapped up in our own busy lives to even think about it. Yet, a dog happily awaits with fervent joy in order to greet you with their tail wagging, lick your face with kisses, and anticipates being scratched behind the ears as he/she sees his/her owner stepping through the front door. Of course, they don't do it because they have to; instead, they want to as they exude similar human characteristics as we do. In other words, it's in their nature to be happy, sad, to miss, love, care, comfort, and protect the ones they love.

In retrospect, life is considerably more enjoyable when you have the company of a pet by your side. A pet who has a unique personality all their own and it shines forth so much so he/she will make you laugh to no end. On the other hand, they will unintentionally cause sadness as they either pass away or have to be put down leaving you to endure the immense impact of what is considered to be in your mind a tragic loss, which may have been recent for some of you. In any case, love knows no bounds when it comes to the animals you think of as your own children because they're that special to you. In the end, whether the pet you have is a cat, dog, hamster, birds, snake, horse, pig or whatever the case may be you know them by just three simple words...man's best friend.

UNLEASHED

March 4, 2013

Paulo Coelho once said, ~When we least expect it, life sets us a challenge to test our courage and willingness to change; at such a moment, there is no point in pretending that nothing has happened or in saying that we are not ready. The challenge will not wait. Life does not look back. A week is more than enough time for us to decide whether or not to accept our destiny.~ If you think about it, challenges come in many different forms to where it most definitely tests one's courage and willingness to not only move on but let go of the past as well. For it can be a tough situation indeed to move forward inevitably leaving the past behind. Yet, with encouragement, as well as support from those who love/care about you the journey itself will certainly feel far less frightening, especially for a female intern working for Gulf Coast's hit radio station.

Without a doubt, when you look up the word versatile her picture is right next to it with a list of impressive credentials underneath. Thinking about it further, what makes this particular female intern such a jack of all trades on morning radio is her overall tenacity in allowing herself to endure pain of any kind when it involves crazy stunts. Essentially, it's her "if boys can do it girls can do it better" mentality that has earned her the respect of many who wouldn't have the cojones to actually do it themselves. Hey, whether it's matching the gross factor in puke art against MTV's Bam Margera, being voluntarily shot at with a paintball gun, having her hair cut by Qtip, etc. she has the potential to set the bar for future female interns to be insane enough to possibly follow in her footsteps.

As I said before, versatile comes to mind regarding this remarkable woman who isn't just a one trick pony, so to speak. You see, there lies within her a deadly verbal arsenal and if handed a mic she will spit out stinging rhymes of epic proportions the likes of which Slim

Shady himself would not just be proud of but be downright in awe of. Of course, it's because of her sick rap skills she has been deemed with the moniker Slim Lady, which is a homage to the no nonsense, music award winning rapper. Let me tell you something ladies and gentlemen, a woman of her caliber who can work the mic and not to mention work sleepless nights as a DJ is considered a deadly 1-2 combo that has those in the social media industry taking notice.

Let me ask you this question to the listeners of 97.5 WABD, do you honestly believe this fiery blonde intern has a destiny to fulfill in regard to making it in the world of reality tv to the point of becoming a star herself? The answer is yes. True, she has the determination, drive, and fortitude to go after a spot that was potentially offered by the powers that be of Redneck Island who contacted her. A chance of a lifetime to prove, if chosen, mind you, how much of her inner redneck she can channel against other rednecks. Plus, she'll be fortunate enough to meet The Texas Rattlesnake Stone Cold Steve Austin...but I digress. What it primarily comes down to is confidence because each and every one of us knows you have it within you to hopefully show America what we in the Gulf Coast already know.

In retrospect, there comes a point in every person's life when an intervention is most sorely needed, and it is currently being done by Rachel "Blondie" Jones and Producer Heather Bright to their fellow friend/employee Alyssa Ann Honea. Granted, it started off a bit rough with Beyonce's Single Ladies dance, but she was able to pull it off making all of us around the Gulf Coast proud. In any case, it oftentimes takes a tremendous amount of trust to put your life in the hands of your friends after suffering utter heartbreak. However, she has and hopefully relationship rehab will bring back the old Alyssa everyone has been so accustomed to seeing in person, watching on YouTube, and listening on the radio. In the end, when it's all said and done, I say this to the single men of the Gulf Coast: be afraid...be very afraid because soon a new, revitalized Alyssa will be unleashed.

HOLD YOUR BREATH
March 8, 2013

Someone once said, ~Love is like a bomb. It's a very powerful force which is fragile enough to make you...or break you. It has the power to hang one's happiness and anger on a very uneven scale. It's too bad happiness is the lightest of the two.~ In some aspect, love is like a bomb as it has the capacity to have you in a way become an explosives disposal expert of sorts so much so your life will never be the same, which is a good thing. In any case, it's a truly risky and not to mention heart stopping situation indeed when you encounter a guy/girl who one's genuinely interested in. Why? Essentially, you want to, in all intents and purposes carefully cut/disarm the seemingly deadly wires in a positive way in order to potentially leave not only your heart completely blown away, so to speak, but theirs as well.

If you think about it, one should most definitely err on the side of caution when it comes to defusing the live wire known as the human heart, especially in regard to women. You see, the female species tends to not just have 1 main trigger to disarm/cut but countless triggers unbeknownst to the guy in question who thinks he has it all figured out. Thinking about it further, the triggers themselves are considerably more complicated to handle as they're considered to be emotional and quite certainly mental as well. In other words, being able to disarm/cut the right wires regarding matters of the heart is easier said than done because there are so many unknown variables men don't see coming to where they end up finding themselves experiencing more than just getting blasted into oblivion.

As I mentioned before, the female species tends to not just have one main trigger to cut/disarm but countless triggers within the bomb that is their own heart. True, the wires in a woman's heart don't just represent their thoughts, feelings, and emotions. For they are also a representation of key aspects concerning a relationship such as honesty, respect, faith, hope, trust, understanding, security, contentment, intimacy, compassion, communication, etc. What it primarily comes down to is having a considerable amount of time, effort, patience, and a really steady hand, in a manner of speaking, to individually cut/disarm each one knowing full well one wrong move could spell absolute doom.

Let me ask this question to those who are in the dating scene, have you ever been in a situation where you knew the wires in your heart weren't cut/disarmed properly prompting you to personally watch the guy/girl's efforts to blow up in their face? I think it's safe to say we know someone or in fact are that someone who knew immediately the date wasn't going to go well because of something he/she said or did causing you to seek shelter within yourself to avoid the unfortunate blast radius created by the sheer stupidity of the guy/girl. Without a doubt, every person wants to meet/ date/fall in love/marry someone who they want to find themselves seeing an immediate countdown ticking up towards a worthwhile future rather than down whereby a potentially worthwhile relationship is inevitably established.

In retrospect, love or true love for that matter is a tricky explosive to figure out. Granted, there are a number of people who are fortunate enough to not be blown to smithereens as they were able to find/ properly handle the right wires in a now significant other's heart. Hey, it can oftentimes be purely out of dumb luck that a once scary ordeal in the beginning has ultimately become an excellent memory to reflect back on together. Of course, whether or not your eyes are closed when you cut/disarm the wire in which you finally laid it out all on the line involving him or her makes one's experience that much more intense. In the end, you sometimes just have to say a prayer, hold your breath, and then simply go for it hoping for the explosion of true happiness instead of utter heartbreak.

FAITHFULLY

March 12, 2013

Someone once said, ~When you're truly in love, being faithful isn't a sacrifice, it's a joy.~ Without a doubt, love and faithfulness is considerably rare these days to have when it comes to a potential and/or significant relationship. Yet, both most definitely do exist as there are a number of perfect examples involving couples who haven't sacrificed what being faithful means in order to experience absolute true happiness. In any case, it's a simple concept indeed to be lovingly faithful to one person for the rest of your life so much so it puts a smile on not only your face just thinking about it, but theirs as well. Unfortunately, for some guys/girls the reality of being with one person for a lifetime truly scares them to no end, which it shouldn't because of how much joy it will certainly bring into their lives.

Let me ask this question to each and every one of you, what does being faithful mean to you? By definition, faithful means a long continued and steadfast fidelity to whatever one is bound to be a pledge, duty, or obligation. I think it's safe to say every person wants to experience a type of fidelity where the guy/girl's heart will never stray and forever be yours. True, to be bound together in love by way of heartfelt words/vows and a wedding ring signifying a longstanding faithfulness is worthy of being absolutely memorable, as well as worthwhile. Let me tell you something, so few get the chance to experience what most feel who are jaded today due to constant utter heartbreak is merely pure fantasy but in actuality it's quite real.

If you think about it, there is a deluded mindset in which two people agree on having an open relationship and yet establish some sort of faithfulness for one another. Granted, there may possibly be enjoyment of partaking in the best of both worlds, but the relationship suffers because of one of the main keys or should I say vital thing that is sacrificed...respect. The lack of respect given to one another shows that even though you're together there is an immense disconnect, to where both of you will never have a clear understanding, for that matter of the true meaning of joy. You see, it's a sad state of affairs for those in open relationships sacrificing important aspects of love/true love he/she are deserving of whereas for others they cherish and hold on to it knowing full well how lucky they are to have it.

For the question can be asked to those who are either in a committed relationship, engaged or married for that matter, how/when did you know you wanted to be 100% faithful to the man/woman you love with all your heart? Thinking about it, the question itself has many difference answers and at the same time they all are important when it pertains to matters of the heart. Of course, to be faithful mentally, personally, physically, spiritually, and not to mention emotionally shows a strong bond established in every sense of the word to the point where you're left with no uncertainly whatsoever concerning how your heart will never be betrayed. What it primarily comes down to is the desire of wanting to work together to have such a strong commitment instead of being it just one sided.

In retrospect, there comes a point where it's hard to believe people have the ability to stay faithful. Women, more often than not, believe this to be true evident by their own past experiences concerning the guys they've dated, been in a significant relationship with, or been married to. However, one has to remind the female species not all guys are like this and aren't the best representation of men who have in their life a strong male role model to go by...but I digress. Ultimately, it's just a matter of meeting the right guy/girl who proves to you how serious being faithful is and they just aren't plain words or actions to him or her. In the end, when you do finally stand in front of/meet your best friend for life you'll somehow know and believe he'll/she'll be faithfully bound to you always.

INSANITY AT ITS BEST

March 13, 2013

Johann Wolfgang von Goethe once said, ~We do not have to visit
the madhouse to find disordered minds; our planet is the mental
institution of the universe.~ Without a doubt, one could very well
consider Qtip and Blondie In The Morning radio show not only a
madhouse, but a mental institution of Alice In Wonderland type
proportions. Thinking about it, the radio personalities of the Gulf
Coast's hit music station 97.5 WABD are definite comparisons to
certain characters, one of which is most definitely The Mad Hatter.
You see, when it comes to this particular character his cup of tea,
so to speak, is making people not only laugh with his own sense of
web-based insanity but leaves you wondering what's in store next
for a guy who certainly has a method to his madness.

As I said before, there is certainly a method to his madness
because quite frankly you never know what he's going to pull out
of his hat, in a manner of speaking. Of course, you can't help but
be entertained with amusement by his antics when it involves
talking/dressing up like a pirate, dressed up dancing like a Mayan
in absolute cold weather, dancing in oversize pajama pants, joining
in on the fad of pouring milk over himself, and not to mention
running for President leading him to debate over the radio listeners
in the Gulf Coast. What it primarily comes down to is the sheer
commitment/passion he delivers to the characters he brings
life to so much so he doesn't break it whatsoever, which shows
tremendous amounts of dedication to his craft.

If you think about it, laughter isn't always the case for someone who
causes people to wonder if he's completely lost his mind or possibly
already has. In any case, he does indeed have a serious side when it
pertains to helping the teenage population with relatable problems/
situations involving dating/relationships. Thinkteen.org is an

organization in which the graduates of the University of Alabama....
Roll Tide...take part in asking teens what advice they would give
for a particular guy/girl pertaining to relationships. True, it's an
excellent organization to be associated with and you're able to make
a difference in some way. Hey, you have to give a tip of the hat to
someone who even though is certifiably insane, he helps assist/
brings attention to a helpful cause.

Let me ask you this question to those who have met in person or
personally know the man I dubbed the Mad Hatter, do you think
he has the potential to go even farther taking the insanity level
far beyond where it's capable of going? In other words, will he be
able to top himself when it involves the memorable antics, and
will it live up to the expectations, we the listeners have grown to
enjoy? Truth be told, I think he does and I, along with the listeners
of WABD think or should I say wholeheartedly believe so too. Let
me tell you something ladies and gentlemen, he wasn't given the
2012's promotions tech award for nothing and hopefully he'll
continue to receive more awards in the coming future.

In retrospect, the enigma that is Nicholas Walter Fox is both
insane and a genius. Granted, he plays off his fellow Wonderland
characters The March Hare(Qtip), The Cheshire Cat(Blondie), The
White Rabbit (Intern Alyssa), The Caterpillar(Producer Heather)
see Wiki Adventures In Wonderland and the radio listeners all
around the Gulf Coast. I think it's safe to say the best is yet to come
for Nick and many of us who are listening on the radio, watching/
subscribed to his YouTube channel, or hanging out on location
within the Gulf Coast know he's saving the ultimate antic for last.
In the end, you know you're in for a treat when Nick Fox is live on
the radio in a studio or somewhere in the Gulf Coast in costume
because it's insanity at its best.

ON FIRE

March 14, 2013

Helen Keller once said, ~Life is either a daring adventure or nothing. To keep our faces toward change and behave like free spirits in the presence of fate is strength undefeatable.~ Let me ask you this question t those who are avid listeners of Qtip and Blondie in the Morning, among the 5 individuals behind the mic who do you consider to be more of an absolute free spirit? I think it's safe to say the answer would most definitely be unanimous if you have ever met in person or listened to this free-spirited woman on a semi-daily basis then you know who I'm talking about. For it's always an entertaining and certainly adventurous situation indeed for any listener on the radio as they are taken for one wild ride, so to speak, when you hear her speak so much so you can't help but smile.

If you think about it, every radio personality started out with humble beginnings and when it comes to this down to earth blonde she began as a YouTube contestant vying for a spot on the old 97.5 WABB Morning Show with John and Johnna. Essentially, she was a fresh faced and energetic young woman who back then pressed forward toward change which could clearly be seen in the desire/determination in her eyes. For its that desire/determination for change in which she would slowly but surely gain the love of not only the Gulf Coast audience, but practically the entire male species as well. Listen, you can't deny she has a winning personality that truly shines forth not just by the sound of her voice, but in person as well whether it's in location or simply somewhere out in public.

Without a doubt, one thing that hasn't changed is her passion for her two cats Big Frank and Domino. True, the proud and protective mother of two make felines is easily offended when Big Frank is referred to as fat leading her to strike back. Oftentimes, the target in her proverbial crosshairs sits directly across from her every morning jabbing at the unfortunate fact her big boy is a bit on the husky side. In any case, the emotional bond she has with her two cats is undeniable to the point where she nearly/has shed tears talking about the both of them as if they are her own kids. Let me tell you something, the love she has for them gives her a considerable amount of strength and despite being given the moniker "crazy cat lady" by Q-Tip, she continues to speak proudly of them no matter what.

For the question can be asked to the ladies of the Gulf Coast who are currently suffering utter heartbreak, would you at a drop of hat take part in a creation she and a teacher/producer formed in order to help a friend/intern stuck in a rut? Of course, the answer would be yes because quite frankly their success rate is 100%. Granted, they've only had one client, so to speak, but it's a success nonetheless with the woman known as Slim Lady back to her old self once again. However, something tells me many heartbroken women who are unable to move past their exes could very much pay for the experience of going through her ingenious 5 step boot camp. Hey, who knows it could be a very successful business venture if she ever decides to leave the radio business behind.

Rachel "Blondie" Jones. A woman who can look proudly back on where she started from to where she is now in her career and possibly not have any regret. Yet, when it comes to her love life she's still hoping to meet Mr. Right who is truly deserving of a woman who many believe is the Gulf Coast hit music station's sweetheart. In other words, the radio version of America's sweetheart Julia Roberts. In addition, she is a fiery ball of awesome who has taken it upon herself to introduce available single males and females to the Gulf Coast in a segment well known as Hotties Of The Week. In the end, as long as there is loving support for this incredible woman who is absolutely priceless her star will never burn out and this girl will be on fire for years to come, , which is a song by 2001's Best-selling artist/R&B artist Alicia Keys.

THE BRIGHT SIDE
March 18, 2013

Brahma Kumaris once said, ~To be a teacher means to touch the heart rather than the head. Teaching others means being subtle and explaining in such a way that the mind opens because the heart has understood. The one who truly teaches inspires rather than just becoming the one who teaches others. There is the recognition of the positivity that is in each one and so no comparisons are made with others. Once we are able to look at the positivity in another individual and have the pure desire of enabling progress within that person, we are able to feel love from him. This is like a parent's love where love for the child is that which makes him grow. We become a teacher who inspires rather than the one who teaches.~ Without a doubt, the power of positivity is being taught and shared by a female radio producer throughout the Gulf Coast.

As I said before, the power of positivity is being taught and shared by a female producer throughout the Gulf Coast. For it's this 97.5 WABD producer who is most definitely a public servant when it comes to teaching the impressionable young minds of children. It's a noble and sometimes thankless profession but if you have the patience, as well as caring fortitude to make a positive impact in any way on each of their lives such as this woman is striving for then my friend it show on her part the desire to make an absolute difference in a child's mental/social/behavioral upbringing. In any case, you can't help but admire her dedication and determination to teach / inform the future generation, but the entire Gulf Coast as well in regards to what listeners possibly have weighing on their mind.

Oftentimes, being taught and retaining positivity is certainly a life lesson, especially when it comes to the online dating scene. True, this proud college graduate is on several dating websites and has admitted it freely on air many times to everyone who listens to the show every morning. Yet, it's an unfortunate situation indeed knowing her prospective dates haven't gone the way she wanted, which isn't her fault by any means whatsoever. Thinking about it, one may dwell on it to no end focusing on the negative; instead she is focused on the positive and moving on to the next potential date who will quite possibly bring to her heart true happiness someday. Essentially, it's a sentiment countless Q-Tip and Blondie In The Morning/97.5 WABD collectively hope also because we got your back supporting you every step of the way.

If you think about it, certain segments within the show are spawned to become a whole new creation by way of social media known as Twitter. You see, it had its humble beginnings when this plucky producer began tweeting positive, uplifting messages to unfortunate souls who were feeling down to the point where it was put on YouTube for others to see if you're a follower of hers of course. Granted, it started off simple, meaning, and heartfelt but they eventually have become larger than life to where she has put her own flair and style into each message. Personally speaking, I look forward to what is in store with her daily positive YouTube messages because you never know what you're going to get or who may show up for that matter.

In retrospect, Heather Bright is considered one of the important cogs that helps the Gulf Coast's favorite hit morning radio station run smoothly. In a sense, it's the person behind the scenes who helps keep the two cogs otherwise known as Q-Tip and Blondie along with Nick Fox, Intern Alyssa, Scott Adams, and not to mention Crazy Dale running on full cylinder, in a manner speaking. What it primarily comes down to is positive teamwork because quite frankly if one cog doesn't work properly then something is surely off, which can be heard and somehow felt live on the air. In the end, heed the YouTube message of positivity Ms. Bright gives every morning because they'll teach you something and if you're unable to then look on the bright side, you at least got a cyber hug from her.

THAT'S FUNNY

March 20, 2013

Mary Hirsch once said, ~Humor is a rubber rubber sword - it allows you to make a point without drawing blood.~ If you think about it, every person has a different way of expressing humor whether it be dry, cynical, sarcastic, morbid, sick and twisted, etc. You see, when it comes to a certain mail radio personality from St. Louis now residing in the Gulf Coast, the listening audience receives a mixed bag of humor. For it's a type of mixed bag humor in which you can totally laugh at because one knows what he's speaking of is the truth; on the other hand, there are those moments where you laugh in absolute disbelief regarding the shock value of what is said on air. Hey, he has the proverbial rubber sword in hand known as the mic and it's just a matter of how hard he'll in all intents and purposes slap you with his own off the cuff style humor.

Without a doubt, one of the many things you can find humorous about one half of an incredibly awesome morning radio duo is the fact he's a diehard Kenny Chesney fan. It's a comical situation indeed knowing on any given morning the conversation or topic at hand can most definitely take a quick turn out of nowhere, putting the focus on Mr. Chesney. Thinking about it further, whether it's a concert in or near the Gulf Coast, a CD coming out, an appearance on a certain tv show, or whatever the case may be you'll surely hear about it because he's that big of a loyal fan. I think it would be safe to say if it were up to him when he eventually passes away he would like to be buried in a Kenny Chesney coffin with built-in speakers playing his songs.

As said before in the above mentioned quote humor is a rubber sword allowing you to make a point without drawing blood. This fits him to a T. Essentially, the keeper of Screwy News will sometimes wield his rubber sword of humor towards the listening audience, myself included, which is at times a backhanded compliment. True, the humorous verbal barbs be slaps us with, in a manner of speaking, are in jest and not to be taken seriously most of the time because quite frankly the entire Gulf Coast is practically used to it by now. Oftentimes, the listeners who call in not only get the brunt of being amusingly sliced and diced without any blood being spilled but have been hung up on live on the air. Let me tell you something, if he's done that to you then consider it an honor, especially if you're a first-time caller but long-time listener.

Let me ask this question to each and every person who listens to the Gulf Coast's hit music station, do you truly believe the man who continually calls Blondie's cat Big Frank fat will end up one day on the receiving end of a live on the air massive beat down? Truth be told, I believe so and the rest of the listening audience would agree with me knowing how absolutely sensitive she is when it comes to her big boy's weight. Granted, she may not seem the violent type but if he continually jabs/provokes her all-the-while enjoying every second of it he knowing full well it gets under her skin she'll one day Hulk up and go on a rampage of epic proportions. Of course, if that ever happens may God have mercy on this man's soul because it will take more than just the entire Morning/97.5 WABD crew to stop her.

In retrospect, Glenn Johnson otherwise known as Q-Tip is one of a kind when it comes to morning radio personalities. He is surrounded by 3 beautiful single women on a semi daily basis and for any guy that would be considered a treat but for him it's torture. In any case, one may recall he started out employed by a rival music station as their stunt guy but he would inevitably cross over to the other side a few years later bringing along his brand of humor working with 97.5 WABB. For it's there, he would meet his future best friend for life Cherish Lombard. Fast forward a few years and he's at the helm of one of the most awesome morning radio shows in the Gulf Coast. In the end, Q-Tip is the type of guy who never expresses an all gut busting laugh but you'll hear two familiar words he always utters to where it has become his signature reply when he finds something hilarious...that's funny.

AGE OF THE GEEK
April 2, 2013

Actor Dominic Monaghan once said, ~The term "geek" to me is like you having a passion, interest in something that is unabashed and you don't care if people think it's not cool. You think it's cool and that's your thing.~ Without a doubt, when you think about having a passionate interest you don't necessarily consider this 97.5 WABD radio personality a geek judging by the outside exterior. However, on the inside beats the heart of one of the geekiest people not only residing in the Gulf Coast, but a guy who I consider a friend. Granted, it may not seem cool to a select number of people who don't listen to the hit music station or know him personally; yet, its cool to the listening audience such as myself who is indeed a fellow geek as well in regard to being a fan of a well-known movie franchise. In any case, his geeky interests fall into 3 categories: sippy cups, sports, and Star Wars.

Let me ask you this question, what do you personally own that has essentially become a part of you to the point where you've possibly named it? I think it's safe to say it may be considerably geeky for the rather hulking 6th member of the WABD team but at the same time has a considerable soft spot for something he's been using to drink out of, which is a well-known fact for those who know the back story. For it's at times a humorous situation to the point where his fellow radio mates have ragged him about the seemingly odd relationship shared with it. Unfortunately, the aforementioned sippy cup was replaced with a new one and even though it may possibly have been a difficult transition to part ways with, he knows how truly reliable it was for him.

If you think about it, a person can most definitely be considered a passionate sports geek, especially if you're from Detroit such as this individual. You see, his loyalty and blood bleeds the Detroit teams of Tiger Baseball and Red Wings Hockey evident by the jerseys he consistently wears. True, he may appear to be a jock, but when you talk to, hear him on the radio, and/or read his FB statuses he'll mention player stats, history, as well as anything that interests him concerning the sports of Detroit, Michigan. Of course, he's also the emcee of the Pensacola Ice Flyers and keeps the audience not only thoroughly entertained but informed too. Let me tell you something, many would wholeheartedly agree he's doing an awesome job and is absolutely having fun at the same time.

For the question can be asked to the ladies of the Gulf Coast, do you think owning a Darth Vader costume is considered an attractive quality in your own personal dating/relationship list? Women, more often than not, wouldn't think it's attractive but when the guy owning it does the g thing(gym) in order to keep himself fit I would fair to guess they'll check it off on their list as a positive. As I said before, he's a fellow Star Wars geek who I know after having a conversation with him concerning if he ever gets married some day and needs a hobby, he would build his own R2D2 unit. Plus, during a recent Star Wars themed Ice Flyers game he was able to take video and a pic with R2. So, take note ladies if any of you one day are lucky enough to marry this guy just know what you'll be getting yourself into.

In retrospect, Scott Adams or just known as Scotty by his friends, is a geek and will proudly proclaim it. Thinking about it, you have to give it up for a dude who geeks out over certain YouTube clips, old Japanese tv series on DVD like Ultraman, or whatever the case may be because it shows how geeky he can be. Personally speaking, it's an honor to call him a friend and a fellow Star Wars enthusiast despite owning a Darth Vader costume. Who am I to judge since I own a Yoda costume myself...but I digress. Ultimately, geeks stick together, and you can always count on him to show his geekiness whether on the radio or in person. In the end, the age of the geek is at hand and it's a safe bet Scotty will be at the forefront leading the charge.

SOMEWHERE I BELONG

April 9, 2013

Someone once said, ~It's scary to find someone that makes you happy. You start giving them all of your attention because they're what makes you forget everything bad that's going on in your life. They're the first person you want to talk to in the morning and the last one before you sleep just so you can start and end your day with a smile. It all sounds great to have that someone, but it's scary to think about how easily they could just leave and take that happiness away too when they go.~ If you think about it, we all want to experience that innate sense of belonging in regard to matters of the heart. For it's most definitely a comforting and at the same time scary situation indeed to know that type of true happiness is out there to the point where you can't help but smile.

As I said before, we all want to experience that innate sense of belonging in regard to matters of the heart. Thinking about it further, it's a place within one's heart not too many individuals have the fortunate opportunity to not only think and feel they absolutely belong when it comes to love/true love but know as well. Why? What it comes down to is allowing yourself to become fully vulnerable/exposed and opening up to a guy/girl who you're deathly afraid of hurting you, in a good way of course. You have to face what you're most afraid of when you're potentially standing in front of someone special...sharing your feelings. Essentially, it gives a person the chance to tap into a place you never really get a chance to express verbally, especially if you're a guy.

Without a doubt, the emotional and mental turmoil one goes through during their time of painful sadness can certainly be tortuous. True, it takes time to break on through to the other side of a broken heart in order to fully heal, as well as feel once again. Hey, it's a sad and oftentimes frustrating state of affairs when you find yourself completely far away from where you think/want to/know you belong concerning being in a long lasting, worthwhile relationship. Granted, there will be bumps and not to mention setbacks involving relationship road that will be considered obstacles hindering your journey back to having a permanent rather than a temporary smile with a guy/girl who you are truly deserving of and vice versa.

Let me ask this question to those who are living the single life and/or are in the dating scene, how many of you are in a possibly potential relationship leading you to feel as if you're not an emotional nomad anymore traveling, so to speak, every which way but to the one place you so want to be at. I think it's safe to say there are a certain number of people who so want to stop themselves from making a costly mistake by walking away from a dream come true. You see, it's the unfortunate utter heartbreaks experienced in the past have brought tears of sadness but it's one's present tears being shed are in large part to the joy of feeling like you're no longer banished or should I say exiled from within your own heart.

In retrospect, to have someone in your life who will never leave sticking with you no matter what gives you a sense of home. A home where there is never the fear of him/her leaving you, which is far from your mind because you're focusing more on the positives than the negatives. Let me tell you something, if you're in a significant relationship where he/she has helped make you forget every bad thing that has happened or is happening around/near/to you then kudos my friend. In the end, there comes a point where all the emotional and mental turmoil/ sadness/sorrow you've been through will be well worth it so much so you think to yourself while in his/her warm, loving embrace I'm finally somewhere I belong.

UNSTOPPABLE

April 14, 2013

3X Olympic Beach Volleyball winner Kerri Walsh-Jennings once said, ~You touch every other ball and, if you screw up, you only have one person to back you up. You can't hide in the corner.~ In some aspect, matters of the heart regarding being in a significant relationship is like the sport of Olympic beach volleyball. Essentially, it's you and your partner literally, as well as metaphorically on the so-called grandest stage up against the very skilled/top opponent known as love. For it can most definitely be a tough and not to mention exhausting situation indeed taking on not only a crafty, seasoned veteran, but each other too when areas in the sandy relationship court aren't working out as planned. Let me tell you something, that's when partners dig deep, set aside their differences, rely on and trust each other even more.

Without a doubt, it takes team effort to be on the top of the proverbial medal stand, so to speak, knowing full well hard work, determination, blood, sweat, tears have been given to be there achieving a goal. In a sense, it's that way with significant relationships as two people work together in acquiring important/pivotal points by signaling and setting up one another to serve/hit/spike the volleyball representing the couple's heart. Thinking about it further, the volleyball, otherwise known as the couple's heart, is a representation of the following aspects shared: trust, respect, faith, loyalty, honor, intimacy, communication, understanding, forgiveness, happiness, joy, etc. True, it will gradually become easier rather than harder to settle into a groove with your partner so much so a much stronger bond will certainly be established.

As said before, it takes team effort to establish a strong

partnership where unfortunately mistakes don't affect the focus both of you have. However, it's a sad state of affairs when continuous service errors/mistakes occur causing problems in the seemingly cohesive unit shared to where there is an absolute inability to focus. You see, the lack of focus will inevitably lead to a slowly deteriorating partnership whereby anger, bitterness, resentment, distrust, lack of faith/communication/respect/ teamwork, etc. come into play. Unfortunately, there comes a point where the team is no longer a team as there is simply just one or both individuals selfishly yelling out loud one word... mine. I think it's safe to say we know of a relationship in the past or in fact currently part of a relationship like this and there is absolutely no teamwork whatsoever.

Let me ask you this question to those who are in a significant relationship, do you and your partner give 100% no matter how difficult the challenges are? Oftentimes, having someone in your life who'll fight for every point with you instead of against is totally amazing. A special someone who won't doesn't have an ego accepting all the glory as he/she knowingly didn't put every ounce of their being into the match. To have a guy/girl who isn't afraid to get dirty and have every bit of sand in places that it shouldn't be in lets you know he/she is a keeper. Hey, to share the court with your best friend for life who is doing everything in his/her power just short of putting one's body on the line to make those unbelievable saves when it counts so the game isn't over yet brings absolute worthwhile comfort to your heart.

In retrospect, the Olympics are every 4 years but when it comes to the partnership that is marriage it's all year round. Sadly, a gold medal isn't won but you do win the pure satisfaction of putting your heart/soul into a relationship one can look back on and be proud of in the latter years of life. Additionally, you're representing your better half, which is the best feeling in the world. In other words, you can smile knowing everything was left on the sandy court without any regrets to think back on. Of course, you both have fans in the form of friends and family who are supportive and will continually cheer win or lose. In the end, when you have a partner who is a team player, can communicate with you verbally/nonverbally, and tells you "we got this" when the matches in life get intense, you're not just a force to be reckoned with, you're unstoppable.

I WANT IT THAT WAY

April 21, 2013

Someone once said, ~Love who your heart wants, not what your eyes want. Don't worry what others say or think. This love is yours, not theirs.~ If you think about it, it's not so much who your heart wants but rather what your heart wants when it comes to absolute true happiness. For it can most definitely be a heartwarming and not to mention comforting situation indeed when you know with 100% surety the type of relationship you want based on the inward qualities of a potential significant other instead of the outer. Essentially, the qualities of that type of relationship you truly want may not necessarily match with those who are into the superficial standards whereby a temporary desire is unfortunately experienced and not a permanent, worthwhile bond. A bond that is genuinely honest and real so much so it's considered to be a rarity to have these days.

Without a doubt, we all want the same thing regarding matters of the heart and even though the circumstances may be inherently different we're all universally connected when it pertains to love/true love. True, one may be perceived as envious, jealous, and a little bit selfish in wanting what a handful of people are lucky enough to have. To be perfectly honest, you have every right to feel that way because of experiencing firsthand the heartache, as well as frustration of a guy/girl's selfishness and disregard of providing only for himself/herself, which is sadly an unwanted character trait. In any case, being a giver and not a take is a tremendous quality to have and for many women it's one of the main attributes they've been wanting in a man who although seems like a mere fantasy, he's really existing somewhere in the world.

As I said before, the qualities/traits you truly wanted may not necessarily match with those who are into the superficial standards whereby a temporary desire is unfortunately experienced and not a permanent, worthwhile bond. Thinking about it further, superficial individuals tend to find it humorous that people like myself are wanting a relationship with more substance with a deep-rooted connection built on trust, faith in God, respect, honor, loyalty, intimacy, understanding, commitment, etc. Of course, you have to find the humor in their humor because it's these individuals who are continually establishing empty, meaningless relationships with no future whatsoever. Let me tell you something, stay true to everything you want that's pure, genuine and real within your heart and don't allow yourself to doubt/second guess/compromise your personal decision by others because it will all be worth it for you someday.

Let me ask you this question to the single people out there, when it involves your own heart what do you want? Granted, it's a seemingly simple question and yet it can oftentimes leave a person searching for a meaningful, well thought out answer as it relates to a rewarding future. Personally speaking, as a single guy I want first and foremost a relationship where we both have a servant's heart for God. You see, it's through Him that I will eventually have everything I ever wanted when I do fall in love. Hey, the rest will inevitably fall into place as she hopefully is a fan of Star Wars, enjoys insane activities such as skydiving, will accept me for being a die-hard pro wrestling fan, etc. In other words, I would like to meet a woman who is just as dorky/weird/insane/nerdy/geeky as I am and if it just so happens, she is absolutely beautiful, well then that's a plus in my book.

In retrospect, love metaphorically sees every want within the human heart and not with one's eyes. Fortunately, fulfilling all you've ever possibly wanted can come to fruition as it takes massive amounts of patience and trusting in God's plan through prayer. A perfect example is couples who have been married for more than 40/50/60 years and are still going strong. In a sense, they have what those of us who are living the single life dream of wanting/having. I think it's safe to say each one of us has witnessed moments where a surprise kiss on the cheek by the elderly husband totally lights up the face of his elderly wife. Truth be told, you can't help but smile knowing the fire between them after so many years will never die out. In the end, it's the longevity of a elderly married couple who have set the proverbial benchmark for how a relationship should be to the point where it causes you to think to yourself or say out loud, I want it that way.

IT WON'T BE LIKE THIS FOR LONG

April 24, 2013

Someone once said, ~They say that from the instant he lays eyes on her a father adores his daughter. Whoever she grows up to be, she is always to him that little girl in pigtails. She makes him feel like Christmas. In exchange, he makes a secret promise not to see the awkwardness of her teenage years, the mistakes and the mistakes she makes on the secrets she keeps.~ Without a doubt the father-daughter relationship is considered to be a dynamic, special bond between the two of them, especially right when she's held in his arms at birth. For it's most definitely an impactful situation indeed for any proud papa who will automatically swear a personal oath to protect his baby girl from being hurt not just from the outside world, but by what he considers public enemy #1...boys/guys.

Let me ask you this question to you ladies out there, do/did you have your father wrapped around your little finger to the point where you can basically get away with anything? Thinking about it, daughters at a very early age are instilled with the power of the Jedi mind trick allowing them to manipulate the situation whatever it may be to their way. In other words, using the dark side of the force to their advantage...but I digress. In any case, that's how the relationship will and forever always be as daddy's little girl will truly hold a special place in his heart. Of course, stress and headaches are certainly going to be experienced once boys come into the picture but more specifically the wrong boys who cause dads to clean their guns more often than usual.

As I said before, stress and headaches are certainly going to be experienced for dear old dad once the wrong kind of boy begins to lurk around the corner, so to speak. I think it's safe to say the teenage years are what every father dreads as their precious munchkin have grown into a young lady. True, most or pretty much all fathers would like nothing more than to not only protect them from young adolescent teenage males who he knows have one thing on their mind, but also protecting her/them from being emotionally hurt suffering their first heartbreak. You see, fathers can't stand to see their daughter cry knowing full well a boy/guy is responsible and even though they can't put the fear of God into the boy/guy in question he can just be there to help turn those tears into a smile.

For the question can be asked to all you dads who have daughters, what is the greatest fear you have when she no longer dating the wrong guy? If your answer is when she begins dating the right guy, then you would absolutely correct. Essentially, a father's job has always been to intimidate the boys/guy who he views are not right for his daughter and will have pure enjoyment doing it. Unfortunately, the fun will come to an end when he finally meets the guy who no matter how hard he tries to dislike him he can't help but approve of the smartest choice she has ever made. Yet, it leaves him to also realize he's no longer going to be the #1 man in her life as she's eventually going to live a life of her own after being under his protective wing for so many years.

Joseph Addison said, ~Certain is it that there is no kind of affection so purely angelic as of a father to a daughter. In love to our wives there is desire; to our sons, ambition; but to our daughters there is something there are no words to express.~ Oftentimes, there are no words to describe the love he has for his daughter. A man who when she was born could literally hold her within the palm of his hand. A grizzly bear who instantly turns into a teddy bear when being hugged by his little ankle biter. The special moments sitting on one's lap, being called her hero, finding her own identity as a teenager, the "I hate you/you're embarrassing me phase", the constant state of panic when she's out with her friends, etc. In end, to all the dads out there keep the moments you have with you daughter(s) close to your heart because you know it won't be like this for long, which is a song by Hootie and Blowfish frontman/2009's New Artist Award from the Country Music Association Darius Rucker.

ONE MORE SHOT

May 5, 2013

Someone once said, ~Life is like a camera. Just focus on
what's important and capture the good times, develop from
the negative, and if things don't work out - just take another
shot.~ In some aspect, life is most definitely like a camera in the
context where it captures moments of our lives and places then
one's internal album otherwise known as our memory banks.
Thinking about it, as the metaphorical photographer of our
lives each of us want to be photographed at our very best but it
unfortunately doesn't work out that way. For it can certainly be
a sad, frustrating, and embarrassing situation indeed when life
itself takes a snapshot of a particular moment in time you weren't
ready for. Yet, at the same time the snapshot taken is considered
to be an absolute learning experience.

Without a doubt, we live in a digital age where you no longer have
to wait to get your picture developed. You see, in an instant a
photo can be digitally taken and viewed in a matter of seconds. In
a sense, life gives us the opportunity to capture moments with not
just old friends, but new ones as well. Hey, its the stranger(s) we
meet on a semi-daily basis on any given time at any given place
that leads to life snapping a metaphorical snapshot, so to speak,
of a possibly worthwhile developing friendship. Granted, it starts
off as mere strangers, then acquaintances, and eventually moving
on to great friends after a substantial amount of time hanging
out together. Let me tell you something, each one of us distinctly
remembers that first initial snapshot concerning one's best friend
and how the bonds of friendship developed from there.

As I said before, it can certainly be a sad, frustrating, and
embarrassing situation indeed when life itself takes a snapshot
of a particular moment in time you weren't ready for. Yet, at the

same time the snapshot taken is considered to be an absolute learning experience, especially in regard to one's professional career. I think it's safe to say we've all been in a situation where something happened at work either involving a project, a co-worker, or even your boss for that matter to where you're given the pink slip or made the decision to quit. If you think about it, nobody ever really wants to reflect back on the mental images life took showing all the plethora of emotions tied to the unwanted memory of the past. However, it's a blessing in disguise as the mental image of an unwanted memory brings about laughter and a smile knowing you're now in a far better career venture.

Let me ask you this question to those who are in the dating scene, when it comes to life snapping away at matters of your own heart, are there more pics showing disappointment or worthwhile true happiness. True, living the single life can be difficult because the fact of the mater is it's oftentimes hard to get a good focus on meeting the right guy/girl. Of course, photos can or have been taken upon meeting a potential Ms./Mr. Right and that's when an attempt to get a clear picture of the relationship happens when established. Unfortunately, for some people the photo taken by life with that supposed special someone isn't/didn't quite come out as clear due to relationship issues causing a deletion then retake. However, for others it becomes much clearer with every photo taken with their best friend for life, so much so a bright future is seen between the two of them.

In retrospect, not every moment captured by life will be a happy one. Essentially, there are going to be times where you desperately want to photoshop in real life out the forgettable parts of your internal memory album leaving only the awesome ones in. Sadly, that's not how life works as it continually snaps 24/7 the bad moments along with the good. What it primarily comes down to is how you deal with the bad snapshots of life regarding friendships, career, and love/true love. As mentioned before, laughing and smiling reflecting back on the now torn up images of the bad moments shows you've let go and moved on from the past. Hey, when you finally do, you'll look forward to capturing special moments with someone you're absolutely deserving of. In the end, like a camera taking pictures we're all provided the chance in life to take one more shot when you think/know the last one didn't turn out as well.

A SOFT TOUCH

May 9, 2013

Someone once said, ~Love is like a sunburn. You can feel it coming but you let it happen anyway, even though in the end, you know it hurts.~ If you think about it, getting a sunburn is considerably similar to matters of the heart. How so? Essentially, both are most definitely considered to be a delicate and not to mention painful situation indeed to handle so much so nobody wants to end up getting burned literally, as well as figuratively. Unfortunately, it doesn't necessarily work out that way as countless individuals have experienced/are now experiencing the sunburn known all too well as either utter heartbreak or true happiness. For its certainly a painfully stinging situation indeed lasting for quite some time to the point where one hopes for or finally receives some sweet, soothing relief.

As I said before, love and a sunburn are considerably similar in the sense that both are a delicate and painful situation to handle so much so nobody wants to end up getting burned literally, as well as figuratively. In other words, both hurt but not if they're correctly handled in a way to where it leaves you with a lasting positive smile instead of an unwanted negative wince on your face. What it primarily comes down to is being in a relationship with a guy/girl who is able to "apply" the right amount of sunscreen protection, so to speak, in order to protect one's heart. Trust. patience, understanding, honesty, faith, love, honor, respect, understanding, contentment, intimacy, commitment, etc. are a representation of what any person wants to in all intents and purposes be applied to their own heart by someone special.

Without a doubt, the one thing every person tries to avoid when having a sunburn is being touched because of how sensitive particular areas of one's body are. In some aspect, when a person finds themselves feeling heartbroken, he/she can truly be personally, mentally, and emotionally sensitive to where it's absolutely painful if a specific memory touches their heart/mind. I think it's safe to say there are many of you out there who are quite possibly experiencing this right now as the memories of a past love are slapping/hitting your heart to no end causing you to wince immensely. You see, those memories are viewed as an irritating nuisance and you want nothing more than the tortuous inner turmoil you're going through to peel away, in a manner of speaking, like one's own skin once it begins peeling.

Let me ask you this question concerning getting a sunburn, how many absolutely enjoy peeling away the dead, burnt skin away from particular areas of your body that were exposed to the sun after a period of time has passed? Of course, the dead skin that you're inevitably peeling away represents the anger, hatred, bitterness, frustration, confusion, grief, heartache, self-doubt, etc. Thinking about it further, it hopefully allows your heart to gradually return to the softness of what it was before it in all intents and purposes got beaten down by the harsh toxic rays of a relationship that badly burned you. True, the feeling after peeling away every negative aspect of one's past relationship is tremendously refreshing, giving you the opportunity to soak up the rays of love/love from a guy/girl you are most deserving of.

In retrospect, you have to be careful in love because it exposes you mentally, personally, and emotionally within your heart. Granted, you don't want to become so badly burned, you end up focusing more on the pain rather than wanting to experience the ultimate satisfaction of finally being happy. Sadly, there are men and women who are refusing to let go of the pain and continuing to hold on to the skin that's been peeled away instead of throwing it away. Ultimately, I tip my hat to those who are taking every opportunity with their fresh new skin to put themselves out there knowing full well they're somewhat afraid, which is understandable. In the end, for those living the single life such as myself you hope to meet someone who quintessentially gives you a nice, even tan all over your heart; if mistakes in the relationship occur that could possibly burn it he/she completely surprises you by simply handling it with a soft touch.

I GOT YOU

May 18, 2013

John Scott once said, ~It seems we are capable of immense love
and loyalty, and as capable of deceit and strategy. It's probably
the shocking ambivalence that makes us unique.~ Without a
doubt, there is most definitely a unique difference when it comes
to meeting/being with a genuinely real guy/girl who has the
immense capability of being absolutely loyal in regard to being in a
significant relationship. The unique difference is the rarity of truly
experiencing a type of unwavering loyalty in which he/she solidly
stands by your side to the point where you find yourself in amazed
disbelief. Hey, to personally that innate sense of loving loyalty can
bring about or has brought a smile to your face knowing full well
he/she will never leave your side.

If you think about it, men and women have the capacity to
love and be loyal with every fiber of their being to one person.
Unfortunately, it's not the case nowadays as a number of
individuals experienced for themselves in the past or recently the
harsh, painful reality of being betrayed. So, what has been lost?
Thinking about it, what's lost is not having any idea what the
true meaning of loyalty is anymore. You see, the true meaning
of loyalty regarding matters of the heart is holding strong to the
valuable/cherished standards of what makes being in a relationship
so worthwhile. Trust, patience, faith, honor, respect, honestly,
understanding, communication, commitment, etc, are key aspects
that if continually kept alive instead of ignored will thrive because
of the strength within the bond of loyalty shared with each other.

As I said before, to meet a genuinely real guy/girl who is uniquely
different from all the rest and exudes unwavering loyalty can leave
you feeling a mixture of amazed disbelief. True, it certainly can be
a shock to the system experiencing something one may not be used

to so much so you want to pinch yourself. Sadly, betrayal and love are synonymous with each other to where it's an all-too-common occurrence for many as the deceit and atrocities oftentimes done in secrecy by a past love. In some aspect, it's like a knife plunged deeply into one's own heart by him/her. Essentially, that knife is/ can be considered both a strength, as well as a weakness and it takes having a special someone who'll you'll put 100% trust in to be able to finally remove the utter heartbreak you've been holding on to for quite some time.

Let me ask this question to those who have been betrayed in the past or recently, do you personally believe there are men and women still adhering to the concept of loyalty concerning love/true love or it's merely a lost ideal? My answer is yes and quite frankly one can't have the deluded that once you're in a relationship he/she is going to cheat/betray you, which will mess with you not only mentally but emotionally also. Women, more so than men, tend to think this way and it can cause or already has caused complications in a potential relationship. However, the cycle of mistrust can be broken, and the lost ideal can gradually be found once again. How? What it primarily comes down to is him/ her proving to you how trustworthy he/she is by simply standing by your side every step of the way rather than behind you.

In retrospect, love and loyalty can be a difficult combo to find or even have these days. Granted, a person can have love but without loyalty and everything else in between that's important is not considerably unique. Essentially, every relationship is the same but it's the special uniqueness that makes the loving loyalty shared between two people far different from everyone else. The betrayal of your own fears, doubts, frustration, confusion, etc. plays a pivotal role when your own heart is on the line and yet you risk it in hopes he/she doesn't walk away when things around get crazy/tough. In the end, you know you're standing at the fringe of true happiness bonded in the strength of loyalty when he/she will not only be there for you sometimes without even being asked but says three comforting words bringing a smile to your heart if/when you fall...I got you.

WORDS OF LOVE
May 21, 2013

Someone once said, ~The game of scrabble is a lot like love. You spend time thinking and trying to make sense of the pieces in front of you. It's hard and easy. Arguments happen. Sometimes you get so frustrated you want to flip the board. When it's all said and done you hope the words you've been given spelled out a win.~ If you think about it, the game of scrabble and love are synonymous with each other as there are certain aspects that have innate similarities. You see, it can most definitely be a tough situation indeed finding/searching for the right individual tiles jumbled up within your own heart to metaphorically place on the so-called scrabble board of someone else's heart. Essentially, it's the challenge of being able to form the words you want to express and score points, so to speak, in your favor.

Let me ask you this question to those who play scrabble, do you always get the letters you want in order to easily spell out the word. The answer is no and in some aspect, it can be considerably difficult to find/search for the potential words you want to express whereas for others it seems as if it comes naturally. Of course, one just has to work that much harder to make a good impression without sounding completely stupid or making any kind of sense whatsoever as well. Unfortunately, it happens and if you're truly, as well as, genuinely interested in that particular guy/girl your brain shuts down causing you to become considerably tongue tied. For the most part, you work with what you got by being yourself and hope your words aren't questioned/challenged.

Without a doubt, part of what makes playing scrabble so competitive is having the words being spelled out challenged by the people you're playing with. As said before, the game itself can lead to arguments and in a sense, it's that way when it pertains to matters of the heart too. Oftentimes, one questions/challenges not only the words, but the actions of a guy/girl who's potentially interested in him/her leading you to put your guard up. True, he/she may have the truest intentions in mind and yet your past history tells a different story as the scrabble board representing your heart has spelled out the following words: bitterness, betrayal, anger, hate, frustration, confusion, heartbreak, etc. Hey, it those particular words you don't have to look up in a dictionary because it comes from personal experience.

For the question can be asked, have you ever gotten to the point where you ended up flipping the board because you were getting frustrated? Thinking about it further, an individual can become absolutely frustrated concerning the dating scene or relationships in general to where It leads them to flip their heart, in a manner of speaking, causing all tiles to fly off the quintessential board of the human heart. In any case, it's the pieces representing faith, trust, hope, patience, joy, understanding, etc. end up in all intents and purposes scattered about leaving you to lose much more than points...your sanity. Let me tell you something, we've all gone through it and you just have to pray to God for continued strength all-the-while reading the scrabble words of His wisdom found within The Bible.

In retrospect, every person wants to play the scramble game known as love/true love. However, instead of playing against it's playing with someone putting together deep meaningful words to one another such as sanctification, contentment, commitment, loyalty, family, forever, and/or best friend for life. Ultimately, it's those previous words mentioned and many others that are considered to be triple word scores of true happiness. What it primarily takes is a positive team effort and being keenly aware of the words being placed from heart to heart not only verbally, but non-verbally also. In the end, to those who are in significant relationships I say to you I hope for continued success in finding the letters that form the words of love you both express every day even into the latter days of life.

THE OKLAHOMA STANDARD

May 22, 2013

Childhood icon Fred Rogers once said, ~When I was a boy and I would see scary things in the news, my mother would say to me, 'Look for the helpers. You will always find people who are helping.'"~ Without a doubt, the tragedy that happened in Moore, Oklahoma was devastating and not to mention a truly heartbreaking situation indeed as it left a town not only in absolute ruins, but a substantial amount of lives lost. Sadly, some of those lost lives were young children and there are still 6 people who are unaccounted for. It most definitely tugs at the proverbial heartstrings lives have been completely turned upside down. However, an immense tragedy such as this certainly brings together a hurting community, as well as the entire nation watching on television too.

As I said before, a number of the lives lost were young children, 2 of them being infants. Fortunately, the number could have been much higher if it weren't for the heroic teachers of Briarwood and Plaza Towers Elementary School who put their lives on the line to protect their students. I think it's safe to say we've all had the picture of two teachers tightly holding/carrying a student to safety thoroughly ingrained into our memory banks. True, a photo can speak a thousand words and when it comes to that particular photo it causes you to be rendered speechless to the point where tears are shed. Of course, there are tears of sadness but at the same time tears of joy as love who were thought to be lost were thankfully found alive, which is considered to be an absolute miracle.

If you think about it, you have to be thankful to God for the prayer filled miracles of countless kids and adults who were trapped within the rubble of schools/homes. Essentially, countless stories can be told of people/families huddled in a closet, in a storm shelter, or whatever the case may be riding out the monstrous tornado. The stories are unbelievable as one man on the news who suffered no injuries considered himself lucky and described how the tornado itself sounded like a loud freight train. Yet, the personal accounts of the teachers like Sherrie Biddle who instructed her students to put their backpacks over their heads as a safety precaution while situated in the middle of the classroom leave you feeling a mixture of proud disbelief.

Let me ask you this question to those who have been watching the aftermath on the news, do you find yourself wanting to help in any way? You see, what it primarily comes down to money as countless individuals including movie/sports celebrities have stepped up giving large financial donations to the Red Cross or what they can to help rebuild a fallen community. In some cases, social media such as Facebook can be a helpful tool as Leslie Hagelberg created a page in order to help tornado victims reunite items that were blown away as far Mississippi. The said page is called: Pray for Oklahoma - https://www.facebook.com/groups/MAY192013OKTORNADODOCSPICS/ Hey, we are all united as one and do what we can.

Oklahoma Gov. Mary Fallin said, ~We jump in and do what needs to be done and do it quickly and keep in mind that people need our help. And when we do everything we can to make it happen.~ In retrospect, Gov. Fallin did in fact take quick action and was no stranger to awful calamities, one of them being the Oklahoma City Bombing in 1995. In any case, what occurred in the aftermath was a woman taking charge holding together her composure as she stood in the middle of a debris field late at night watching dozens of first responders digging for trapped children in a building that once was Plaza Towers Elementary School. In the end, Gov. Fallin proclaimed they're going to come out of this as stronger people with a much stronger resolve as they've done in the past, which is what she refers to as The Oklahoma Standard.

MADE TO BE BROKEN

June 5, 2013

Ogden Nash once said, ~You are only young once, but you can stay immature indefinitely.~ If you think about it, getting older doesn't necessarily mean becoming or quite possibly staying a mature adult. For it's most definitely an interesting situation indeed to find yourself at a stage in one's life where you're expected to eventually outgrow the juvenile antics of your youth, especially if you're a guy. However, it doesn't turn out that way as he/she continues to have that never grow up mentality. In any case, the older each of us gets we tend to forget or should I say lose our mischievous and rebellious nature that is our own inner child because of that not so fun word called responsibility. Fortunately, immaturity isn't lost on those who still think of themselves as young at heart.

As I said before, getting older doesn't necessarily mean becoming or quite possibly staying a mature adult. True, we've been given responsibilities that need to be taken care of such as going to work to earn a paycheck but there are times we can ignore it in order to simply have fun. In any case, earning a paycheck and having fun can coincide with each other otherwise known as the office prank. The clever and hopefully harmless prank against one's office mates can certainly alleviate/break up much of the boredom on a seemingly long day. You see, whether it's on spur of the moment or a well planned out taking days, weeks, or even months you take absolute pleasure in the sheer amusement of either hearing and/or watching your handiwork become a complete success.

Without a doubt, getting older in the context of being a senior citizen does have its advantages as you're able to get away with a lot more things. Hey, even though age has caught up with them, so to speak, they're very youthful inside and as it has been said many times before "what keeps you young." Of course, you can't help but laugh and smile knowing the elderly basically are having fun to the point of possibly turning heads for their own amusement due to their juvenile mischief meant for the young. Skydiving, rapping, or whatever the case may be. What it primarily comes down to is not letting the trivial things in life bring them down, which is considered a fairly well known trade secret inevitably learned later on down the road.

Let me ask you this question, do you think immaturity and love are absolutely synonymous with each other even in the latter part of life. I think so. Oftentimes, the beginning stages of a budding relationship cause two seemingly normal, mature, level headed adults turn into giddy school kids. Thinking about it further, a perfect example would be senior citizens or one's own grandparents who act like they struck teenagers around each other so much that you tend to be embarrassed/shocked by their public displays of affection. Granted, embarrassment and shock are experienced but the fact of the matter is you so want it to be you someday with that certain special someone regarding true happiness. In other words, a guy/girl you just want to grow old and immature with.

In retrospect, every person has the right to have that type of Pee Wee Herman mentality when it comes to breaking away from being a mature adult. I think we all know someone or in fact are that someone who will always be considered immature despite becoming a relatively responsible human being. For a certain number of people it's an absolute requirement as it involves a particular profession and the people he/she serves. Ultimately, each of us may be grown ups on the outside with our set of responsibilities and rules but on the inside it's a whole different story. In the end, it's certain things in life that give us the opportunity to let loose our inner child run causing it to ramped because as it has been said before about the rules of getting older... they can be made to be broken.

IN YOUR OWN SKIN

June 19, 2013

Eustace Budgell once said, ~Love and esteem are the first principles of friendship; it is always imperfect if either of these two are wanting.~ As said before, love and esteem are the principles of friendship, especially when it comes to matters of the heart. For its most definitely an uplifting situation indeed to have your self-esteem be metaphorically built up by someone who you're in a potential and/or significant relationship with. Of course, when it is you can't help but have a smile on your face, but within your heart as well. Essentially, you feel better about yourself personally, physically, mentally, and not to mention emotionally as well due to how positive rather than negative he/she has been in your life.

If you think about it, when you experience the overwhelming sense of being comfortable within yourself by a special someone one has a much stronger and healthier self-esteem. I think it would be safe to say there's a glow that shines forth witnessed by others causing you to become more confident inwardly, as well as outwardly. Women, more so than men, exude this shining glow when they're with a guy who truly treats her right in every aspect, inevitably making her happy. It's her happiness that brings out her inward beauty leading to self-confidence gained outwardly. Hey, when everything is working together personally, physically, mentally, and emotionally there is a swag of positivity that can't be denied.

Without a doubt, one's self esteem can take a very brutal hit in the aftermath of a big break up so much so you're unable to be comfortable within your own skin. Sadly, it's an unfortunate situation quite a number of people have been or are going through because of past relationships. Thinking about it further, it befuddles the mind of how big of a douche a person can be for causing a guy/girl to have a deluded mindset concerning their own physical appearance. True, an ex has the uncanny ability to place a seed of doubt in a woman's mind leaving her to question her worth not just as a woman, but as a human being also. Let me tell you something ladies, if you were ever in a relationship with said douche, he didn't realize how special and beautiful you absolutely are.

Let me ask you this question to those in a significant relationship, does your best friend for life continually build up instead of tearing down your self-esteem? You see, to have a man/woman accept you for who you are, imperfections and all, definitely gives you the greatest feeling one can ever have. In other words, it's considered a breath of fresh air filling one's heart with joy and contentment. Granted, there may be aspects you want to change within reason and it's a decision that lies with you alone. Fortunately, you have the support of your loving partner who will stand by you no matter how you feel about or look at yourself when experiencing those types of days. What it primarily comes down to is being able to accept you're imperfectly perfect to someone who brings you absolute true happiness.

In retrospect, self-esteem is considerably valuable because it allows you to think and cope with challenges involving love/true love. Oftentimes, you have to remind yourself you are worthy of having someone fall in love with you and it always starts with embracing/loving who you are. However, there may be difficulty in that as past relationships caused you to think differently to where a skewed perception has you believing otherwise. Ultimately, a strong self-esteem combined with a positive personality will bring about shared success and fulfillment in a worthwhile relationship you're deserving of. In the end, it's just a matter of growing in every sense conveying a positive outlook and with your bf/gf/husband/wife by your side you won't ever be uncomfortable in your own skin.

ALL IN

June 24, 2013

Someone once said, ~Love is like playing a game of high stakes
poker. Either you're given the right cards from the deck or you
don't. You clear your hand and then you just wait another round.
In the end, the right card will help you win the game.~ In some
aspect, when it comes to matters of the heart each one of us
has taken or are taking the risky gamble of putting ourselves
out there in regard to that certain someone special. For it can
most definitely be considered a high stakes situation indeed
knowing what all you're putting on the line in order to hopefully
experience a worthwhile, lasting relationship. Essentially, you
have to for all intents and purposes play smart, have patience,
don't tip your hand, and above all else hope have the luck of the
draw on your side.

Without a doubt, being able to have a solid poker face is one of
the main aspects that measures how great a poker player you are.
In other words, not showing any kind of emotion whatsoever
so as to not express to your opponent(s) whether you're at an
absolute disadvantage or have a tremendous advantage. In a
sense, it's that same poker face one puts on regarding a potential
relationship and knowing full well the emotional/mental roller
coaster being endured inside isn't a reflection of what's been
seen pertaining to the proverbial tells given off by one's body
language. Hey, every person has been or is quite possibly going
through it attempting to remain calm, cool, and collected outside
all the while completely freaking out on the inside.

If you think about it, in the game of poker there are times where it
becomes a psychological battle between two players in the form
of a bluff. A bluff is defined as a bet or raise made with a hand
which is not thought to be the best hand. In any case, every person

has or is currently finding themselves in a verbal/nonverbal bluff situation involving a guy/girl's signals, if any, and to whether or not make the move forward towards the possibility of true happiness. True, it's risky nonetheless to make the move knowing full well you may possibly misinterpret their verbal/nonverbal bluffs causing utter embarrassment on one's part. However, it's what love/true love is all about as you try to read him/her to the point where you end up just going with your gut instinct.

Let me ask you this question to those who watched the movie Maverick starring Mel Gibson, do you remember what he did in order to win the $500,000 prize money? If you answered, take the card that he was given to where he doesn't look at it, feels it, closes his eyes, then tosses it for his opponent to see. It turns out to be the Ace of Spades, which beats out a straight flush to his royal flush. Thinking about it, when it comes to establishing a heart-to-heart connection you sometimes just have to close your eyes and toss your heart on the table towards him/her and hope for the best. Of course, you may lose everything in the process; but on the other hand, you took a big risk, so much so you won something far more valuable, as well as priceless, it can be shared together for years to come.

In retrospect, the cards we hold in our hands as we play for the biggest prize of them all...a man/woman's heart. You see, the individual cards are a representation of trust, honor, loyalty, respect, faith, understanding, patience, compassion, contentment, happiness, joy, commitment, etc. Granted, it seems as if it's difficult nowadays to see those particular cards because they've experienced in the past of having some, most, or all of it hidden under a guy/girl's sleeve. A low-down dirty cheat if you want to be more specific...but I digress. In the end, to every person living the single life like myself we hope to meet our best friend for life who we will know with 100% surety that when the chips are down, we'll be all in.

SPEAK TO ME
July 7, 2013

Sara Paddison once said, ~Have the courage to be sincere, clear, and honest. This opens the door to deeper communication all around. It creates self empowerment and the kind of connection with others we want in life. Speaking from the heart frees us from the secrets that burdens us. These secrets are what make us sick or fearful. Speaking truth helps you get clarity on your real heart directives.~ Without a doubt, one of the key aspects in being in a worthwhile, long-lasting relationship is the exchange of open and deep communication. For it's most definitely a heartwarming situation indeed for any person to have someone they can truly confide in, especially when it's their best friend for life. Hey, to have a confidant such as that in which you can speak freely with, without any fear whatsoever can leave you smiling from ear to ear.

Let me ask you this question to those in a significant relationship, does there continue to be open communication between the two of you to the point where there is an absolute deeper understanding of each other? You see, being able to have an open dialogue with your partner gives one the opportunity to continually learn/know more about him/her and vice versa. As I said before, there is much deeper understanding when you're opening yourself mentally, personally, spiritually, and not to mention emotionally in regard to their/your past, present, as well as future. True, there is an innate fear of revealing too much but if it's done with gradual ease and not all at once to where it overwhelms him/her then you're doing it the right way.

If you think about it, having a lack of open communication has the propensity to not only put a strain on a significant relationship, but can tear it apart also without even uttering a single word. Of course, the exchange of verbal arguments leads to things being unfortunately said in the heat of the moment due to anger and that in turn initiates the silent treatment. Granted, women are more than likely to initiate it and truth be told they are Jedi masters at it. In any case, nothing is solved because you're both stubborn, nobody takes the initiative to save face and apologize in order to have a possible clear path of open dialogue. Thinking about it further, even though one may not have started the verbal war of words causing mental and emotional pain, an attempt is made to make amends because he/she is worth it.

For the question can be asked to the women concerning the man you married, was it difficult or easy for you to have an open discussion from the time you met until now? I think it's safe to say it's difficult for guys to express themselves emotionally because from the time we're young we've been taught to internalize our thoughts, feelings, and emotions. In other words, expressing ourselves regarding matters of the heart shows weakness...but I digress. However, to freely talk with and share openly with him/her how you're thinking and feeling about the guy/girl you love frees one of the burdens weighing down on their shoulders. The fears, worries, doubts, and whatever else are being lifted away causing you to be a much happier person, which is what every person living the single life wants to experience for themselves.

Dinah Craik said, ~Oh the comfort, the inexpressible comfort of feeling safe with a person, having neither to weigh thoughts nor measure words, but pouring them all right out, just as they are-chaff and grain together-certain that a faithful hand will take and sift them, keep what is worth keeping, and with the breath of kindness blow the rest away.~ In retrospect, the relief, contentment and security you feel when you know full well the person you're speaking to involving everything shared between the two of you is kept in the vault brings joy to your heart.

Ultimately, you don't have to worry about him/her breaking your confidence because in the end, when you're having a bad day or just simply want to talk you know you'll never be uneasy when you hear the following three words: speak to me.

BEAM ME UP
July 12, 2013

Marcel Proust once said, ~The real voyage of discovery consists in seeking not new landscapes, but in having new eyes.~ In some aspect, love or true love for that matter is like going on a voyage boldly going where every person now in a significant relationship has gone before and for those living the single life such as myself want to find ourselves at. Of course, one may not necessarily be traveling the vast reaches of the final frontier of outer space in a starship vessel known as the U.S.S. Enterprise; but each of us are for all intents and purposes at the helm of our own heart navigating ourselves through the seemingly vast final frontier of one day finally experiencing absolute true happiness. For it can most definitely be a tough and frustrating situation indeed exploring/seeking out what others have easily discovered for themselves.

Without a doubt, every Star Trek aficionado knows about/heard the spoken intro to the tv series always stating a 5 year mission to explore strange new worlds, seeking out new life/civilizations, and not to mention boldly going where no man has gone before. Thinking about it further, it truly feels more than just a 5-year mission in regard to being a single guy/woman exploring the oftentimes strange world of the dating scene. A world where you want to seek out or even better be seeked out by that one special life form out there who makes matters of the heart absolutely logical to you rather than illogical. Hey, as easy as it sounds the reality of it all is the dating scene is brutally scary filled with alien type creatures much scarier than the Gorn

If you think about it, utter heartbreak and Star Trek II are synonymous with each other as it pertains to dealing with one's inner emotions expressed outwardly. What do I mean? I think it's safe to say the aftermath of a breakup leads to dealing with so many painful thoughts, feelings, and emotions swirling around not only in your head, but heart as well. Essentially, it can be all rolled into one big volatile mixture of anger and depending on how great a scale you've been personally, mentally, and emotionally affected; you end up just wanting to scream out his/her name like Kirk did screaming out the name of Khan. True, it may not solve anything, scream their name so loud it possibly echoes out into space but at least you're able to hopefully relieve some much-needed aggression out of your system.

Let me ask you this question to you ladies who are in a worthwhile significant relationship, do you or are you able to see some, most, or all the Star Trek characters in your forever best friend? You see, if you really take close observation you'll notice hints of the cunning, confident leadership of James T. Kirk mixed in with Jean Luc Picard. A combination of Spock and Lt. Commander Data where the lack of emotion tends to be replaced with illogical reasoning and facts concerning pop culture/video game references relevant to him. The security and protectiveness of Worf with the fun, loving mentality of Q. The loyalty and passion of Dr. McCoy along with a possible dose of Sulu's sophisticated culture and the intellectual prowess of Jordi LaForge. The naivety of Chekov, Scotty's ability to handle solutions in fixing problems, and lastly the patient wisdom of Commander Riker are what quite possibly any wants to see in their husband.

Alexander Smith said, ~Love is but the discovery of ourselves in others, and the delight in the recognition.~ In retrospect, being able to discover the meaning of love is considered to be THE best feeling one can ever experience for themselves. What it primarily comes down to is opening your eyes and being able to see in every sense of the word who is there for you and it doesn't take Jordi's visor to filter out who is genuinely real concerning their intentions. Granted, we all don't want to become wearing the metaphorical red shirt and unfortunately become the poster child for failed/dead relationships. In the end, to my fellow single peeps I say to you each one of us will or may one day make that epic discovery of the heart to where you smile from ear to ear, look up to the heavens, and say beam me up.

LIKE IT OR NOT
July 21, 2021

Jaron Lanier once said, ~Pop culture has entered into a nostalgic malaise. Online culture is dominated by trivial mashups of the culture existed before the on set of mashups, and by fandoms responding to the dwindling outposts of centralized mass media. It is a culture of reaction without action.~ Without a doubt, on any given day each one of us does/says/involved in something that is referenced to pop culture so much so it's part of our everyday lives. In other words, the part of the human condition to the point where it becomes an automatic response to any particular situation in life and more often than not you don't realize how much it has affected you. Hey, it defines us as a generation depending on which ear we all grew up in don't you think?

As I said before, pop culture is part of the human condition to the point where it becomes an automatic response to any particular situation in life and more often than not you don't realize how much i has immensely affected you. True, it's thoroughly ingrained in the way we live our loves and it's something we can't necessarily escape from no matter how hard one tries. For example, we all have movie quotes that have been downloaded in our brain to where we automatically spit out a line when something is said or done warranting a needed amusing zinger. For it's most definitely a comical situation indeed when you find yourself listening to someone say something so incredibly ridiculous your automatic response is to possibly retort with a memorable movie line such as "Hello McFly."

If you think about it, a particular individual can elicit a reaction as well, especially if that person is considered to be a pop culture icon. I think it's safe to say Arsenio Hall is a name we're all familiar with. The mere sight of him leads fans of his to rotate their fists in a forward circular motion all-the-while barking out loud. Once again, an automatic response every time he makes an appearance, whereby showing how big of an impact he still has after so many years out of the spotlight. Thinking about it further, his popularity is quite possibly larger now than it was back, causing it to become increasingly stronger. Essentially, he was and continues to be a pop culture icon who hasn't lost the connection with not only the viewing audience, but his loyal fan base too.

Let me ask you this question about pop culture and loyal fan bases in regard to past tv shows, how many of you would give your own money to bring it back on the big screen? Of course, the show with the best and loyal fans can certainly be debated to the ground. However, you can't dispute the heart and loyalty of the Veronica Mars fans who lobbied hard to get the pop culture that aired from 2004-2007 up on the big screen. A kickstarter was created for fans to primarily fund the movie and it was a complete success racking up over $5.5 million dollars. You see, if it weren't for the passion and loyalty of the fans the movie wouldn't have been made and coincidentally it's those same fans/backers who are lucky enough to take part in the movie.

In retrospect, there are so many people, places, or things that reference pop culture that they'll always have a special meaning to each one of us. The house from the tv show Full House continues to be an awesome tourist attraction after all these years. Fashion trends involving haircuts such as "The Rachel" from the hit tv show Friends have played an influential role for women when it pertains to the hot hair style of the decade. When it comes to music, the reformation of the boy band New Kids On The Block and touring no less. Granted, not every person, place, or thing is pop culture worthy, but they unfortunately stick in our conscientious minds. In the end, it will and forever always be the passion and loyalty of die-hard fans who will keep pop culture alive and thriving whether we like it or not.

ROUGH AROUND THE EDGES

July 27, 2013

Claridad Lacon once said, ~Life is like a book, waiting to be filled with interesting stories that can make you cry when needed to let go of something that doesn't need to be held on to. To make you laugh. Laugh to yourself when you make a mistake but learn from it. To enlighten you for the things that you don't understand yet. Finally, to test you if there is faith in you and hope in the time of when you think that there is nothing that you can do.~ If you think about it, life is indeed like a book as each one of us are primarily the author of our own individual stories. Humor, action, drama, tragedy, and everything in between all intertwined within one's ongoing living autobiography that continues to be a work in progress.

Without a doubt, we all tend to live our lives with an all-intensive purpose open book mentality, especially now with the advent of social media allowing others a glimpse into one's life. In any case, when it comes to our friends they inevitably take part in helping write out our story. Thinking about it further, who better than to contribute shared memories than those who more than likely know us more accurately than we know ourselves. Granted, moments and situations can very well be embellished by them, causing those "reading" our living autobiography to be on the edge of their seat, so to speak, because of how truly compelling it is. Hey, it's totally impossible to make this stuff up knowing it's real life with your own personal first-hand accounts of what happened.

As said before, we're primarily the authors of our own individual stories, so much so a person is able to change the course of their story in regard to one's professional career. Oftentimes, like any story it takes a major turn to where it not just affects your life, but possibly those around you too. In other words, an epic plot twist in which something so unexpected happens it changes the course of the story to where it was originally intended to go. A major life event that leaves you at a momentary loss for words such as a job promotion, being fired, being overlooked in one's job, stabbed in the back by a friend/co-worker, or whatever the case may be. So, how many plot twists have occurred while climbing the ladder of success?

Someone said, ~ Love is like an endless book. For every page you turn something that's new, but little happens. Every new chapter something bigger happens. Unfortunately, you can't tell what's happening next. There's no glossary to turn to, no index to look through and no summary of what happens in the end. Love is a mystery, and you just have to turn one page at a time.~ You see, the chapters regarding love/true love have already been filled out for a certain number of lucky people. However, for those living the single life such as myself it's either yet to be written or we keep finding ourselves starting over because he/she couldn't creatively inspire us anymore. Of course, one continues to write from the heart until we finally fill in, in a manner of speaking, the chapters with inspiring words of true happiness for others to read.

In retrospect, we've all heard the saying don't judge a book by its cover. Granted, not every person's life may seem boring and unfulfilling on the surface; but once you in a sense sit down, open the book, and take the time to read what he/she is all about you end up having a far better understanding of his/her story. Essentially, the story we are all individually living isn't by all means perfect and not to mention done by any stretch of the imagination. Essentially, we learn from the past to succeed in the present for a better future. Ultimately, when you take a look inside your book it is there full of bent corners, torn/missing pages, words or should I say moments highlighted/marked out, and the cover faded. In the end, the book of life we're currently writing is considered rough around the edges, and may not necessarily be deemed a best seller, but it's ours, nonetheless.

THE RIGHT TIME
August 8, 2013

Someone once said, ~The words I Love You. Say it when you feel the time is right to say it. Sometimes it's said back and other times it takes a little while for them to say it back. Other times they completely flip out. People say it after three weeks. Some never say it but know it. Others say it after two years. It's a very big thing. So make sure the time is right for you to say it.~ Let me ask you this question, when it comes to being in a newly formed relationship is or should there be a time limit set in saying the words I love you to the point where a break up occurs if it doesn't happen? For it's most definitely a question that raises eyebrows as it deals with an individual's high expectations concerning three impactful words in hopes of cementing their dream of experiencing true happiness.

Without a doubt, establishing a time limit in regard to expecting a potential future mate is considered to be a deluded mindset, especially if it's in the early stages of a relationship. True, we've all imagined a well thought out timeline of events involving our own future, especially when it pertains to matters of the heart. Women, more often than not, tend to put a time limit on such things as getting married and having a family, which isn't all that surprising. However, what is surprising is to establish a set time limit on saying the words I love you and not to mention breaking off the relationship when it's not said brings about a morbidly skewed concept of their version of love/true love. So ladies, do you know or is someone like this who I'm describing?

As I said before, it certainly raises eyebrows as a person has seemingly high expectations concerning hearing three impactful words in hopes of cementing their dream of experiencing true happiness. Of course, to continually wait and expecting those three specific words to come from his/her mouth early in a relationship may very well not only cause one to lose their sanity but endure absolute disappointment as well when the words aren't uttered from his/her lips. Thinking about it further, the yearning to verbally hear it at a particular point and time in their fledgling relationship possibly shows the lack of loving security/self-esteem on their part is missing for one's life. In other words, being able to hear those words from a potential future mate sadly validates the expectations selfishly set for themselves.

For the question can be asked to you ladies who are now or have been in a significant relationship for quite some time, do you vividly remember when and how long did it take for your husband/bf to say to you the following three words: I love you? Essentially, it's primarily different for each individual but similar in the sense that it was hopefully a memorable moment one can reflect back on and smile from ear to ear. Granted, it probably doesn't matter if the setting wasn't considerably romantic like standing in line getting tickets for the movie because the sole importance was the two of you sharing that special moment together. Hey, for any woman to be totally surprised or in some cases be completely thrown off by the words I love you only if it's genuinely real and the guy took his time to eventually say it.

In retrospect, to become overly obsessive in wanting to hear what is considered to be the three most important words you can say to someone you love shows you shouldn't be in a relationship. You see, if you feel the need for verbal self-gratification of knowing for sure he/she actually loves you and establishes an "or else" clause within it then you're portraying a lack of maturity on your part. What it primarily comes down to is being in a relationship without any high expectations or set ultimatums in mind because you'll set yourself up to fail miserably. Essentially, once you do you'll get everything you've ever wanted from those three little words. In the end, never find yourself anticipating/waiting for/establishing a deadline for the right time in having I love you said to you because to be perfectly honest there is no right time.

CHALLENGE ACCEPTED

August 11, 2013

Someone once said, ~Love isn't always perfect. It isn't a fairytale or a storybook. And it doesn't always come easy. Love is overcoming obstacles, facing challenges, fighting to be together. Holding on and never letting go. It is a short word, easy to spell, difficult to define. Impossible to live without. Love is work, but most of all, love is realizing that every hour, every minute and every second was worth it because you did it together.~ Without a doubt, being able to face challenges in regard to matters of the heart is most definitely part of what makes a truly significant relationship. For it can certainly be a tough and frustrating situation indeed to put in the work in order to keep an imperfectly perfect partnership together. However, if he/she is well worth it you'll happily take up the challenge.

If you think about it, challenges and love/true love are oftentimes never easy because you have to come face to face with the absolute unknown. I think it's safe to say when it comes to the absolute unknown pertaining to the challenge of true happiness you'll metaphorically look into the eyes of your own fears, doubts, frustrations, anger, etc. You see, it's those just previously mentioned that can hold you back from taking the next step forward inevitably moving past one of many challenging relationship obstacles. What it primarily comes down to is having the desire, fortitude, and determination to want to be a part of something so wonderfully special you'll thank God as you look back at all at what you've been able to accomplish together whether it be good or bad.

As said before, love is not only about overcoming obstacles and facing challenges; but its also involves fighting to be together. Unfortunately, there are some people who tend to give up too easily when facing the seemingly overwhelming obstacles in the face of potentially establishing a significant relationship. Sadly, it's an unfortunate situation concerning how particular guys, as well as girls give into the fear, doubt, frustration, anger, etc. and end up taking the pathetic/cowardly option of not facing the challenges that lie before them. Granted, one could have very well looked forward to the endless possibilities/opportunities, but have found himself/herself reflecting back on painful regrets. Let me tell you something ladies and gentlemen, it's these kinds of individuals who don't deserve to be in a relationship because they do everything in their power to avoid difficult challenges to where they eventually bail on such things as commitment.

Let me ask you this question to those who are in a potential and/or significant relationship, does your best friend for life help challenge you in every way and vice versa? Thinking about it further, to have someone in your life who mentally, personally, emotionally, and spiritually challenges you shows a person how much of a big influence he/she is to you. In other words, being the guy/girl who even though causes the loved one to become irritated/annoyed he/she has the innate ability to be supportive by continually pushing, encouraging, and motivating in a deeply positive way. Granted, the end result may not necessarily turn out how one wanted but at least you tried knowing full well your husband/bf/wife/gf has been by your side every step of the way.

Anthony Robbins said, ~Some of the biggest challenges in relationships come from the fact most people enter a relationship in order to get something. They're trying to find someone who's going to make them feel good. In reality, the only way a relationship will last is if you see your relationship as a place that you go to give and not a place that you go to take.~ In retrospect, what one can challenge themselves is by consistently showing/giving their trust, faith, honesty, integrity, unwavering hope, constant communication, deep understanding, 100% full commitment, etc. Of course, it will be hard and yet it's so worth it. In the end, to those living the single life such as myself we'll finally meet "the one" who wants to be challenged in every sense of the word and once we do, we'll smile saying the following two words: challenge accepted.

KILLER INSTINCTS

August 19, 2013

Someone once said, ~Always believe in you. Listen to your heart. Trust your instincts. Know you can see your own strength. Dream it. Dare it. Do what you are afraid of. Keep the faith. Keep the faith. Follow your vision and remember anything is possible if you only believe.~ If you think about it, there can most definitely be at times a tough situation indeed to go with and trust your instincts, especially when it pertains to matters of the heart. Hey, any person can easily be fooled by the actions and/or words of a supposed loved one to the point where one suffers an utterly painful heartbreak. However, if a guy/girl truly believes their instincts are absolutely genuine concerning the possibility of a bright future one should take a leap of faith; but at the same time always stay mentally, as well as, emotionally alert.

Without a doubt, you certainly have to attain a level head in regards to the instincts involving the one thing that can not only cause you to become weak in every sense of the word, but leads you to question the belief you have in yourself as well: love/true love. In any case, being thoroughly self aware and not to mention having a keen eye/ear of any warning signs help thwart the possibility of potential heartbreak. True, there are a number of individuals whose instincts have been perfectly spot on and are experiencing a worry/stress free long lasting, worthwhile significant relationship. Essentially, the reason why is they've been able to instinctively ascertain the guy/girl who strengthens him/her personally, mentally, physically, and emotionally. For it's considered to be a difficult task to undertake for those living the single life and yet a lucky few are enjoying loving success instead of metaphorically kicking themselves in the heart.

As said before, attaining a level head involves your own instincts regarding something so powerful that it can not only lead you to become weak in every sense of the word, but leads you to question the belief in yourself. Unfortunately, some people's instincts are either faulty to where it leads to self-sabotage or not completely listening to it knowing full well they're setting themselves up for an incredibly heartbreaking fall. Granted, all the warning signs can plainly be seen with their own two eyes, and they end up ignoring because he/she doesn't act by verbally questioning what's clearly wrong, whereby putting their own personal happiness in jeopardy. You see, the painful impact of sadness, anger, bitterness, frustration, etc. will hurt far worse if not handled immediately rather than letting it continue knowing that in the back of your mind, you're much more deserving of someone special to where it leaves. a real smile on your face inside of a fake one.

Let me ask you this question to those who are in significant relationships, what were your initial instincts when it involved meeting your best friend for life for the first time? Oftentimes, first impressions are key and your instincts are tremendously heightened taking into account everything from topics of discussion shared to the way the person is acting. Women, more so than guys, rely on their intuitive instincts to evaluate whether a not a guy is potentially worth their time so much so they assess within seconds if they're absolutely interested. Of course, their instincts can steer them wrong, in a manner of speaking, as the so-called Mr. Right is in fact Mr. Wrong, which can also apply to guys as well. What it primarily comes down to is honing in on and being keenly aware of the most valuable aspect you have that tends to go on the fritz from time to time...common sense.

Honore de Blazac said, ~Love has its own instincts in finding the way to the heart; as the feeblest insect the way to its flower with a will which nothing can dismay nor turn aside.~ In retrospect, trusting your instincts is one big part of the equation, so to speak, in the proverbial enigma that is relationships. Faith, honesty, integrity, understanding, commitment, communication, hope, etc. along with trust help in establishing whether the gut feeling about that guy/girl is either correct or totally wrong. Ultimately, listen to the little voice in your head and your heart because 99.9% of the time it's right. However, it doesn't hurt to seek counsel by praying to God and talking with gal pals/best buds who always have your back. In the end, love is a very powerful force that can turn you topsy turvy in a negative or positive way, but if you have some killer instincts working for instead of against you then my friend, you'll be able to mentally maneuver the right path to true happiness.

THIS IS WHY WE CHOP

September 6, 2013

Retired/future hall of famer Chipper Jones of the Atlanta Braves once said, ~I think the legacy is what it is. We've won 14 straight division titles. We know how special that is. We're going to keep doing our thing whether we win or lose the postseason. It's not going to change the fact that we've won 14 straight division titles.~ Without a doubt, the Atlanta Braves have come a long way from being considered a mediocre afterthought in the late 80's to an absolute strong contender now to the point where they've made a huge impact, especially in the 90's. For it's most definitely a memorable situation indeed to any die hard fan who has been through their ups and downs with the team so much so loyal fans such as myself consider ourselves part of the prolific baseball team.

As I said before, there are certainly countless memories to choose from concerning the early history of the Bravos in the 90's. Thinking about it, one memory that tends to stick out is the great rivalry established with the Los Angeles Dodgers for the top spot in the division when it was merely the east and west during that particular era. In any case, it was considered a David vs. Goliath type battle between the two teams as the Braves truly fought their way from being known as the worst team in baseball to finding themselves in first place. True, clutch hitting played a role in their rising success; but what made such a significant impact at the time was the pitching staff. Glavine, Maddux, Avery, Smoltz, and Merker along with a revolving door of closers gradually elevated them to premier pinnacle status.

Without a doubt, every fan of the Braves knows what I'm saying when I mention the words Sid Slide. Essentially, it's a memory that has been deeply ingrained not only in our minds, but hearts as well. The setting was the bottom of the 9th at 92' NLCS in Atlanta Fulton County Stadium against the Pirates. Stan Belinda on the mound, Francisco Cabrera at the plate, and a not so swift footed Sid Bream representing the winning run on second base. It's a play that would live in utter infamy in a good way of course with the late Skip Carey calling the play. When it was all said and done, Sid Bream would be forever encapsulated as the guy who chugged his way with full force and inevitably slid his team to the World Series against the Minnesota Twins. Let me tell you something, I was so emotionally invested in the game that night, I couldn't watch and went to bed only to find out later they would go to the World Series.

Let me ask you this question to my fellow Braves fans, how did you react/feel when they finally won their first World Series in 95'. Personally speaking, I went through a mixture of emotions but mostly happiness as I literally jumped off my couch as the final out was caught letting the celebration begin. Glavine was in the zone as he pitched a superb game with David Justice providing the lone home run and the defensive play of the night went to Javy Lopez, throwing out an Indian player at first base. Of course, I had a smile the following day as I watched Sportscenter repeatedly just watch and listen to our guys celebrate a deserving title knowing they've fallen short in the past.

In retrospect, there have been other memories that still to this day stick with any Braves fan. The combined no hitter against the San Diego Padres by Merker, Wohlers, and Pena. Who can never forget the outstanding catch by Otis Nixon to the right center field wall hit by Pirate's player Andy Van Slyke to preserve the 13 game winning streak in 92'. Of course, the debut of Chipper Jones in 93' and sadly his goodbye season in 2012. Ultimately, the Braves today are on the verge of clinching their division with ease and hopefully a World Series visit once again and a newly built Waffle House in Turner Stadium is partly responsible for that. In the end, I say to my fellow Braves fans this is why we chop for a team who never quits till the end, which is why they have as of now 22 comeback walk off wins under their belt.

ABOUT THE AUTHOR

Dante Abundo Jr was born in Subic Bay, Philippines. He grew up with a military father who is happily retired from the Navy and has been spending quality time with his wife of 48 years. Dante lives in the Sunshine State of the Florida Panhandle. When he's not working, he enjoys in his spare time a number of activities such as drawing, traveling, playing video games, watching anime, and writing. You can find him on social media: Facebook, Instagram, Twitter, YouTube etc.

Visit The Inner Sanctum:
http://yodaisms.blogspot.com

www.ingramcontent.com/pod-product-compliance
Lightning Source LLC
Chambersburg PA
CBHW062148080426
42734CB00010B/1610